MARY, THE HELP OF CHRISTIANS

Mary, Help of Christians

MARY
··⦿[HELP OF CHRISTIANS]⦿··

and the
Fourteen Saints
Invoked as Holy Helpers

Instructions, Legends, Novenas and Prayers
with
Thoughts of the Saints for Every Day in the Year

compiled by
Rev. Bonaventure Hammer, O.F.M.

To which is added an Appendix on the
Reasonableness of Catholic Ceremonies and Practices
by Rev. John J. Burke

2014
ST. AUGUSTINE ACADEMY PRESS
LISLE, ILLINOIS

Imprimi Permittitur.

  FR. CHRYSOSTOMUS THEOBALD, O.F.M.,
  Minister Provincialis.
  Cincinnati, Ohio, die 30, Martii, 1908.

Nihil Obstat.

  REMY LAFORT, S.T.L.,
  Censor Librorum.

Imprimatur.

  JOHN M. FARLEY,
  Archbishop of New York.

NEW YORK, March 4, 1909.

This book was originally published in 1909
by Benziger Brothers.
This edition ©2014 by St. Augustine Academy Press.
All editing by Lisa Bergman.

ISBN: 978-1-936639-29-8

Preface

THE contents of the following pages are based on the Catholic doctrine of the veneration and invocation of the saints, and of the efficacy of the prayer of intercession. The legends of the individual "Holy Helpers" were compiled from authors whose writings have the approval of the Church.

In compliance with the decrees of Pope Urban VIII of 1625, 1631, and 1634, the compiler formally declares that he submits everything contained in this little book to the infallible judgment of the Church, and that he claims no other than human credibility for the facts, legends, and miracles related, except where the Church has otherwise decided.

—THE COMPILER.

Mary, conceived without sin, pray for us.

Contents

PART III
The Fourteen Holy Helpers

PART IV
Novenas to the Holy Helpers

PRAYERS OF PETITION AND INTERCESSION

PART V
General Devotions

PART VI

Thoughts and Counsels of the Saints for Every Day of the Year

PART VII

Reasonableness of Catholic Ceremonies and Practices

Contents

PART I

The Veneration and Invocation of Saints, and the Efficacy of Prayer

"Remember your prelates who have spoken the word of God to you; whose faith follow, considering the end of their conversation" (Heb. 13:7).

"Wherefore I beseech you, be ye followers of me, as I am also of Christ" (1 Cor. 4:16).

Mary Queen of Heaven, pray for us.

CHAPTER I

The Veneration and Invocation of Saints

*I*N THE Creed of the Council of Trent, which the Catholic Church places before the faithful as the Rule of Faith, we read: "I firmly believe that the saints reigning with Christ are to be venerated and invoked."

The Church therefore teaches, first, that it is right and pleasing to God to venerate the saints and to invoke their intercession; and second, that it is useful and profitable to eternal salvation for us to do so.

The veneration of the saints is useful and profitable to us. Men conspicuous in life for knowledge, bravery, or other noble qualities and unusual merits are honored after death. Why, then, should Catholics not be permitted to honor the heroes of their faith, who excelled in the practice of supernatural virtue and are in special grace and favor with God? That this veneration is profitable to us is evident from the fact that the example of the saints incites us to imitate them to the best of our ability.

The veneration of the saints is not only in full accord with the demands of reason, but we are, moreover, enjoined explicitly by Holy Scripture to venerate the memory of the holy patriarchs and prophets: "Let us now praise men of renown, and our fathers in their generation" (Ecclus. 44:1). "And their names continue for ever, the glory of the holy men remaining unto their children" (Ecclus. 46:15).

Reason and Holy Scripture, then, are in favor of the veneration of the saints. We find it practised, therefore, also in the early Church. She was convinced from the very beginning of its propriety and utility. As early as the first century the memorial day of the martyrs' death was observed by the Christians. They assembled at the tombs of the sainted victims of pagan cruelty and celebrated their memory by offering up the Holy Sacrifice over their relics. We know this not only from the testimony of the earliest ecclesiastical writers, as Origen, Tertullian, and St. Cyprian, but also from the history of St. Ignatius the Martyr (d. 107), and of St. Polycarp of Smyrna (d. 166). Over one hundred panegyrics of various saints written by St. Augustine are still extant.

And why should it not be right and useful to invoke the *intercession* of the saints? Everybody deems it proper to ask a pious friend for his prayers. St. Paul the Apostle recommended himself to the prayers of the faithful (Rom. 15:30), and God Himself commanded the friends of Job to ask Him for His intercession that their sin might not be imputed to them (Job 42:8). How, then, can it be wrong or superfluous to invoke the intercession of the saints in heaven? The saints are *willing* to invoke God's bounty in our favor, for they love us. They are *able* to obtain it for us, because God always accepts their prayer with complacency.

That they really hear our prayer and intercede with God for us is clearly shown by many examples in Holy Scripture. And if, according to the testimony of St. James (v. 16), the prayer of the just man here on earth availeth much with God, how much more powerful, then, must be the prayer of the saints, who are united with God in heaven in perfect love and are, so to say, partakers of His infinite goodness and omnipotence?

A most striking proof of the efficacy of the prayers of the saints is the numerous miracles wrought and the many favors obtained at all times through their intercession. Among these miracles are a great number whose authenticity was declared by the Church after the most scrupulous and strict investigation, as the acts of canonization prove.

That the invocation of the saints was a practice of the early Church is proved by the numerous inscriptions on the tombs of the Roman catacombs preserved to this day. We read there, for instance, on the tomb of Sabbatius, a martyr, "Sabbatius, O pious soul, pray and intercede for your brethren and associates!" On another tomb is inscribed, "Allicius, thy spirit is blessed; pray for thy parents!" And again, "Jovianus, live in God, and pray for us!"

We have also the testimony of one of the greatest thinkers and Protestant philosophers, Leibnitz, for the claim that the veneration and invocation of the saints is founded in reason, on Holy Scripture, and on the tradition of the Church. He writes: "Because we justly expect great advantage by uniting our prayers with those of our brethren here on earth, I can not understand how it can be called a crime if a person invokes the intercession of a glorified soul, or an angel. If it be really idolatry or a detestable cult to invoke the saints and the angels to intercede for us with God, I do not comprehend how Basil, Gregory Nazianzen, Ambrose, and others, who were hitherto considered saints, can be absolved from idolatry or superstition. To continue in such a practice would indeed not be a small defect in the Fathers, such as is inherent in human nature—it would be an enormous public crime. For if the Church, even in those early times, was infected with such abominable errors, let any one judge for himself what the Christian faith would eventually come to. Would not Gamaliel's proposition, to judge whether Christ's religion be divine or human from its effects, result in its disfavor?"

But whilst the Catholic Church practises and recommends the veneration and invocation of the saints, she does not teach us to honor and invoke them as we do God, nor to pray to them as we do to Him. She makes a great distinction.

The veneration of the saints differs from the worship of God in the following:

1. We *adore* God as our supreme Lord. We *honor* the saints as His faithful servants and friends.

2. We *adore* God for His own sake. We *honor* the saints for the gifts and prerogatives with which God endowed them.

Therefore there is a difference between the prayer to God and the invocation of the saints. We pray to God asking Him to help us by His omnipotence: we pray to the saints to help us by their intercession with God.

Our veneration of the saints should consist, primarily, in the imitation of their virtues. It is truly profitable only when we are intent upon following their example; for only by imitating their virtues shall we share their eternal bliss in heaven. A veneration which contents itself with honoring the saints without imitating their virtues is similar to a tree that produces leaves and blossoms but bears no fruit.

The saints themselves desire that we should follow their example. Each of them, so to say, exhorts us with St. Paul, "Be ye followers of me, as I also am of Christ" (1 Cor. 4:16). There is no age, no sex, no station in life for which the Catholic Church has not saints, whose example teaches us to avoid sin and to observe faithfully the commandments of God and the Church at this or that age, or in this or that station. Therefore the principal object of our invocation of the saints ought to be the obtaining of their help in following their example. Thus we shall move them to come to our aid all the more readily.

CHAPTER II

Efficacy of the Intercession of the Saints

*N*OTHING is more consoling and comforting than the assurance that in the saints of heaven we have powerful protectors and advocates with God. Through their intercession they obtain for us from Him the grace to lead a virtuous life and to gain heaven.

However, is there any reasonable doubt that the saints are able to render us such a service? In virtue of the communion of saints, which comprises the Church militant on earth, the Church suffering in purgatory, and the Church triumphant in heaven, all members of the Church are members of one body, whose head is Christ. Hence the saints are united with us in spirit, though separated from us in body. United with Christ, they are imbued with a superior knowledge, and through Him, the All-Knowing, they know everything that concerns us, and for which we have recourse to them in prayer.

Our confidence in the intercessory power of the saints is founded on their relation to God and to us. As friends of God they have influence with Him now, even more than during their sojourn on earth, because their intercessory power is one of their glorious prerogatives in heaven. Their love of God and their charity for their fellow-men, and the zeal for the salvation of souls resulting therefrom, together with their conformity with Christ, induces them to use their influence readily in our favor. Because God dispenses His gifts according to His own adorable will, it may please Him to grant a certain favor at the particular intercession of a certain saint; hence it is not superstition to invoke His aid in such cases. Moreover, we justly place our confidence in saints whom we have selected to be our special patrons, or who were given us as such by ecclesiastical authority.

By the intercession of the saints the mediatorship of Christ is not set aside or restricted. The power of intercession, the intercession itself, and its invocation are an effect of the grace of Christ; therefore He remains our only mediator. God remains Our Lord and Father, although men share in His lordship and paternity; for all power and authority comes from God, who is pleased to operate in His creatures through other creatures. Hence, only a dependent mediatorship can be ascribed to the saints. Whoever admits that the living can pray for each other can not denounce the intercession of the saints as an usurpation of the mediatorship of Christ. The saints are not the authors and dispensers of grace and heavenly gifts, but they are able to obtain them for us from God.

The saints, moreover, do not only pray for mankind in general, but for their clients in particular. As co-reigners with Christ, the denizens of heaven have knowledge of the conditions and events of His kingdom; hence the saints

may pray for us individually; therefore it is permissible
and profitable for us to invoke them. It is obvious that the
knowledge of individual occurrences does not mar the bliss
of the saints. How they gain this knowledge is not clear to
the spiritual authors; but most of them incline to the view
that they attain it by direct divine mediation. God reveals
our condition and our invocation to the saints.

Can we doubt the willingness of the saints to aid us by
their intercession? According to St. Paul, charity is the
greatest of all virtues. If, then, the saints, whilst on earth
loved their fellow-men, cared for and prayed for them,
how much more will they do so now, when their charity is
perfected? They, too, were pilgrims on earth, who had to
suffer the adversities and miseries of life and therefore know
by experience how sorely in need of divine assistance we
poor mortals are. Persons who have themselves experienced
trials have more compassion for the adversities of others.
Therefore it is certain that the saints have compassion on
us, that they wish our prayers to be heard and bring them
before the throne of God. "The saints," says St. Augustine,
"being secure of their eternal welfare, are intent upon ours."
Holy Scripture establishes this beyond doubt, saying that
the saints bring the prayers of the faithful before the throne
of God (Apoc. 5:8).

Or is there any one that doubts the *efficacy* of the
saints' prayer with God? At any rate, we must concede
that their prayer is more effectual than ours; for they are
confirmed in justice, and therefore friends and favorites of
God, whilst we are sinners, of whom Holy Scripture says,

"The Lord is far from the wicked, and He will hear the prayers of the just" (Prov. 15:29). On this subject, let us hear St. Basil in his panegyric on the Forty Martyrs: "You often wanted to find an intercessor: here you have forty who intercede unanimously for you. Are you in distress? Have recourse to the holy martyrs. Rejoicing, do the same. The former that you may find relief, the latter that you may continue to prosper. These saints hear the mother praying for her children, the wife invoking aid for her sick or absent husband. O brave and victorious band, protectors of mankind, generous intercessors when invoked, be our advocates with God!"

There is no doubt, then, that during our earthly pilgrimage the saints are our intercessors with God. True, we know that there is One who guides our destinies and whose providence watches over all; but who would not choose, also, to have a friend already abiding with God, sharing His bliss and confirmed for ever in His grace, and who therefore is in a position to aid us, and certainly will do so if we invoke Him?

The following is an example illustrating the power of the saints' intercession with God:

Basilides was one of the guards that led St. Potamiana to a martyr's death. Whilst the rest of the soldiers and the crowd of spectators insulted the holy virgin, he treated her with great respect and protected her from the assaults of the rabble. The martyr thanked him for his kindness, and promised to pray for him when she came into God's presence. A few days after her death the grace of God touched

Basilides' heart, and he professed himself a Christian. His comrades at first imagined that he was jesting. But when he persevered in the confession of the Faith, he was brought before the judge, who sentenced him to be beheaded next day. Taken to prison, he was baptized, and at the appointed time, executed.

What else but the intercession of the saint whom he had befriended obtained for this heathen the grace of the Faith and martyrdom? Convinced of the power of the intercession of the saints, Origen writes: "I will fall on my knees, and because I am unworthy to pray to God on account of my sins, I will invoke all the saints to come to my aid. O ye saints of God, I, filled with sadness, sighing and weeping, implore you; intercede for me, a miserable sinner, with the Lord of mercies!"

CHAPTER III

For What the Intercession of the Saints May and Should be Invoked

*I*T IS obvious that there are objects to attain for which we ought not to pray. We shall try to specify them as follows:

1. *We may not pray for things that are evil or injurious in themselves, or injurious on account of circumstances.* Amongst these are comprised all those that are opposed to the salvation of the person praying, or of some one else. It is contrary to the very idea of prayer that God should grant to His creature anything evil, anything that is in itself, and not only by abuse, harmful. Prayer, according to the rules of morality, must have for its object only the attainment of whatever is good and profitable, and only then is it heard by God.

2. *Things completely indifferent are not comprised in the efficacy of prayer. Hence prayer imploring for temporal goods is heard only inasmuch as they relate to the salvation of souls.* Reason, as well as faith, teaches us that God orders all His actions first for the promotion of His glory, and secondly for the salvation of souls. Matters, therefore, that are either in general, or

on account of circumstances, positively indifferent, must be excluded from the general plan of God's providence when there is question of His positive agency, and not simply of His permission. It is obvious that temporal goods, such as health, wealth, etc., are classed with things indifferent, in as far as they are not connected with the moral order.

Thus considered, the various goods of the temporal order do, or at least may, under certain conditions, cooperate unto man's salvation, and then they belong to the supernatural order. As such, the efficacy of prayer in their regard must be judged according to the principles applying to the latter.

3. *All those things which any one can obtain himself without extraordinary effort, are not comprised within the scope of prayer.* This restriction results from the very nature of prayer. Obviously, prayer is not the only means by which man can obtain those things which, on the one hand, he momentarily does not possess, and which, on the other hand, are necessary or advantageous for his supernatural life. As a rule, man can, by labor and application, procure his sustenance. Persons unable to work can have recourse to the charity of their fellow-men, and will, as a rule, find the necessary assistance. In regard to salvation, it must first be ascertained whether in many or at least in some cases, the faithful co-operation with the graces which God gives to all men is not sufficient.

Considered from this view, we may, and even must, in a certain sense say: When there is question of attaining specified goods and specified graces, prayer is often not the primary, but only the secondary and subordinate means. From this premise follows that God in His wise providence does not have regard for our prayer when we easily can help ourselves, either by our own exertion and industry, or by the faithful cooperation with graces already received, or by the reception of the holy sacraments. This self-evident idea is expressed in Holy Scripture as follows, "Because of the cold the sluggard would not plow; he shall beg therefore in the summer, and it shall not be given him" (Prov. 20:4). For this reason formal miracles are, as a rule, not to be expected from the efficacy of prayer. God ordained the world and its course in such a manner, that mankind in general and each individual in particular can be provided, without the intervention of a miracle, with all things necessary for their temporal and eternal welfare.

Theologians, therefore, teach that to ask God for a miracle, generally, is the same as to tempt Him. This rule, however, admits of exceptions. And if we may, in exceptional cases, ask for miracles, we may, logically, expect them; for miracles in general are not excluded from the plan of divine Providence. They are rather an essential part of the existing order of God's government of the world. At most we may say: As miracles of their nature belong among the extraordinary manifestations of Providence, they are not obtained by the prayer of each and every one, but only in exceptional cases.

However, if we consider how feeble and helpless man's nature is, even with the assistance of divine grace, we may not apply the above principles too strictly. This, for the following reason: Cases in which we can not help ourselves with the aid of the grace given us are rare. Therefore God gives us, in reward of our confident prayer, not only that which is strictly necessary, but also that which is profitable and conducive to our welfare. This being so, the logical deduction is, that God is willing to hear our prayer not only when we, of ourselves, are totally incapable of helping ourselves, but also when great difficulties beset us in this our self-help. Hence, in a certain sense, we may maintain that in the work of our salvation prayer and its efficacy must be considered, together with the sacraments, as one of the chief means, and not as a mere accessory.

This limitation of the main principle is founded on the generality of the divine promises concerning the hearing of prayer, and on the great goodness and bounty of God in which these promises originated. When man, making use of all the means placed at his disposal, can not help himself, a cry for help is sent to Heaven is not presumptuous or unreasonable, and therefore the hope of being heard is not unfounded or in vain.

CHAPTER IV

The Qualities of Prayer

*F*OR greater convenience of explanation, we condense the various qualities of prayer taught by theologians as conditions of its efficacy into the following four: (1) Devotion; (2) Confidence; (3) Perseverance; (4) Resignation to the will of God.

Treating of prayer, some theological authors demand, above all, the intention of praying. This intention is indeed so necessary that it does not belong to the qualities or attributes of prayer, but to its very essence. For whosoever has not the intention or will to pray may recite a formula of prayer with the greatest attention, yet does not really and truly pray.

Again, the teachers of the spiritual life tell us that prayer must be "in the name of Jesus." This being a condition insisted upon by our divine Lord Himself, it also belongs to the essence of prayer. It means that we offer up our prayer to God in the name of Jesus His Son, that is, with reference to Him and in the firm confidence that we shall be heard on His account and because of His promises. Again, to pray in the name of Jesus means to pray according to His manner and in His spirit.

We now proceed to explain the qualities of true prayer:

1. *Devotion.*—What is meant by devotion in prayer? Devotion in prayer means: (a) that our prayer must be *attentive*; that is, the person praying must direct his thoughts as uninterruptedly as possible to his prayer, *viz.*, to the formula he uses to state the object of his desires, and above all to God, to whom his prayer is directed. (b) The person praying must know and acknowledge his own needs, and that of himself he has no claims whatsoever on God, and thus engender in himself sentiments of true humility. (c) These sentiments must, moreover, embrace reverence for God and the acknowledgment of dependence on Him, thus giving to prayer the character of piety. (d) All this must culminate in full abandonment to God, the Giver of all good things. This abandonment is an essential part of our divine cult.

As to the question whether devotion, and what grade of it, is necessary in prayer, and whether prayer without it loses its entire efficacy, and especially its imploring efficiency, it is evident that prayer without devotion is ineffective; it is simulation. An example of this, that is, of a man pretending to pray and not praying in reality, is given us in the parable of the Pharisee and the Publican (Luke 18:10-12). To determine accurately what grade of devotion, that is, what degree of attention, humility, and piety is necessary to render prayer from a formality into a reality, is possible only when all the circumstances, dispositions, and qualities of mind of the person praying can be taken into account. Suffice it to remark that when all the other conditions, together with the intention of praying, combine, strict but reliable theologians declare that the true essence of prayer is compatible with a less degree of attention and recollection.

2. *Confidence.*—There is no doubt but that strong confidence, or the firm hope of being heard, contributes much to the perfection of prayer and renders it especially effective. Therefore confidence, like devotion or attention, must be reckoned among the essential qualities or attributes of prayer. For it is inconceivable that a rational being should resolve on presenting a petition when he has not the least hope of its being granted. In this case his petition would be entirely useless, and therefore irrational. Again, it is inconceivable that God should have regard for a prayer or the petition of a man who has absolutely no confidence in His mercy. A prayer without confidence is hypocrisy, rather than true and sincere supplication. If we address a petition to God without the confidence that He can and will grant it, He must rather feel offended than honored thereby. How, then, shall He feel moved to grant us new benefits? If we nevertheless receive them, it is the effect of His bountiful goodness, and not the result of our sham prayer.

Therefore, to be effective, our prayer must be inspired by confidence. The apostle St. James inculcates this, saying: "But let him ask in faith, nothing wavering; for he that wavereth is like a wave of the sea, which is moved and carried about by the wind. Therefore let not that man think that he shall receive any thing of the Lord" (James 1:6-7). By these words the apostle designates not a common and ordinary confidence, but one firm and steadfast. At the same time he speaks in general; that is, his words have reference not only to extraordinary petitions, but to everything for which we are accustomed to pray.

Moreover, the explicit and positive promises made by Christ in regard to prayer manifestly have the purpose of inspiring the person praying with firm confidence and the sure hope of being heard. If, then, our prayer be wanting in this quality, we do not pray in the spirit of Christ, nor in the terms in which we ought to pray, and can not claim the fulfilment of His promises.

3. *Perseverance.*—To understand properly in how far perseverance is a quality of prayer, we must, above all, know what may be the objects of our prayer. Of these there are three classes. To the first class belong those cases in which a person needs divine help at the present moment or at least at a time definitely near, and seeks it through prayer. Such a petition would be, for instance, to obtain the necessary and effective aid of divine grace for overcoming an existing transient temptation, or the conversion of a certain sinner approaching death. To the second class belongs the avoidance of temporal evils, or of continuous temptations, or the conversion of a certain sinner now in good health. To the third class belong such benefits which can be granted only for a later period, perhaps at the hour of death. The grace of final perseverance is the foremost among these.

Having stated the preliminary conditions, the answer to the question of perseverance in prayer is:

(a.) Inasmuch as our prayer is directed toward the attainment of benefits of the first class, that is, of graces which we need immediately, perseverance can obviously not be an essential condition of our prayer. Either we can not attain our object by prayer, or a transient prayer which has the other necessary qualities must suffice for its attainment. The first supposition is contrary to the divine promises; therefore the alternative must stand.

(b.) When there is question of benefits and graces of the second and third class, we must concede that perseverance or continuance in prayer is neither impossible, nor is it unreasonable. God is willing to grant us His almighty help, but at the same time He desires that we, being convinced of its necessity, implore it all the more eagerly, and thereby become more worthy to receive it when He shall be pleased to grant our petitions. Therefore

4. *Resignation to the will of God* is a necessary condition for the efficacy of our prayer. This quality of our prayer needs no lengthy explanation; its application to prayer is self-evident.

Finally the petition for a certain benefit, in order to be reasonable and permissible, must include the following two attributes: (a) The object prayed for must not be harmful, but profitable; (b) it must not be opposed to the will of God.

Conclusions.—Careful observation will convince us that prayer is often wanting in one or more of the above qualities. Often that which one seeks to obtain by prayer is not promotive of God's glory and of the salvation of souls, even considered from a human point of view, much less in the designs of Providence.

In cases where the object of prayer in itself presents

no difficulties, it is often defective for want of devotion or perseverance. But oftenest our prayer is wanting in confidence and trust, which want originates in the feeble faith of the person praying, or in too little reliance on the promises of Christ and in the merits of His redemption. Thus there is nothing to surprise us if we are not heard.

Again, we must never forget that very many, and generally the most precious gifts of divine grace are bestowed secretly. Remember the many and great benefits conferred daily and hourly by God on mankind, universally and individually. Considering them, it is presumption to maintain that in a special case the prayer of the Church, or of a community, or of an individual, was not granted. The opposite is fully proved by the goodness, bounty, and mercy which God shows so profusely to us.

We must, moreover, never lose sight of the principle that the promises made to prayer concern directly only the supernatural order of salvation. To the goods of the temporal order they are applicable only relatively. If we, therefore, experience that our prayers relative to temporal things remain unheard, we must, instead of doubting the divine promises, be firmly convinced that the attainment of the object for which we prayed was, under the circumstances, not conducive to our real welfare. We must, moreover, be convinced that God, in order not to leave our petition ungranted, conferred on us some other real benefit.

Finally, when the refusal of our prayer is clearly and unmistakably established, the reasons for this may be the following: (a) Perhaps the person praying was wanting in effort, or in cooperation with graces formerly received, a deficiency which can not be repaired by prayer alone. (b) Or the prayer itself is wanting in one or the other necessary qualities, especially in confidence. (c) God does not intend to refuse the desired grace, but, for reasons of His own, delays it. (d) God gives us in place of what we asked some other grace more salutary to us.

PART II

Mary, the Help of Christians

Novenas in Preparation for the Principal Feasts of the Blessed Virgin

"Holy Mary, aid the miserable, assist the desponding, strengthen the weak, pray for the people, plead for the clergy, intercede for the devout female sex. Let all who have recourse to thee experience the efficacy of thy help!"

—HOLY CHURCH.

Rules for the Proper Observance of Novenas

BY ST. ALPHONSUS LIGUORI

1. THE soul must be in the state of grace; for the devotion of a sinful heart pleases neither God nor the saints.

2. We must persevere, that is, the prayers for each day of the novena must never be omitted.

3. If possible, we should visit a church every day, and there implore the favor we desire.

4. Every day we ought to perform certain specified acts of exterior self-denial and interior mortification, in order to prepare us thereby for the reception of grace.

5. It is most important that we receive holy communion when making a novena. Therefore prepare yourself well for it.

6. After obtaining the desired grace for which the novena was made, do not omit to return thanks to God and to the saint through whose intercession your prayers were heard.

On the Manner of Reading the Meditations and Observing the Practices

*H*OLY SCRIPTURE says, "Before prayer prepare thy soul; and be not as a man that tempteth God" (Eccles. 18:23). Therefore place yourself in the presence of God, invoke the assistance of the Holy Ghost, and make a most sincere act of contrition for your sins. Offer up to God your will, your intellect, and your memory, so that your prayer may be pleasing to God and serve to promote your spiritual welfare.

Then read the meditation slowly, reflecting on each point of the thought or mystery treated, and consider what you can learn from it, and for what grace you ought to implore God. This is the principal object to be attained by mental prayer.

Never rise from your prayer without having formed some special resolution for practical observance. The practices at the end of each consideration in the following novenas will aid you to do so. Finally, ask for grace to carry out effectively your good purposes, and thank God for enlightening your mind during the meditation.

INTRODUCTION

Mary, the Help of Christians

NO CATHOLIC denies that Our Lord Jesus Christ is the only mediator through whose merits we became reconciled to God. Nevertheless, it is a doctrine of our faith that God willingly grants us grace if the saints, and especially the Blessed Virgin Mary, the queen of saints, intercede for us. If the saints, during their life on earth, were so potent with God that through their prayers the blind obtained sight, the deaf hearing, and the dumb speech, that the sick of all conditions were healed, the dead restored to life, and the most obstinate sinners converted; if thousands of other miracles in the order of nature and of grace were performed through their intercession; what, then, will not *she* obtain for us from God, whose virtue and merits transcend those of all the saints, and who did more for the greater honor and glory of God than they all? Mary is the queen of saints not only because she is the Mother of the Most High, but also because her sanctity is more perfect than theirs, and she therefore thrones above them all in heaven. Hence the favor with which God regards her, and consequently the power of her intercession with Him is so much the greater.

If Mary's sanctity thus impressively illustrates the potency of her intercession, the contemplation of her dignity as the Mother of God does still more so. Mary brought forth Him who is the Almighty. She calls Him her Son, who by the word of His omnipotence created from out of nothing the whole world with all its beauties, and who can call into being countless millions of other worlds. She calls Him her Son, whose throne is heaven and whose footstool is the earth, who governs all nature with almighty power and reveals His name to mankind through the most astounding miracles. In a word, Mary calls Him her Son, whose omnipotence fills heaven and earth; and this great, almighty God, who honors her as His Mother and has wrought in her such great things, will He not heed her word of intercession, and hear her pleading for those who have recourse to her? On earth He was subject to her. Her intercession moved Him to exercise His omnipotent power at the wedding feast at Cana; and now, when He has glorified and raised her up so high He would let her invoke Him in vain? No, it is inconceivable that God should not hear the prayers of His Mother!

The holy Fathers and Doctors of the Church vie with each other in proclaiming the power of Mary's intercession with the Heart of her divine Son. Some say that having been subject to her on earth, He desires to be so in heaven, inasmuch as to refuse her nothing she asks. Hence St. Bernard calls her the "Intercessory Omnipotence."

Indeed, when all the angels and saints in heaven join in supplication to God, their prayers are but those of servants; but when Mary prays her intercession is that of His Mother.

Therefore we can not sufficiently thank God for having given us in Mary so powerful an advocate. St. Bernard aptly says: "The angel announces, 'thou hast found grace before God.' O supreme happiness! Mary shall always find grace. And what else could we wish? If we seek grace, let us seek it through Mary; for what she seeks, she finds. Never can she plead ineffectually."

God, then, who in His infinite mercy has been pleased to provide for all our needs, desires through Mary to console us, to comfort us, to remove all distrust, to strengthen our hope. How consoling to him who calls upon God in sore distress, or implores His pardon for sins committed, is the thought that at the throne of divine Mercy he has in Mary an advocate as mighty as she is gracious, who supplements his great unworthiness by her sublime dignity, and who makes good the defects of his prayer by her intercession! Therefore St. Bonaventure exclaims: "Verily, great is Our Lord's mercy! That we, through fear of our divine Judge, depart not forever from Him, He gave us His own Mother for our advocate and mediatrix of grace."

I.

Novena in Honor of the Immaculate Conception of the Blessed Virgin Mary

INDULGENCES

TO ALL the faithful who by themselves or with others, in church or at home, with at least contrite heart and devotion, shall make this novena: (1) 300 days indulgence for each of the nine days; (2) a plenary indulgence on one day of the novena or of the eight days following it. (Pius IX, January 5, 1849.)

Conditions: Confession, communion, and prayer, according to the intentions of the Holy Father.

Remark.—Whenever, in the following pages, an indulgence is said to be granted "under the usual conditions," these conditions are the same as above.

Note.—The above indulgences may also be gained for making the novena at any other time of the year, and are not attached to any prescribed formula of prayer. The same applies to all other novenas in honor of the Blessed Virgin.

✄ FIRST DAY ✄

The Predestination of the Blessed Virgin Mary

PREPARATORY PRAYER

*I*N THY conception, O Virgin Mary, thou wast immaculate; pray for us to the Father, whose Son Jesus, conceived in thy womb by the Holy Ghost, thou didst bring forth.

Indulgence. 200 days, every time. (Pius VI, November 21, 1793.)

MEDITATION

*H*OLY Church, our Mother, purposely gathered into the season of Advent everything which might contribute to assist us in preparing for the coming of the Redeemer. Purity of heart is the most necessary and helpful requirement for receiving God worthily, and for participating in the fruits of our Redemption through Christ. To remind us of this, Holy Church celebrates the feast of the Immaculate Conception of the Blessed Virgin Mary, this primary feast of purity, in Advent.

The Church, moreover, intends to remind us that the coming of Christ, our promised Redeemer, depended on the consent of the Blessed Virgin. The Redeemer could not appear before she was born of whom He was to be born. The aurora must precede the rising sun. Thus also Mary, the spiritual aurora, had to be conceived and born before the appearance of the Sun of Justice in this world.

PRACTICE

*I*N MARY appeared the woman who was to crush the serpent's head, who was to repair by her willing co-operation with God's designs the damage wrought by the disobedience of our first parents, and who was to become our mother and mighty advocate with God.

The designs of God concerning Mary were fully accomplished. God also has designs concerning us. Our life was planned by Him from all eternity, and we were destined to co-operate with Him harmoniously and conscientiously in working out our salvation. Have we corresponded with God's designs? Did we not oppose them by yielding to our evil inclinations and passions? What a disparity between God's intentions concerning us and our own co-operation, between His merciful designs and our cowardly resistance to them!

PRAYER OF THE CHURCH

O GOD, who through the immaculate conception of the Virgin didst prepare a worthy dwelling-place for Thy divine Son; grant that, as in view of Thy Son Thou didst preserve her from all taint, so Thou wouldst vouchsafe unto us that cleansed from all sin by her intercession we too may arrive at Thine eternal glory. Through the same Christ our Lord. Amen.

Litany of Loreto (p. 301).

PRAYER

*B*EHOLD, Virgin immaculate, at thy sacred feet I bow, while my heart overflows with joy in union with thine own, because from eternity thou wast the Mother-elect of the eternal Word, and was preserved stainless from the taint of Adam's sin. Forever praised, forever blessed be the Most Holy Trinity, who in thy conception poured out upon thy soul the riches of that matchless privilege. I humbly pray thee, most gracious Mother, obtain for me the grace to overcome the bitter results of original sin. Make me victorious over them, that I may never cease to love my God.

Hail Mary, etc.

EJACULATION

O Mary, conceived without sin, pray for us who have recourse to thee!

Indulgence. 100 days, once a day. (Leo XIII, March 25, 1884.)

✎ SECOND DAY ✎

Mary's Immaculate Conception

PREPARATORY PRAYER (p. 30).

MEDITATION

*A*CCORDING to the definition of Pope Pius IX, the immaculate conception of the Blessed Virgin Mary is that privilege by which she was preserved, in view of the merits of our Saviour Jesus Christ, from original sin in the first moment of her conception.

By solemnly proclaiming the dogma of Mary's immaculate conception, the Church confirmed anew the fundamental principles of Christianity which in our times are so frequently attacked, derided, or forgotten. God reserved the solemn proclamation of this dogma, which seemingly has no practical bearing on the Christian life, for our age, to recall to our mind the doctrines resulting from it.

PRACTICE

*T*HE most important of these doctrines is that of original sin, which to-day is rejected by many as a debasement of human nature, and is forgotten by others as having no practical influence on our moral state. By the promulgation of the doctrine of the immaculate conception of the Blessed Virgin Mary, the Church solemnly declares and defines as an article of faith, that the Blessed Virgin

Mary is conceived without the stain of original sin by a special privilege and grace of God. If, then, Mary's sinlessness is an exception, the general rule remains in force, and all other human beings enter this world in the state of original sin.

Thus, by the proclamation of the dogma of the immaculate conception, the Church combats human pride and sensuality, the foremost vices of the age.

PRAYER OF THE CHURCH (p. 31).

Litany of Loreto (p. 301).

PRAYER

*M*ARY, unsullied lily of heavenly purity, I rejoice with thee, because at thy conception's earliest dawn thou wast full of grace and endowed with the perfect use of reason. I thank and adore the ever-blessed Trinity, who gave thee such high gifts. I am overwhelmed with shame in thy presence, to see myself so poor in grace. O thou who wast filled with heavenly grace, impart some portion of it to my soul, and make me share the treasures of thy immaculate conception.

Hail Mary, etc.

EJACULATION (p. 32).

⟡ THIRD DAY ⟡

Mary, the Victrix of Satan

PREPARATORY PRAYER (p. 30).

MEDITATION

*T*HE immaculate conception of the Blessed Virgin
Mary inaugurated the fulfilment of the divine
promise made to our first parents in paradise in the words
addressed to the serpent: "I shall put enmities between thee
and the woman, and thy seed and her seed; she shall crush
thy head" (Gen. 3:15). Mary is the woman in whom Satan
never had a part. Her intimate connection with God was
announced by the angel: "Hail, full of grace; the Lord is
with thee." Now was fulfilled the saying of the Psalmist,
"The Most High hath sanctified His own tabernacle. God
is in the midst thereof, it shall not be moved: God will help
it in the morning early" (Ps. 45:5-6). Mary was chosen to be
the glorious tabernacle of the Son of God "in the morning
early," that is, in the first moment of her existence. God
called her into being that she might assume the exalted
dignity of the Mother of His Son, and therefore granted
her the singular privilege of exemption from original sin.
In her were fulfilled Solomon's prophetic words of praise,
"Thou art all fair, O my love, and there is not a spot in
thee" (Cant. 4:7). It was in view of her Son's merits applied

to her beforehand that God thus produced in her the image of the new man regenerated in the Holy Ghost.

PRACTICE

*T*HE spirit of darkness holds mankind enslaved, but one human being escapes him. A destructive fire lays waste the whole earth, but one tree remains unscathed. A terrible tyrant conquers the whole world, but one fortified city repels his assaults. This human being retaining liberty, this tree escaping destruction, this city repelling the enemy's attack is the Blessed Virgin Mary.

Will the almighty and merciful God, who has accomplished such great things in Mary, who has selected her for His Mother, not listen to her prayers when she intercedes for us? St. William of Paris exclaims: "No other created being can obtain for us so many and so great graces from God as His Mother. By the all-powerful might of her intercession He honors her not only as His handmaid, but also as His Mother." Therefore we ought not be surprised when the holy Fathers maintain that a single sigh of Mary is more effective with God than the combined intercession of all the angels and saints. If, then, Mary's power is so great, she will surely hear us when we invoke her help in our combat with Satan. Having conquered him herself, she will also help us to conquer him.

PRAYER OF THE CHURCH (p. 31).

Litany of Loreto (p. 301).

PRAYER

*M*ARY, thou mystical rose of purity, my heart rejoices with thine at the glorious triumph which thou didst gain over the infernal serpent by thy immaculate conception, and because thou wast conceived without stain of original sin. I thank and praise with my whole heart the ever-blessed Trinity, who granted thee this glorious privilege; and I pray thee to obtain for me strength to overcome all the wiles of the infernal foe, and never to stain my soul with sin. Be thou mine aid; make me, by thy protection, victorious over the common foe of our eternal welfare.

Hail Mary, etc.

EJACULATION (p. 32).

❧ FOURTH DAY ❧

Mary without Actual Sin

PREPARATORY PRAYER (p. 30).

MEDITATION

*M*ARY conceived without sin is the most blessed daughter of the eternal Father, the real and true Mother of the divine Son, the elect spouse of the Holy Ghost. But in the world, in what condition do we behold her? She dwells not in a splendid palace; she is not surrounded by a retinue of servants ready at every moment to do her bidding; she is not exempt from trials and suffering. On the contrary, she is poor; she lives in obscurity, and suffered so much on earth that, without shedding her blood, she merits to be styled the queen of martyrs. Her heart was transfixed with the sword of sorrow. Mary is not exempt from tribulations and adversity; but one thing God does not permit to touch her, *i.e.*, sin. Hence Holy Church applies to her the words, "Thou art all fair, O my love, and there is not a spot in thee" (Cant. 4:7).

PRACTICE

THOUGH we were not preserved from sin like Mary, yet God in His ineffable goodness and mercy granted us the grace to be cleansed from sin and to be clothed with the garment of sanctifying grace in Baptism. No treasure of the world can be compared with this prerogative. But as we bear this grace in a fragile vase, we must be most careful to protect and preserve it in ourselves and others from all danger. Let the Blessed Virgin Mary be our example. Well knowing the inestimable value of the grace conferred upon her, she guarded it with the greatest care. Although exempt from concupiscence and "full of grace," she was so distrustful of herself as if she were in continual danger. How much more, then, must we use precaution to preserve in ourselves and in others this treasure of grace, since we feel in ourselves constantly the law of the flesh, which resists the law of the spirit, and urges us on to evil, whilst the world and the devil never weary in placing snares for us in order to accomplish our ruin. Therefore let us have recourse to Mary, and invoking her aid bravely resist all temptations.

PRAYER OF THE CHURCH (p. 31).

Litany of Loreto (p. 301).

PRAYER

*M*IRROR of holy purity, Mary, Virgin immaculate, great is my joy while I consider that, from thy immaculate conception, the most sublime and perfect virtues were infused into thy soul, and with them all the gifts of the Holy Ghost. I thank and praise the Most Holy Trinity, who bestowed on thee these high privileges. I pray thee, gentle Mother, obtain for me grace to practise virtue, and to make me worthy to become partaker of the gifts and graces of the Holy Ghost.

Hail Mary, etc.

EJACULATION (p. 32).

FIFTH DAY

Mary, Full of Grace

PREPARATORY PRAYER (p. 30).

MEDITATION

SATAN'S relation to God as His child was severed by sin. The beautiful image of God imprinted on man's soul was disfigured by it. But with the immaculate conception of Mary, a being full of grace, an object of God's supreme complacency entered this world. After the lapse of four thousand years God, in His wisdom, power, and love, for the first time again created a human being in that state in which He had originally created our first parents. Mary, from the first moment of her existence was, in virtue of the sanctifying grace infused into her soul, most intimately united with God, and endowed with the most precious gifts of heaven. Because she was predestined to become the Mother of the Redeemer of mankind, it was befitting that she should unite in herself all the gifts becoming to such an ineffable dignity. Hence she surpassed in grace and holiness all other created beings, and was consecrated a worthy temple of the incarnate Word. Therefore she was saluted by the angel as "full of grace," and the Church, in our behalf, addresses the Almighty: "O God, who through the immaculate conception of the Virgin didst prepare a worthy dwelling-place for Thy divine Son; grant, that, as in view of the death of that Son Thou didst preserve her from all taint, so Thou wouldst vouchsafe unto us that, cleansed from all sin by her intercession, we too may arrive at Thine eternal glory."

PRACTICE

*T*HE world considers men according to their rank and station, their wealth and knowledge. God recognizes in them but one difference, that caused by the presence or absence of sanctifying grace in their soul. A soul in the state of sanctifying grace is God's friend; without it, His enemy. A man dying in the state of sanctifying grace is sure of eternal bliss. Therefore we ought to prize this grace above all else, and do everything in our power to preserve it. St. Leo exhorts us, "Recognize, O man, thy dignity! As thou hast received divine grace, beware of returning to your former sinful condition by a wicked life."

PRAYER OF THE CHURCH (p. 31).

Litany of Loreto (p.301).

PRAYER

*M*ARY, bright moon of purity, I rejoice with thee, because the mystery of thy immaculate conception was the beginning of salvation for the race of man and the joy of the whole world. I thank and bless the ever-blessed Trinity, who thus did magnify and glorify thee; and I beg of thee to obtain for me the grace so to profit by thy dear Son's death and passion, that His precious blood may not have been shed in vain for me upon the cross, but that, after a holy life, I may reach heaven in safety.

Hail Mary, etc.

EJACULATION (p. 32).

❧ SIXTH DAY ❧

Mary, Our Refuge

PREPARATORY PRAYER (p. 30).

MEDITATION

WE CARRY the precious treasure of sanctifying grace in a frail vessel. Our inclination to evil remains with us, and continues to impel us to that which is forbidden. On whom shall we call for aid? Call on Mary! She is conceived without sin. She, the lily among thorns, who never lost God's friendship, is our advocate. Let her, who was found worthy to become the Mother of our Redeemer, inspire you with trust and confidence. The Church invokes her as the refuge of sinners, and under no other title does she show her love for us more convincingly and her power with God more efficiently.

PRACTICE

WE MAY trust confidently in Mary's intercession and aid in all temptations and trials, if we but have recourse to her. Therefore St. John Damascene writes: "Come to my aid, O Mother of my Redeemer! Thou art my help, my consolation in life. Come to my aid, and I shall escape unscorched from the fire of temptation; amongst a thousand I shall remain unharmed; I shall brave the storms of assault unwrecked. Thy name is my shield, thy help my armor, thy protection my defense. With thee I boldly attack the enemy and drive him off in confusion; through thee I shall achieve a triumphant victory." In all temptations, therefore, let us have recourse to Mary and through her intercession we shall overcome them.

PRAYER OF THE CHURCH (p.31).

Litany of Loreto (p. 301).

PRAYER

*M*ARY immaculate, most brilliant star of purity, I rejoice with thee because thy immaculate conception has bestowed upon the angels in paradise the greatest joy. I thank and bless the ever-blessed Trinity, who enriched thee with this high privilege. O let me, too, one day enter into this heavenly joy, in the company of angels, that I may praise and bless thee, world without end.

Hail Mary, etc.

EJACULATION (p. 32).

☙ SEVENTH DAY ❧

Mary, the Mother of Chastity

PREPARATORY PRAYER (p. 30).

MEDITATION

*H*OLY Scripture and the Fathers agree in the statement that the Blessed Virgin Mary made the vow of perpetual virginity. For when the Archangel Gabriel brought God's message to the immaculate spouse of St. Joseph, that she was to become the Mother of the Most High, she asked, "How shall this be done, because I know not man?" (Luke 1:34). Indeed, Mary would not have been, in the full and most excellent sense of the word, the "Virgin of virgins," had she not from her own free choice vowed her virginity to God.

During the whole Christian era there have been heroic souls who made the vow of perpetual chastity, consecrating themselves to God. Trusting in the powerful protection of the immaculate Virgin, they persevered in their resolve to bear this priceless treasure before God's throne despite the dangers of the world, the temptations of concupiscence, and the assaults of hell, and with the help of the queen of virgins they achieved a triumphant victory.

PRACTICE

SINCE the fall of Adam our senses are in rebellion against the law of God. "I see another law in my members, fighting against the law of my mind, and captivating me in the law of sin" (Rom. 7:23). Chastity is the virtue which causes us the greatest struggles. St. Augustine says: "The fiercest of all combats is the one for the preservation of chastity, and we must engage in it every day." Fierce as this combat is, the aid which Mary gives her children to achieve victory is all-powerful. She sustains them by her maternal love and protection. Those who lead a chaste life receive the Divine Spirit, are happy in this life, and will receive a special crown in heaven.

Among the means for the preservation of chastity, the following are specially recommended: The assiduous and constant practice of self-denial; the frequentation of the sacraments; the daily invocation of Mary for her aid and protection; scrupulous avoidance of the occasions of sin. St. Chrysostom writes: "He errs who believes that he can overcome his sensual propensities and preserve chastity by his own efforts. God's mercy must extinguish nature's ardor." Have recourse to the intercession of the immaculate Virgin and rest assured that you will obtain this mercy.

PRAYER OF THE CHURCH (p. 31).

Litany of Loreto (p. 301).

PRAYER

*M*ARY immaculate, rising morn of purity, I rejoice with thee, gazing in wonder upon thy soul confirmed in grace from the very first moment of thy conception, and rendered inaccessible to sin. I thank and magnify the ever-blessed Trinity, who chose thee from all our race for this special privilege. Holy Virgin, obtain for me utter and constant hatred of all sin above every other evil, and let me rather die than ever again fall into sin.

Hail Mary, etc.

EJACULATION (p. 32).

✍ EIGHTH DAY ✍

The Image of the Immaculate Conception

PREPARATORY PRAYER (p. 30).

MEDITATION

*C*HRISTIAN art represents the Immaculate Conception as follows: The Blessed Virgin appears standing on a globe, about which is coiled a serpent holding an apple in its mouth. One of Mary's feet rests upon the serpent, the other is placed on the moon. Her eyes are raised toward heaven; her hands are either joined in prayer, or she holds a lily in her right, and places the left on her breast. Her dress is white; her ample mantle is of blue color. A crown of twelve stars encircles her head. These emblems typify in a most striking manner Mary's power and glory. "And a great sign appeared in heaven. A woman clothed with the sun, and the moon under her feet, and on her head a crown of twelve stars" (Apoc. 12:1).

PRACTICE

*T*HE representation of the Immaculate Conception is very instructive. (1) Mary appears standing on the globe. This signifies that being human, she belongs to the earth, and yet is exalted above the world and sin; also, that she trampled under foot earthly possessions, vanities, and joys. (2) A serpent is coiled about the globe, bearing an apple in its mouth. This reminds us of the fall of our first parents, and of the consequences of their sin. (3) Mary's foot rests on the serpent, indicating that she never was under Satan's dominion, but was preserved from sin in the first moment of her existence. (4) Mary stands on the moon. The moon, on account of its changes, is an emblem of inconstancy. We see it at Mary's feet, to be reminded that we ought to be constant in faith and virtue. (5) Mary wears a crown, to indicate that she is a queen. The crown is composed of twelve stars: she is the queen of heaven. (6) Mary's dress is white, to denote her spotless purity and innocence. (7) She folds her hands in prayer, reminding us to imitate her example. (8) Or she holds a lily in her right hand, to indicate her virginity and chastity, and the sweet odor of her virtues. (9) Mary's mantle is blue, which color is emblematic of humility. Its folds are ample, to remind us that all who have recourse to her find a secure refuge in all dangers and necessities.

Therefore let us invoke her intercession in the words of Holy Church: "We fly to thy patronage, O holy Mother of God. Despise not our petitions, and deliver us from all danger, O ever glorious and blessed Virgin!"

PRAYER OF THE CHURCH (p. 31).

Litany of Loreto (p. 301).

PRAYER

*O*SPOTLESS sun! O Virgin Mary! I congratulate thee. I rejoice with thee because in thy conception God gave thee grace greater and more boundless than He ever shed on all His angels and all the saints, together with all their merits. I am thankful and I marvel at the surpassing beneficence of the ever-blessed Trinity, who conferred on thee this privilege. O make me correspond with the grace of God and never abuse it. Change this heart of mine; make me now begin to amend my life.

Hail Mary, etc.

EJACULATION (p. 32).

❧ NINTH DAY ❧

The Feast of the Immaculate Conception

PREPARATORY PRAYER (p. 30).

MEDITATION

*E*ARLY in the Christian era the feast of Mary's immaculate conception was observed in several countries. St. Anselm, Bishop of Canterbury, introduced it in England. A great number of Popes favored the doctrine of Mary's absolute sinlessness, and the adversaries of the Immaculate Conception were bidden to be silent and not publicly assert or defend their view. In 1477, Pope Sixtus IV prescribed the feast of the Immaculate Conception to be observed in the whole Church, and made it obligatory on priests to recite the special canonical office and to use the Mass formula published for the purpose. In 1846, the bishops of the United States assembled in plenary council in Baltimore elected the Blessed Virgin under the title of her immaculate conception Patroness of the Church in their country.

Finally, Pope Pius IX, after consulting with the bishops throughout the world, and having implored the Holy Ghost for His guidance in prayer and fasting, promulgated, on December 8, 1854, the dogma which teaches that the Blessed Virgin Mary was in her conception, by a special grace and through the merits of her divine Son, preserved from the stain of original sin. This doctrine was received throughout the world with ineffable joy; and, indeed, no one who loves the Blessed Virgin can help rejoicing at this her most glorious privilege.

The invocation, "Queen conceived without the stain of original sin," was added to the Litany of Loreto. In 1866, at the Second Plenary Council in Baltimore, the feast of the Immaculate Conception was raised to the rank of a holyday of obligation for the Church of the United States.

PRACTICE

*J*N THE inscrutable designs of His providence God ordained that the mystery of the immaculate conception of the Blessed Virgin Mary should be proclaimed an article of faith as late as the middle of the nineteenth century. But, then, its proclamation was attended by circumstances that undeniably proved that the Holy Father in pronouncing the dogma had been inspired and guided by the Holy Ghost.

Let us praise God and thank Him for bestowing this glorious privilege on our beloved Mother, and let us often invoke her under her favorite title, the Immaculate Conception. St. Alphonsus Liguori tells us that the devotion to this mystery is especially efficacious in overcoming the temptations of impurity. Therefore he was accustomed to recommend to his penitents thus tempted to recite three times every day the Hail Mary in honor of Mary immaculate. And the Venerable John of Avila assures us that he never found any one who practised a true devotion to the Immaculate Conception of Mary, who did not in a short time obtain the gift of that virtue which renders us so dear to her immaculate heart.

PRAYER OF THE CHURCH (p. 31).

Litany of Loreto (p.301).

PRAYER

O LIVING light of holiness, model of purity, Mary immaculate, virgin and mother! As soon as thou wast conceived thou didst profoundly adore thy God, giving Him thanks that in thee the ancient curse was revoked, and blessing came again upon the sinful sons of

Adam. O make this blessing kindle in my heart love for God; and do thou fan this flame of love within me, that I may love Him constantly and one day in heaven eternally enjoy Him, there to thank Him more and more fervently for all the wondrous privileges conferred on thee, and to rejoice with thee for thy high crown of glory.

Hail Mary, etc.

EJACULATION (p. 32).

II

Novena in Honor of the Nativity of the Blessed Virgin Mary

ꙮ FIRST DAY ꙮ

The Birth of Mary

PREPARATORY PRAYER

WE FLY to thy patronage, O holy Mother of God. Despise not our petitions in our necessities, and deliver us from all dangers, O ever glorious and blessed Virgin!

MEDITATION

MARY is born! The dawn announcing the coming salvation of mankind is at hand. The deep significance of Mary's birth is expressed in the words of the Church: "Thy birth, O virgin Mother of God, has brought joy to the world; for from thee is to come forth the Sun of Justice, Christ our Lord, to dispel the curse and bring the blessing, to conquer death and bring us everlasting life.

On this day a light broke forth to brighten the paths of men through all time. Let us, then, rejoice in Mary's coming."

Equally expressive and touching are the reflections of that great Doctor of the Church, St. Augustine: "The day has dawned, the long-wished-for day of the blessed and venerable Virgin Mary. Well may this earth of ours rejoice and be glad for having been honored and sanctified by the birth of such a virgin."

PRACTICE

*L*ET us, then, rejoice in Mary's coming. Let us hail the birth of her who attained the dignity of mother without losing the high privilege of a virgin. Let us imitate her holy life, that she may become our intercessor before the throne of her Son, our judge and redeemer. By becoming the Mother of God she became also our Mother. As Mother of the Redeemer she is also the Mother of the redeemed. Richard of St. Lawrence writes: "If we desire grace and help, let us have recourse to Mary and we shall obtain what we desire." For, as St. Alphonsus remarks: "All graces and gifts which God has resolved to bestow upon us He gives us through the hands of Mary."

PRAYER OF THE CHURCH

*G*RANT to us, Thy servants, we beseech Thee, O Lord, the gift of heavenly grace; that to those for whom the delivery of the Blessed Virgin was the commencement of salvation, the commemoration of her nativity may give increasing peace. Through Christ our Lord. Amen.

Litany of Loreto (p. 301).

PRAYER

*M*OST lovely child, who by thy birth hast comforted the world, made glad the heavens, struck terror into hell, brought help to the fallen, consolation to the sad, health to the sick, joy to all; we pray thee with all fervent love, be thou born again in spirit in our souls through thy most holy love. Renew our fervor in thy service, rekindle in our hearts the fire of thy love, and bid all virtues blossom there, which may cause us to find more and more fervor in thy gracious eyes. O Mary, may we feel the saving power of thy sweetest name! Let it ever be our comfort to call on that great name in all our troubles; let it be our hope in dangers, our shield in temptation, and in death our last aspiration.

EJACULATION

O Mary, who didst come into the world free from stain: obtain of God for me that I may leave it without sin!

Indulgence. 100 days, once a day. (Pius IX, March 27, 1863.)

≈ SECOND DAY ≈

Mary, the Elect of God

PREPARATORY PRAYER (p. 52).

MEDITATION

*W*E FIND the explanation of the great prerogatives and privileges which God bestowed upon the Blessed Virgin Mary by reflecting on her singular and glorious predestination. From all eternity she was predestined to become the Mother of His divine Son; therefore, says Pope Pius IX, God loved her above all created beings, and in His special predilection made her the object of His divine complacency. With singular appropriateness we may apply to her the words of Holy Scripture, "I have loved thee with an everlasting love" (Jer. 31:3). The eternal Father regarded Mary as His beloved Daughter; the divine Son honored her as His dearest Mother; the Holy Ghost loved her as His spotless Spouse. "And," says St. Anselm, "they loved each other with an affection unsurpassed by any other."

PRACTICE

*I*NSPIRED by the contemplation of Mary's extraordinary privileges, St. Anselm exclaims: "Thou, O Mary, art more exalted than the patriarchs, greater than the martyrs, more glorious than the confessors, purer than the virgins, and therefore thou, alone, canst achieve more than they can without thee." Let us, then, rejoice that we possess such a powerful advocate in heaven, and let us place implicit trust in her. But let us also co-operate with the graces and favors which she obtains for us. Moreover, let us remember that we grievously offend God and Mary if we abuse what we obtain through her intercession to gratify

our evil inclinations, and that the graces she obtains for us
for our salvation will redound to our ruin if we do not use
them for the glory of God and the promotion of our soul's
welfare.

PRAYER OF THE CHURCH (p. 53).

Litany of Loreto (p. 301).

PRAYER

*W*E HAIL thee, Mary, who, sprung from the
royal line of David, didst come forth to the light
of heaven with high honor from the womb of holy Anna,
thy most happy mother.
Hail Mary, etc.

EJACULATION (p. 54).

⤳ THIRD DAY *⤲*

Mary, the Child of Royalty

PREPARATORY PRAYER (p. 52).

MEDITATION

*A*CCORDING to her lineage, as traced in two
Gospels, Mary numbers among her paternal
and maternal ancestors the holiest and most renowned

personages of the Old Testament. We find amongst them Abraham, the friend of God, the father of Israel and of all the faithful; then David, the man after God's own heart, the inspired Royal Prophet; and Solomon, the wise and mighty king, and the whole line of the kings of Juda. On her mother's side she belonged to the tribe of Levi, and was descended from its noblest and most prominent family, that of Aaron the High Priest, and was therefore a relative of the High Priests of the Old Testament. Thus royal and sacerdotal prestige distinguished Mary's lineage.

PRACTICE

*T*HE Blessed Virgin was not proud of her illustrious ancestry, and not depressed because of the downfall of her family, but applied herself diligently to adhere to the faith and follow the example of her ancestors. Remembering the wicked members of her family, she learned from them that temporal greatness, success, wealth, and glory are more dangerous to virtue than poverty, retirement, and work. Let us imitate Mary's example. Even possessed of the most excellent prestiges of the natural order, of ourselves we are nothing. "What hast thou that thou hast not received? And if thou hast received, why dost thou glory as if thou hadst not received?" (1 Cor. 4:7). Therefore do not overestimate yourself; do not be conceited; do not strive for praise, honors, and high station; be not boastful or arrogant; do not presume on your merits; rather be distrustful of yourself and patiently bear affronts, neglect, and humiliations. However poor you may be, be content with your lot, remembering the words of the Apostle: "They that will become rich fall into temptation, and into the snare of the devil, and into many unprofitable and hurtful desires which draw men into destruction and perdition. For the desire of money is the root of all evils: which some coveting have erred from the faith, and have entangled themselves in many sorrows" (1 Tim. 6:9, 10).

PRAYER OF THE CHURCH (p. 53).

Litany of Loreto (p. 301).

PRAYER

WE HAIL thee, O Mary, heavenly babe, white dove of purity, who, despite the infernal serpent, was conceived free from the taint of Adam's sin. With all our hearts we pray thee to vouchsafe in thy goodness to come down again and be born in spirit in our souls, that, led captive by thy loveliness and sweetness, they may ever live united to thy most sweet and loving heart.

Hail Mary, etc.

EJACULATION (p. 54).

❧ FOURTH DAY ☙

Mary, the Child of Pious Parents

PREPARATORY PRAYER (p. 52).

MEDITATION

*T*RADITION tells us that Mary's parents were called Joachim and Anna. The holy Fathers rival each other in praising the virtue of this holy couple. St. Epiphanius writes: "Joachim and Anna were pleasing in the sight of God because of the holiness of their lives." St. Andrew of Crete remarks: "Joachim was eminent for the mildness and fortitude of his character. The law of God was his rule of life. He was just, and never relaxed in the fervor of his love of God. Anna was no less noted for her meekness, continence, and chastity." St. Jerome relates: "The life of this holy couple was simple and just before the Lord, edifying and virtuous before men." St. John Damascene exclaims: "O happy, chaste, and immaculate couple, Joachim and Ann! You are known, according to the Lord's word, by your fruit. Your life was pleasing in the sight of God, and worthy of her who was born of you."

PRACTICE

*I*T is a great blessing, and one to be esteemed more highly than wealth and high station, to have God-fearing, pious parents. For their sake God is gracious to the children and lavishes His gifts on them. It is certainly a great privilege to be offered up to God immediately after birth by the hands of a pious mother. To have, from childhood up, the example and guidance of virtuous parents is certainly of the greatest importance. St. Chrysostom writes: "The parents' example is the book from which the child learns." A pious bishop was wont to say: "The good example of the parents is the best catechism and the truest mirror that a family can have." If Christian parents imitate the example of Joachim and Ann the blessing of God will rest on them and on their children; for because her parents were so dear to Mary, she will not refuse to join them in their prayers for us.

PRAYER OF THE CHURCH (p. 53).

Litany of Loreto (p. 301).

PRAYER

 E HAIL thee, brightest morn, forerunner of the heavenly Sun of Justice, who didst first bring light to earth. Humbly prostrate, with all our hearts we pray thee to vouchsafe in thy goodness to be born again in spirit in our souls, that, led captive by thy loveliness and sweetness, they may ever live united to thy most sweet and loving heart.

Hail Mary, etc.

EJACULATION (p. 54).

❧ FIFTH DAY ☙

Mary's Supernatural Prerogatives

PREPARATORY PRAYER (p. 52).

MEDITATION

*M*ARY was the masterpiece of God's creation; her soul was the most perfect ever dwelling in a human body. A pious tradition tells us that she possessed the use of reason much earlier than other children. Her intellect was illuminated by supernatural light; her will was exempt from concupiscence. Being preserved from original sin, she surpassed in holiness, from the first moment of her existence, all angels and men. She possessed all virtues in the highest degree, because of her faithful co-operation with sanctifying grace and with the countless actual graces granted to her. She lived in constant communion with God, undisturbed by evil inclinations from within or temptations from without.

PRACTICE

*T*HROUGH the effects of original sin we have lost the supernatural prerogative of original justice, and even after receiving sanctifying grace in holy Baptism we are exposed to many temptations. Our life is a constant warfare. We must, however, not despair in this struggle, for if we are true children of Mary she will come to our aid. In all temptations Mary is the "Help of Christians" if we have recourse to her. But if we wish her to help us, we must not expose ourselves unnecessarily to temptation. "He that loveth danger shall perish in it" (Ecclus. 3:27). This sad experience has come to many. Let us, therefore, avoid the danger and occasion of sin; and whenever evil approaches us in any shape, let us call upon Mary, and we may rest assured that she will assist us. "I shall certainly triumph over my enemies," exclaims St. Alphonsus, "if I place my trust in thee, O Mary, and if thou art my shield and protection against them."

PRAYER OF THE CHURCH (p. 53).

Litany of Loreto (p. 301).

PRAYER

WE HAIL thee, O chosen one! who like the untarnished sun didst burst forth into being in the dark night of sin. Humbly prostrate at thy feet, O Mary, we give thee our homage, and with all our hearts we pray thee to vouchsafe in thy goodness to be born again in our souls, that, led captive by thy loveliness and sweetness, they may ever live united to thy most sweet and loving heart.

Hail Mary, etc.

EJACULATION (p. 54).

❧ SIXTH DAY ☙

Mary, the Joy of the Most Holy Trinity

PREPARATORY PRAYER (p. 52).

MEDITATION

*I*N THE child Mary the eternal Father beheld His unsullied glorious image, which image had been defaced in all other human beings by original and actual sin. What a joy to Him to behold this stainless, immaculate child! And how great must have been the joy of the Son of God at the birth of her who was to be His Mother! From her He was to take that sacred body in which He was to dwell on earth, the blood of which He was to shed on the cross for our redemption, and in which He was to return to heaven to sit at the right hand of the Father. He will call her Mother, and regard her with all the filial tenderness of a child for his mother. She will love Him in return with a true mother's affection and devotion. As the Mother of Sorrows she will weep over His inanimate body taken down from the cross. But like Himself, she will leave the tomb, and reign at His side as the queen of heaven. How great, then, must have been His joy at the birth of this child!

The Holy Ghost, too, rejoiced at Mary's birth. He infused into her the plenitude of His holy love, for she was destined to become the Mother of God. And how Mary will love God, from whom she received so many and so great graces, and whom she is to bear in her arms as her real and true Son! This, her divine Son's love for mankind, will be imparted also to her. Therefore the Holy Ghost rejoices at this child, who received into her heart the fulness of His grace, and shall be the helper of those who have recourse to her.

PRACTICE

*R*AISE your spirit above time and space; try to contemplate well the mystery of Mary's predestination. To make us realize the great privileges conferred upon her, the Church applies to her the words of Holy Scripture, "He that shall find me, shall find life, and have salvation from the Lord" (Prov. 8:35). Only when we consider Mary as the Mother of God, do we arrive at a right conception of her great dignity. Hence St. Bonaventure exclaims, "God might have created a more beautiful world; He might have made heaven more glorious; but it was impossible for Him to exalt a creature higher than Mary in making her His Mother."

PRAYER OF THE CHURCH (p. 53).

Litany of Loreto (p. 301).

PRAYER

*W*E HAIL thee, beauteous moon, O Mary most holy, who didst shed light upon a world wrapped in the densest darkness of sin. Humbly prostrate at thy feet, we give thee our homage, and with all our hearts we pray thee to vouchsafe in thy goodness to be born again in spirit in our souls, that led captive by thy loveliness and sweetness they may ever live united to thy most sweet and loving heart.

Hail Mary, etc.

EJACULATION (p. 54).

⮞ SEVENTH DAY ⮜

The Angels Rejoice at Mary's Birth

PREPARATORY PRAYER (p. 52).

MEDITATION

*D*ESCRIBING God's power and wisdom as shown in creation, Holy Scripture, according to the explanation of the Fathers, introduces Him as saying, "When the morning stars praised me together, and all the sons of God made a joyful melody" (Job 38:7), and by these words intends to convey with what joy the angels praised God's omnipotence on beholding the wonders of creation. What, then, must have been their joy on beholding this new wonder of divine power and wisdom, the child Mary, destined to be their queen. Filled with admiration they exclaimed, "Who is she that cometh forth as the morning rising, fair as the moon, bright as the sun, terrible as an army set in array?" (Cant. 6:9.) And moreover, if, as Our Lord declares, the angels rejoice at the conversion of a sinner, how great must have been their joy at the birth of her who was to be the refuge of sinners and the mother of Him who was to be the Redeemer of sinners? Again, the angels rejoiced at Mary's birth, because she would fill, through the salvation of mankind by her divine Son, the places made vacant in heaven by the apostate angels.

PRACTICE

*G*OOD children rejoice on the birthday of their parents and gratefully remember all the benefits they have received from them. Thus should we, also, celebrate the nativity of the Blessed Virgin by a grateful remembrance of the innumerable graces, individual and general, we received through her intercession. In acknowledging Mary's co-operation with our salvation, Holy Church calls her our mediatrix, and greets her as the "Cause of our joy," because, though we receive grace from Christ, it comes to us through her mediation. What cause, then, have we not for rejoicing at her birth! Again, greeting Mary as the cause of our joy, let us remember the protection she extended to the Church in times of adversity and persecution; let us, furthermore, remember all the graces which, according to the holy Fathers, are dispensed to us by Mary's hands. "Of her plenitude," says St. Bonaventure, "we have all received; the captive liberty, the sick health, the sad consolation, the sinner pardon, the just grace." Therefore the Church invokes Mary as the mother of mercy, the health of the sick, the comforter of the afflicted, the refuge of sinners, the help of Christians, in a word, as the cause of our joy.

PRAYER OF THE CHURCH (p. 53).

Litany of Loreto (p.301).

PRAYER

*W*E HAIL thee, fair soul of Mary, who from all eternity wast God's, and God's alone; sanctuary and living temple of the Holy Ghost; sun without blemish, because free from original sin. With all our hearts we pray to thee, O Mary, to vouchsafe in thy goodness to be born again in spirit in our souls, that, led captive by thy loveliness and sweetness, they may ever live united to thy most sweet and loving heart.

Hail Mary, etc.

EJACULATION (p. 54).

∾ EIGHTH DAY ∾

The Joy of the Just in Limbo at Mary's Birth

PREPARATORY PRAYER (p. 52).

MEDITATION

*F*OR four thousand years the just in limbo sighed for redemption, and sent up to Heaven the plaintive cry, "O that Thou wouldst rend the heavens, and wouldst come down!" (Is. 14:1.) "Drop down dew, ye heavens, from above, and let the clouds rain the just; let the earth be opened and bud forth a Saviour" (Is. 45:8). What joy must have filled the souls of the just when they heard the welcome tidings of the birth of Mary, the virgin Mother of the promised Messias; how great their consolation at the rising of that dawn which preceded the Sun of Justice, whose splendor was to illuminate the darkness of them that sat in the shadow of death!

PRACTICE

A JOY similar to that which filled the captive souls in limbo at Mary's birth now fills the souls in purgatory when we implore her to come to their relief. Contemplating the immense love of the Most Holy Trinity for Mary, we may not doubt but that, by her intercession, she might at once deliver all the suffering souls from their prison, if such were in accordance with God's will. But God's wisdom and providence have decreed otherwise. Therefore Mary does not pray for the release of all souls in purgatory, but recommends them, in conformity with God's will, to His mercy. St. Bernardine of Sienna applies to Mary the words of Holy Scripture, "I have penetrated into the bottom of the deep and have walked in the waves of the sea" (Ecclus. 24:8), and says: "She descends into that sea of suffering and soothes the pains of the poor souls." St. Denis the Carthusian remarks, that when the name of Mary is mentioned in purgatory, the souls there imprisoned experience the same relief as when a sick person hears words of consolation on his bed of pain.

Therefore let us entrust our prayers for the souls in purgatory to Mary. She will present our petitions to God, and thus presented, He will speedily hear and graciously grant them.

PRAYER OF THE CHURCH (p. 53).

Litany of Loreto (p. 301).

PRAYER

*W*E HAIL thee, strong child, who didst put to flight all hell and the powers of darkness. We give thee our homage, and with all our hearts we pray thee to vouchsafe in thy goodness to be born again in spirit in our souls, that, led captive by thy loveliness and sweetness, they may ever live united to thy most sweet and loving heart.

Hail Mary, etc.

EJACULATION (p. 54).

NINTH DAY

The Holy Name of Mary

PREPARATORY PRAYER (p. 52).

MEDITATION

*S*T. ALPHONSUS writes of the name of Mary: "This name was neither invented on earth, nor imposed by human agency. It came from heaven and was given to the Mother of God by divine command." Just as it is a peculiar glory of our Saviour's name, that "God hath given Him a name which is above all names, that in the

name of Jesus every knee should bow of those that are in
heaven, on earth, and under the earth" (Philipp. 2:9), thus
it also behooves that Mary, the most perfect, the most pure,
and most exalted of all created beings, should receive a most
holy, lovely, and powerful name. St. Methodius declares
that the name of Mary is so rich in grace and blessing, that
no one can pronounce it devoutly without at the same time
receiving a spiritual favor. Bl. Jordan exclaims: "Let a heart
be ever so obdurate, let a man even despair of God's mercy,
if he have recourse to thee, O Mary, virgin most clement,
he can not fail to be softened and filled with confidence if
he invokes thy name; for thou wilt inspire him with hope in
God's mercy, pardon, and grace."

PRACTICE

*J*T IS, then, meet and just that we should devoutly
honor and praise the name of Mary. Let us never
mention it except in reverence and devotion. Let us invoke
Mary by it in all dangers of body and soul, mindful of
the words of St. Bernard: "O sinner, when the floods and
tempests of this earthly life overwhelm thee so that thou
canst not firmly set thy foot, turn not away thy gaze from the
light of this guiding star. When the storms of temptation
assail thee, and the rocks and quicksands of vexation and
trial threaten to shatter thy bark of hope, look up to that
bright star in the heavens, and call on the name of Mary.
When the billows of pride and of ambition, when the floods
of calumny are about to submerge thee, look up to this star
and call on the name of Mary. When anger, avarice, and

concupiscence convulse the peace of thy soul, look up to this star and call on Mary. When thy sins rise up like hideous monsters before thy troubled vision, when thy conscience stings thee, when the terrors of future judgment fill thee with deadly anguish, when gloom and sadness overpower thee, when thou findest thyself on the brink of hellish despair, take courage; think of Mary, and thou wilt find from thy own inward experience how true are the sayings of those who tell thee that the name of the Blessed Virgin is 'Star of the Sea,' the name of the Virgin is Mary."

PRAYER OF THE CHURCH (p. 53).

Litany of Loreto (p.301).

PRAYER

WE HAIL thee, beloved child Mary, adorned with every virtue, immeasurably above all the saints, and therefore worthy Mother of the Saviour of the world, who by the operation of the Holy Ghost didst bring forth the incarnate Word. We give thee our homage, and with all our hearts we pray thee to vouchsafe in thy goodness to be born again in our souls, that, led captive by thy loveliness and sweetness, they may ever live united to thy most sweet and loving heart.

Hail Mary, etc.

EJACULATION (p. 54).

III

Novena for the Feast of the Annunciation of the Blessed Virgin Mary

➤ FIRST DAY ➤

The Annunciation

PREPARATORY PRAYER

*M*Y QUEEN, my Mother, remember I am thine own. Keep me, guard me, as thy property and possession!

Indulgence. 40 days, every time. (Pius IX, August 5, 1851.)

MEDITATION

*A*T NAZARETH, a mountain village in Judea, lived poor and in obscurity Mary, the virgin selected by God to become the Mother of His Son. On March 25th she was in prayer in her chamber, and perhaps sent up to heaven the yearning petition, "Drop down dew, ye heavens, from above, and let the clouds rain the just; let the earth be opened and bud a Saviour" (Is. 45:8). Behold, suddenly the chamber is suffused by a heavenly light. The archangel Gabriel stands reverently before her and says, "Hail, full of grace, the Lord is with thee. Blessed art thou among women. And when Mary heard the angel's words, she was troubled at his saying, and thought with herself what manner of salutation this should be" (Luke 1:28, 29).

PRACTICE

THE angel's salutation comprises two titles of ineffable greatness. Mary is called "full of grace," because of her innocence and purity; she is called "blessed among women," because she is the elect Mother of God. Never before was a human being thus greeted. It was God Himself who sent the message to Mary. A good angel now repaired the harm once done by a bad angel. For Lucifer, the fallen angel, seduced Eve to sin and thereby caused the ruin of the whole human race; now another angel, Gabriel, was sent to announce the glad tidings to Mary, that she was to conceive the Redeemer from sin, who was to accomplish the salvation of mankind.

Mary was troubled at the angel's words, and reflected on the meaning of the message. St. Ambrose writes: "Mary was troubled, not because the angel was a heavenly spirit, but because he appeared to her in the form of a youth. Still more was she troubled at the praises spoken to her. She was innocent and humble, and therefore reflected on the meaning of the message. She had always considered herself as a poor and unknown virgin; she deemed herself unworthy of God's grace; therefore she was troubled at the salutation. In that decisive moment she was and remained our model."

PRAYER OF THE CHURCH

*P*OUR forth, we beseech Thee, O Lord, Thy grace into our hearts, that we unto whom the Incarnation of Christ Thy Son was made known by the message of an angel, may, by His passion and cross, be brought to the glory of the resurrection. Through the same Christ our Lord. Amen.

Litany of Loreto (p. 301).

PRAYER

*W*ITH wonder I revere thee, holiest Virgin Mary; for of all God's creatures thou wast the humblest on the very day of thy annunciation, when God Himself exalted Thee to the sublime dignity of His own Mother. O mightiest Virgin, make me, wretched sinner that I am, know the depths of my own nothingness, and make me humble myself at last with all my heart, beneath the feet of all men.

Hail Mary, etc.

EJACULATION

Virgin Mary, Mother of God, pray to Jesus for me!

Indulgence. 50 days, once a day. (Leo XIII, March 20, 1894.)

ᨆ SECOND DAY ᨋ

The Import of the Angel's Salutation

PREPARATORY PRAYER (p. 72).

MEDITATION

"*H*AIL, full of grace!" Mary was greeted as full of grace by the Giver of grace Himself. The angel's salutation meant: "The grace of God has preserved thee from all sin. Neither the stain of original sin, nor the guilt of actual sin, ever obscured the mirror of thy soul. By the special favor of God the most sublime virtues were infused into thy soul."

"The Lord is with thee." From all eternity the Lord was with Mary. He was with her not only as He is with His whole creation, but He was with her in a special manner. The eternal Father was with her from all eternity as with His beloved Daughter. The divine Son was with her from all eternity as with His chosen Mother. The Holy Ghost was with her from all eternity as with His beloved Spouse. This intimate union never was disrupted. Therefore Mary is "Blessed among women," and ever was, and ever shall be the beloved of the Lord.

PRACTICE

*C*ONSIDER how Mary receives the angel's message. She is troubled, she is disturbed at the praise, at the reverence of the angel. What an example of humility! Let us imitate her in this virtue by the acknowledgment before God of our weakness, our unworthiness, our nothingness, and by ordering our whole being accordingly. Humility renders us pleasing in the sight of God and makes us susceptible of His grace. Hence St. Augustine writes: "God resists the proud and gives His grace to the humble. What a terrible punishment for the proud, what a splendid reward for the humble! The proud man resembles a rock, the humble man a beautiful valley. The grace of God descends from heaven like a gentle rain. It can not penetrate the rock of pride, and hence the proud man loses God's grace and love. But in the valley of humility the waters of divine grace can diffuse themselves and fructify the soul of the humble man, so that it may bring forth fruit unto eternal life."

PRAYER OF THE CHURCH (p. 74).

Litany of Loreto (p. 301).

PRAYER

O MARY, holiest Virgin, who, when the archangel Gabriel hailed thee in thy annunciation, and thou wast raised by God above all choirs of the angels, didst confess thyself "the handmaid of the Lord"; do thou obtain for me true humility and a truly angelic purity, and so to live on earth as ever to be worthy of the blessings of God.

Hail Mary, etc.

EJACULATION (p. 74).

❧ THIRD DAY ❧

The Effect of the Angel's Salutation

PREPARATORY PRAYER (p. 72).

MEDITATION

*T*HE effect of the angel's salutation on Mary was striking. Imbued with sentiments quite different from ours, she was troubled at the praise addressed to her. Meanwhile she is silent and considers within herself what might be the meaning of these words. And now the angel calls her by name, saying, "Fear not, Mary, for thou hast found grace with God. Behold thou shalt conceive in thy womb, and shalt bring forth a son, and thou shalt call His name Jesus. He shall be great, and shall be called the Son of the Most High, and the Lord God shall give unto Him the throne of David His father: and He shall reign in the house of Jacob for ever, and of His kingdom there shall be no end" (Luke 1:30-33).

PRACTICE

*L*ET us admire the prudence shining forth in Mary. After hearing the angel's words of praise she was silent and thought within herself what kind of a salutation this was. She is very careful and prudent. On this her conduct St. Thomas Aquinas remarks: "Mary did not refuse to believe, nor did she receive the message with

credulity. She avoided Eve's gullibility and the distrust
of Zachary the high priest." And St. Bernard writes:
"Mary preferred to remain silent in humility, rather than
to speak inconsiderately." Let us strive always to speak
and act with deliberation. Our conversation ought always
to be judicious; for often a word spoken inconsiderately
causes bitter regret. St. Thomas Aquinas observes: "Song
was given to a number of creatures, but human beings
alone were endowed with the faculty of speech, to indicate
that in speaking we should use our reason." And St.
Chrysostom says: "Let us always guard our tongue; not
that it should always be silent, but that it should speak at
the proper time."

PRAYER OF THE CHURCH (p. 74).

Litany of Loreto (p. 301).

PRAYER

I REJOICE with thee, O Virgin ever blessed, because
by thy humble word of consent thou didst draw down
from the bosom of the eternal Father the divine Word
into thy own pure bosom. O draw, then, ever my heart to
God; and with God bring grace into my heart that I may
ever sincerely bless thy word of consent, so mighty and so
efficacious.

Hail Mary, etc.

EJACULATION (p. 74).

✒ FOURTH DAY ✒

Mary's Question

PREPARATORY PRAYER (p. 72).

MEDITATION

*W*ELL versed as Mary was in Holy Scripture, she fully understood the words she had heard and knew their great import. She was destined to become the Mother of the Most High, the Son of God. But there is an obstacle which prevents her from giving immediate assent. She has solemnly vowed her virginity to God. Not knowing how the mystery announced to her was to be accomplished, and intent above all on keeping inviolate her vow, she interrupts her silence by the short but comprehensive question, "How shall this be done, because I know not man?" (Luke 1:34). This is the first word of Mary recorded in the Gospel.

PRACTICE

"*H*OW shall this be done, because I know not man?" Truly a momentous question, proceeding from her knowledge of the great excellence and value before God of virginity, which, before Mary, was unknown to the world.

Let us follow Mary's example and esteem holy purity and chastity above all things. Let us remember how highly

Holy Scripture extols this virtue. "O how beautiful is the chaste generation with glory; for the memory thereof is immortal, because it is known both with God and with men" (Wis. 4:1). St. Athanasius writes: "O chastity, thou precious pearl, found by few, even hated by some, and sought only by those who are worthy of thee! Thou art the joy of the prophets, the ornament of the apostles, the life of the angels, the crown of the saints." Let us therefore carefully guard this inestimable treasure.

PRAYER OF THE CHURCH (p. 74).

Litany of Loreto (p. 301).

PRAYER

MARY, mighty Virgin, thou who on the day of thy annunciation wast found by the archangel so prompt and ready to do God's will, and to correspond with the desires of the august Trinity, who wished for thy consent in order to redeem the world; obtain for me that, whatever happens, good or ill, I may turn to my God, and with resignation say, "Be it done unto me according to thy word."

Hail Mary, etc.

EJACULATION (p. 74).

❧ FIFTH DAY ❧

The Solution

PREPARATORY PRAYER (p. 72).

MEDITATION

*T*HE angel explains to Mary how, without detriment to her virginity, she will become a mother. He says, "The Holy Ghost shall come upon thee, and the power of the Most High shall overshadow thee. And therefore also the Holy which shall be born of thee shall be called the Son of God" (Luke 1:35). St. Bernard remarks: "Let him who can, comprehend it. Who, but that most happy Virgin who was worthy to experience the influence and effect of the power of the Most High and to penetrate this sublime mystery, can understand how the divine Light was poured into the Virgin's womb? The Most Holy Trinity alone co-operated in the sacred act, and it remains an impenetrable mystery to all, except to her who was called to so sublime a destiny."

PRACTICE

*M*ARY did not entertain a single doubt concerning the wonders which the angel announced to her about the coming Messias and His kingdom. She believed with simple faith the words of the heavenly messenger. Only about that which concerned her personally she asked a question. When the wonderful mystery was explained to her, she did not ask how this *can* be done, but only how it *shall* be done. And after the angel had declared to her that she shall conceive by the Holy Ghost, she was fully resigned and announced her implicit belief in these humble words: "Behold the handmaid of the Lord; be it done to me according to thy word" (Luke 1:38). Therefore the Holy Ghost Himself praised her by the mouth of Elizabeth: "Blessed art thou that hast believed" (Luke 1:45).

Let us remain steadfast in the profession of all articles of faith, and let us oppose, like a strong shield, the words, "Nothing is impossible with God," to all attacks of unbelievers, and to all doubts that may arise in our own minds.

PRAYER OF THE CHURCH (p. 74).

Litany of Loreto (p.301).

PRAYER

*M*ARY most holy, I see that thy obedience united thee so closely to God, that all creation never shall know again union so fair and so perfect. I am overwhelmed with confusion in seeing how my sins have separated me from God. Help me, then, gentle Mother, to repent sincerely of my sins, that I may be reunited to thy loving Jesus.

Hail Mary, etc.

EJACULATION (p. 74).

✒ SIXTH DAY ✑

Mary's Consent

PREPARATORY PRAYER (p. 72).

MEDITATION

*W*E ADMIRE the creative word of God, by which heaven and earth were called into existence. But Mary's word, "Be it done to me according to thy word," is even mightier and more efficacious; for it commands the obedience even of the almighty Creator. Without this word of humility and obedience the incarnation of our divine Saviour would not have been accomplished. Mary does not say, "I accept the proposal, I agree to the proposition," nor does she use other words of similar import. She simply says, "Be it done to me according to thy word." It was not her own choice, nor her own decision, but a voluntary, full, and complete surrender to the will of God that the message found in Mary's soul, which was expressed in these words. What a source of consolation to her in the subsequent sorrowful and afflicted stages of her life was this complete surrender to God's will! It comprised the tranquilizing assurance that He to whose designs she submitted, would endow her with the fortitude and strength necessary to co-operate with them.

PRACTICE

*J*UST as our divine Lord Himself became obedient unto death, thus also His incarnation and the motherhood of Mary were the result of obedience. Again, in contemplating the works that in the course of time were undertaken in the Church for the glory of God and the salvation of man, we find that only those were really great, effective, and enduring, which had their beginning, continuation, and consummation in obedience.

Rejoice, then, if it is your happy lot to walk in the safe path of obedience. Avail yourself of every opportunity to submit your will to the will of your Superiors. They are the representatives of God. By obeying them we fulfill His will, not the will of men. St. Bonaventure calls obedience the key of heaven.

PRAYER OF THE CHURCH (p. 74).

Litany of Loreto (p. 301).

PRAYER

*H*OLIEST Mary, if through thy modesty thou wert troubled at the appearance of the archangel Gabriel in thy dwelling, I am terrified at the sight of my monstrous pride. By thy incomparable humility, which brought forth God for men, reopened paradise and let the captive souls go free from their prison, draw me, I pray thee, out of the deep pit into which my sins have cast me, and make me save my soul.

Hail Mary, etc.

EJACULATION (p. 74).

☙ SEVENTH DAY ❧

Mary's Fortitude in Suffering

PREPARATORY PRAYER (p. 72).

MEDITATION

*A*LTHOUGH Mary's consent was free, and freely given, she was clearly convinced and perfectly conscious of the responsibility, the obligations, and the duties involved by that consent, and which she now assumed. Great are the duties and tearful the days of a mother who has to raise her Son, who is also God, to be sacrificed on the cross. Mary assumes with the dignity this responsibility. She consents to conceive the Son of God, to give birth to Him, to nourish Him, to educate Him for the ignominious death of the cross. When she pronounced the words, "Be it done," her eyes were fixed on the distant tragedy of Golgotha, on the cross towering upon its height. Yet she accepts it, together with the dignity of Mother of God.

PRACTICE

*M*ARY, in consenting to become the Mother of Jesus, became not only His Mother, but the Mother of all mankind. She became, for all time, the refuge of sinners, the health of the sick, the intercessor with God for man; she consented to exercise a mother's love for suffering and sinful humanity. But alas, how many of those adopted by Mary as her children under the cross of her dying Son are unworthy of her mother love! How many are rebellious children, who fill her heart with sorrow and anguish! Others, faithless and obdurate, become a reproach to her. Have you, during your past life, always been a good child of this loving Mother? Are you to her an honor or a disgrace, a joy or a sorrow?

PRAYER OF THE CHURCH (p. 74).

Litany of Loreto (p. 301).

PRAYER

*T*HOUGH my tongue is unhallowed, yet, purest Virgin, I presume to hail thee every day with the angel's salutation, "Hail Mary, full of grace!" From my heart, I pray thee, pour into my soul a little of that mighty grace wherewith the Holy Spirit, overshadowing thee, filled thee to the full.

Hail Mary, etc.

EJACULATION (p. 74).

EIGHTH DAY

Mary, the Mother of God

PREPARATORY PRAYER (p. 74).

MEDITATION

*M*ARY'S true greatness consists in her having been chosen the Mother of God. This sublime dignity, pre-eminently her own and shared by no other creature, elevates her to a station inconceivably exalted. Mother of God! St. Peter Damian thus gives expression to his conception of this dignity: "In what words may mortal man be permitted to pronounce the praises of her who brought forth that divine Word who lives for all eternity? Where can a tongue be found holy and pure enough to eulogize her who bore the author of all created things, whom the elements praise and obey in fear and trembling? When we essay to extol a martyr's constancy, to recount his heroic acts of virtue, to describe his devotion to his Saviour's cause and honor, we are supplied with words by facts and occurrences that belong to the province of human experience. But when we undertake to describe the glories of the Blessed Virgin, we are on unknown ground, on a subject transcending all human effort. We fail to find words suitable to portray her sublime prerogatives, privileges, and mysteries."

PRACTICE

*S*T. ANSELM, writing on the motherhood of Mary, says: "It was eminently just and proper that the creature chosen to be the Mother of God should shine with a luster of purity far beyond anything conceivable in any other creature under heaven. For it was to her that the eternal Father decreed to give His only-begotten Son, whom He loves as Himself; and to give Him in such a mysterious manner that He should be at the same time the Son of God and the Son of the Virgin Mary. She must indeed be purity itself, whom the Son of God elected as His Mother, and who was the chosen Spouse of the Holy Ghost, to be overshadowed by Him to bring forth the Second Person of that Most Blessed Trinity from whom He Himself proceeds."

Let us honor the virgin Mother with filial devotion, gratefully greeting her often in the words of the angel, "Hail Mary, full of grace!" Let us remember that God alone is above Mary, and beneath her is all that is not God.

PRAYER OF THE CHURCH (p. 74).

Litany of Loreto (p. 301).

PRAYER

*J*BELIEVE, holiest Mary, that almighty God was ever with thee from thy conception, and is, by His incarnation, still more closely united to thee. Make it thy care, I pray thee, that I may be with that same Lord Jesus ever one heart and soul by means of sanctifying grace.

Hail Mary, etc.

EJACULATION (p. 74).

❧ NINTH DAY ☙

Mary, Our Mother

PREPARATORY PRAYER (p. 72).

MEDITATION

*M*ARY could not consent to become the Mother of the Redeemer without including in her consent those to be redeemed. "She bore one man," says St. Antonine, "and thereby has borne all men again. Beneath the cross of her divine Son she has reborne us to life with great pain, just as Eve our first mother, has borne us under the tree of forbidden fruit unto death. That there be no doubt concerning it, her divine Son made this declaration in His last will." "When therefore Jesus had seen His Mother and the disciple standing whom He loved, He saith to His Mother, Woman, behold thy son. After that He saith to the disciple, Behold thy Mother" (John 19:26-27). She gave up her Son for the redemption of mankind, and He gave us, in the person of His beloved disciple St. John, to her as her children, declaring her our Mother. From that moment we belong to Mary, and Mary belongs to us: "Behold thy Mother!"

PRACTICE

*M*ARY loves us because she loves God, and because God loves us. She loves us as her brethren who share human nature with her. She loves us as her children, whom she has borne to eternal life. She loves us because we are miserable and helpless. True, we offended her divine Son, but she knows our frailty, our blindness, the assaults of the flesh and the devil to which we are exposed; and by all this she is moved to come to our aid.

Do not, however, imagine that this good and amiable Mother will hear your call for assistance if you continue to offend her divine Son with malice prepense. To obtain her aid you must make yourself in a manner worthy of it. This you do by striving to imitate her virtues. Or is there anything in her example that we are unable to imitate? True, we can not attain to her perfection in virtue, but we can copy it to a certain degree. To follow Mary's example there is no need of performing miracles, of having ecstasies, or of doing any other extraordinary deeds. All that is necessary is to persevere faithfully in the ordinary duties of life, and to perform them to the best of our ability.

"Behold thy Mother!" These words of our dying Lord were addressed to the beloved disciple St. John, but were intended for all mankind. Even as Mary never ceases to be the Mother of God, she never will cease to be our Mother.

PRAYER OF THE CHURCH (p. 74).

Litany of Loreto (p. 301).

PRAYER

O HOLIEST Mary, bless me, my heart and my soul, as thou thyself wast ever blessed of God among all women; for I have this sure hope, dear Mother, that if thou bless me while I live, then, when I die, I shall be blessed of God in the everlasting glory of heaven.

Hail Mary, etc.

EJACULATION (p. 74).

IV

Novena in Honor of the Seven Sorrows of Mary

NOTE.—Besides the indulgences granted for every novena in honor of the Blessed Virgin Mary by Pius IX, Pope Leo XIII, January 27, 1888, granted that all the faithful may gain, on the *third Sunday in September*, being the second feast of the Seven Sorrows of Mary (the other is observed on the Friday before Palm Sunday), a plenary indulgence *as often* as they visit, after confession and communion, a church where the Archconfraternity of the Seven Sorrows is canonically established, and pray there for the intentions of the Holy Father. This indulgence is applicable to the souls in purgatory.

☙ FIRST DAY ☜

Devotion to the Seven Sorrows of Mary

PREPARATORY PRAYER

*B*ID me bear, O Mother blessed,
  On my heart the wounds impressed
  Suffered by the Crucified!

Indulgence. 300 days, once a day. A plenary indulgence, on any one day, in each month, to those who shall have practised this devotion for a month, saying besides seven Hail Marys, followed each time by the above invocation. Conditions: Confession, communion, and prayer for the intentions of the Pope. (Pius IX, June 18, 1876.)

MEDITATION

*F*ROM the dolorous way of Our Lord's passion Holy Church selected fourteen incidents to place before us for consideration, which are called the Stations of the Cross. In the same manner the pious devotion of the faithful selected seven events in the life of the Blessed Virgin Mary, and gives itself to their religious contemplation. They are: (1) Simeon's prophecy in the Temple; (2) the flight into Egypt with the divine Child; (3) the loss of the divine Child at Jerusalem; (4) Mary's meeting with her Son bearing the cross; (5) Mary beneath the cross; (6) Mary receives the body of her Son from the cross; (7) the placing of Jesus' body in the tomb.

PRACTICE

"*F*ORGET not the sorrows of thy mother" (Ecclus. 7:29). According to this exhortation of Holy Scripture it is our duty to remember and meditate often on the sorrows of the Blessed Virgin Mary. We ought never to forget that our sins were the cause of the sufferings and death of Jesus, and therefore also of the sorrows of Mary.

Holy Church celebrates two feasts in honor of the sorrows of Mary; she approved of the Rosary and of many other devotions in honor of the Seven Dolors, and enriched them with numerous indulgences. Let us practise these devotions to enkindle in our hearts a true and ardent love for our sorrowful Mother.

PRAYER OF THE CHURCH

*G*RANT, we beseech Thee, O Lord Jesus Christ, that the most blessed Virgin Mary, Thy Mother, may intercede for us before the throne of Thy mercy, now and at the hour of our death, through whose most holy soul, in the hour of Thine own passion, the sword of sorrow passed. Through Thee, Jesus Christ, Saviour of the world, who livest and reignest with the Father and the Holy Ghost, for ever and ever. Amen.

Litany of Loreto (p. 301).

PRAYER

*E*VER glorious Blessed Virgin Mary, queen of martyrs, mother of mercy, hope, and comfort of dejected and desolate souls, through the sorrows that pierced thy tender heart I beseech thee take pity on my poverty and necessities, have compassion on my anxieties and miseries. I ask it through the mercy of thy divine Son; I ask it through His immaculate life, bitter passion, and ignominious death on the cross. As I am persuaded that He honors thee as His beloved Mother, to whom He refuses nothing, let me experience the efficacy of thy powerful intercession, according to the tenderness of thy maternal affection, now and at the hour of my death. Amen.

Hail Mary, etc.

Mother of Sorrows, queen of martyrs, pray for us!

◄ SECOND DAY ►

Mary's First Sorrow: Simeon's Prophecy in the Temple

PREPARATORY PRAYER (p. 91).

MEDITATION

*F*ORTY days after the birth of our divine Saviour, Mary His Mother fulfilled the law of Moses by offering Him to His divine Father in the Temple. "And behold there was a man in Jerusalem named Simeon, and this man was just and devout, waiting for the consolation of Israel, and the Holy Ghost was in Him. And he received an answer from the Holy Ghost, that he should not see death before he had seen the Christ of the Lord. And he came by the Spirit into the temple. And when His parents brought in the child Jesus, to do for Him according to the custom of the law, he also took Him into his arms, and blessed God, and said: Now dost Thou dismiss Thy servant, O Lord, according to Thy word, in peace; because my eyes have seen Thy salvation, which Thou hast prepared before the face of all peoples. A light to the revelation of the gentiles and the glory of Thy people Israel. And His father and mother were wondering at these things which were spoken concerning Him. And Simeon blessed them, and said to Mary His Mother: Behold this child is set for the fall and for the resurrection of many in Israel, and for a sign which shall be contradicted; and thy own soul a sword shall pierce, that out of many hearts thoughts may be revealed" (Luke 2:25-35).

PRACTICE

*M*ARY was familiar with the predictions of the prophets and knew that ignominy, sorrow, and suffering would be her divine Son's portion throughout His earthly career. But to have this secret of her anxious soul thus publicly and solemnly declared by Simeon, was a sharp thrust of that seven-edged sword which was to pierce her loving heart. In spirit she viewed that boundless, surging sea of trials, pain, and death on which her Son was to be tossed about, and was willing to be engulfed in its bitter waters. Her affliction would have scarcely been greater had the death sentence of her divine Son been pronounced then and there and put into execution. What a sorrow, what an affliction, what a trial for such a tender Mother! Well might she exclaim with the Royal Prophet: "My life is wasted with grief, and my years in sighs" (Ps. 30:11). Let us often contemplate this sorrow, and excite our hearts to a tender compassion with the Mother of Sorrows.

PRAYER OF THE CHURCH (p. 93).

Litany of Loreto (p. 301).

PRAYER

I COMPASSIONATE thee, sorrowing Mary, in the grief thy tender heart underwent when the holy old man Simeon prophesied to thee. Dear Mother, by thy heart then so afflicted, obtain for me the virtue of humility and the gift of the holy fear of God.

Hail Mary, etc.

EJACULATION (p. 94).

❧ THIRD DAY ☙

Mary's Second Sorrow: The Flight into Egypt

PREPARATORY PRAYER (p. 91).

MEDITATION

F OR the second time the sword of sorrow pierced Mary's heart when she was commanded to fly into Egypt with her divine Child. Without manifesting undue perplexity or discontent, she hastily gathered a few necessaries for the journey, while St. Joseph saddled the beast of burden. Then taking the infant Jesus into her arms and pressing Him to her throbbing heart, the holy pilgrims set forth into the cold, starry night, away to a foreign land, through the trackless desert, and into a heathen country. Arrived in Egypt, the experience of Bethlehem was renewed; no one gave them shelter.

PRACTICE

*D*URING this second great sorrow, what was Mary's behavior? She was content to fulfil the will of God; she did not ask for reasons, or complain of the fatigues of the journey, but preserved her peace of heart amid all the trials of this severe probation. She is poor, but her poverty does not render her unhappy or querulous. If God sends us trials, we ought not murmur or complain. Following the example of Mary, let us bear them submissively. If we suffer patiently with Mary on earth, we shall enjoy eternal bliss with her in heaven.

PRAYER OF THE CHURCH (p. 93).

Litany of Loreto (p. 301).

PRAYER

I COMPASSIONATE thee, sorrowing Mary, for the anxiety which thy most tender heart underwent during thy flight into Egypt and thy sojourn there. Dear Mother, by thy heart then so sorrowful, obtain for me the virtue of liberality, especially toward the poor, and the gift of piety.

Hail Mary, etc.

EJACULATION (p. 94).

ᔆᕦ FOURTH DAY ᔆᕦ

Mary's Third Sorrow: Jesus Lost in Jerusalem

PREPARATORY PRAYER (p. 91).

MEDITATION

*W*HO can describe Mary's sorrow when, returning from Jerusalem, she missed her divine Son? With St. Joseph she retraced her steps in anxious search of Him whom her soul loved. She went to all her relatives and acquaintances in Jerusalem, but heard no tidings of her lost Child. She passed three long days of anxiety in her search, and this constitutes her third sorrow. Of it, Origen writes: "On account of the ineffable love of Mary for her divine Son, she suffered more by His loss than the martyrs suffered amid the most cruel tortures."

PRACTICE

*I*N MEDITATING on this sorrow of Mary, we ought to remember how indifferent so many Christians are after having lost God by sin. They feel no compunction, no sorrow at having offended Him, and yet they can weep at the loss of a trifle; they shed copious tears when their will is crossed, or when they receive a deserved reprimand; but for the loss of their God they have not a tear. They have lost Him, perhaps years ago, and never make the least effort to find Him. Pray to the sorrowful Mother that she preserve you from such a deplorable fate!

PRAYER OF THE CHURCH (p. 93).

Litany of Loreto (p. 301).

PRAYER

J COMPASSIONATE thee, sorrowing Mary, for the terrors felt by thy anxious heart when thou didst lose thy dear Son, Jesus. Dear Mother, by thy heart, then so agitated, obtain for me the virtue of chastity, and with it the gift of knowledge.

Hail Mary, etc.

EJACULATION (p. 94).

FIFTH DAY

Mary's Fourth Sorrow: She Meets Jesus Carrying His Cross

PREPARATORY PRAYER (p. 91).

MEDITATION

T HE time was at hand when mankind's redemption was to be accomplished. Already the divine Victim of our sins is bearing the instrument of our salvation. Torn by the cruel scourging, crowned with thorns, and covered with blood He proceeds on His way to Calvary, and in this pitiful condition meets His blessed Mother. What a spectacle, what a sight for a Mother such as Mary! Anxious to look upon her, and with one fond glance to thank her for her heroic, unselfish love, He made an effort to change His bowed position beneath the cross, feebly raised His head, and directed toward her one loving glance of ineffable anguish, mingled with grateful recognition and humble resignation. Then the sad procession moves on, Mary following her divine Son on His way to death.

PRACTICE

*W*E, BY our sins, placed into the hands of the Jews and executioners the weapons by which Jesus suffered, and thus we thrust the sword of sorrow into Mary's heart. We repeat this, in a certain sense, as often as we commit a grievous sin, because we thereby number ourselves among those whom the Apostle describes as "crucifying again to themselves the Son of God, and making Him a mockery" (Heb. 6:6). Cardinal Hugo writes: "Sinners crucify, as far as is in them, Christ our Lord, because they repeat the cause of His crucifixion." Doing this, we thrust anew the sword of sorrow into Mary's heart. Let this consideration fill us with hatred for and fear of sin.

PRAYER OF THE CHURCH (p. 93).

Litany of Loreto (p. 301).

PRAYER

I COMPASSIONATE thee, sorrowing Mary, for the shock thy mother heart experienced when Jesus met thee as He carried His cross. Dear Mother, by that heart of thine, then so afflicted, obtain for me the virtue of patience and the gift of fortitude.

Hail Mary, etc.

EJACULATION (p. 94).

❧ SIXTH DAY ❧

Mary's Fifth Sorrow: Beneath the Cross

PREPARATORY PRAYER (p. 91).

MEDITATION

A T THE crucifixion of Jesus the soul of Mary was plunged into a sea of sorrow when she stood three hours under the cross. Writhing in excruciating pain, the Son of God hung upon the tree of disgrace and infamy, yet Mary continued to stand at its foot, tearful, grieving, yet persevering, filled with anguish because she could do nothing to help Him. Another great sorrow befell the heart of Mary when she slowly withdrew her tearful gaze from the face of Jesus, and cast her weeping eyes upon the cold and indifferent world that lay in darkness around and about Calvary. And yet, "When Jesus therefore had seen His Mother and the disciple standing whom He loved, He saith to His Mother, Woman, behold Thy son. After that He saith to the disciple, Behold thy Mother" (John 19:26, 27).

PRACTICE

*T*HESE words, "Behold thy son, behold thy Mother," contain and express the mystery of unbounded love, which Jesus has for all mankind, but more especially for the Church which is appointed and authorized to lead men to salvation. O blessed, O happy bequest! It was not enough for the love of Jesus to have restored heaven to us by His atoning death; He wished also to give us His dearest Mother. And she has always shown herself as such. To each of us individually she was and is a kind and loving Mother. Give thanks to her, bless and praise her for having adopted you as her child, and strive to become worthy of so great a privilege.

PRAYER OF THE CHURCH (p. 93).

Litany of Loreto (p. 301).

PRAYER

I COMPASSIONATE thee, sorrowing Mary, for the martyrdom thy generous heart bore so nobly whilst thou didst stand by Jesus agonizing. Dear Mother, by thy heart then so cruelly martyred, obtain for me the virtue of temperance and the gift of counsel.

Hail Mary, etc.

EJACULATION (p. 94).

✸ SEVENTH DAY ✸

Mary's Sixth Sorrow: The Taking Down of Jesus' Body from the Cross

PREPARATORY PRAYER (p. 91).

MEDITATION

WHO can describe the sorrow and anguish of Mary's heart when the body of Jesus was taken from the cross, when her tearful eyes fell upon His disfigured features! The pure and holy and beauteous form of her Son was a mass of clotted blood and unsightly wounds; and yet, disfigured as it was, there shone in His countenance a clear, calm expression of divine majesty. Now Mary views the wounds of that sacred body; she looks at the gap made in His side by the cruel spear, and can almost see the Sacred Heart of Jesus, all bruised and broken for love of man. Before her vision passes in detail His life and her own. Memory presents to her mind every day and hour of their quiet, happy life at Nazareth. Is it to be wondered, then, that at this bitter moment her sorrow was so great that, as St. Anselm observes, she should have died had she not been sustained by a miracle of divine omnipotence?

PRACTICE

*O*UGHT not the contemplation of the sorrows of our blessed Mother confirm us in patience, in resignation to the will of God in our trials and sufferings? If the Son of God said of Himself: "Ought not Christ to have suffered these things, and so to enter into His glory?" (Luke 24:26); if the most pure and holy Mother of God, despite her great prerogatives and merits, had to suffer a sorrow so ineffable, do not murmur if the word of Christ is addressed also to you: "And he that taketh not up his cross and followeth Me, is not worthy of Me" (Matt. 10:38).

PRAYER OF THE CHURCH (p. 93).

Litany of Loreto (p. 301).

PRAYER

I COMPASSIONATE thee, sorrowing Mary, for the pain thou didst suffer when the body of thy divine Son, taken down all torn and bloody from the cross, was placed in thy arms. Dear Mother, by thy heart pierced through, obtain for me the virtue of fraternal charity and the gift of understanding.

Hail Mary, etc.

EJACULATION (p. 94).

➤ EIGHTH DAY ➤

Mary's Seventh Sorrow: Jesus is Buried

PREPARATORY PRAYER (p. 91).

MEDITATION

*T*HE sacrifice for the redemption of the world was accomplished. "And Joseph, taking the body, wrapt it up in a clean linen cloth, and laid it in his own new monument, which he had hewed out in a rock. And he rolled a great stone to the door of the monument, and went his way" (Matt. 27:59). Mary also took part in the burial of her beloved Son, though the evangelists do not mention her name amongst those who were present on that mournful occasion. Never, most assuredly, was human soul visited by such woe and desolation, as that which overwhelmed hers as she cast a last glance on the precious remains of her dead Son.

PRACTICE

*L*ET us learn of the sorrowful Mother at the tomb of her divine Son submission to God's holy will in all things, but especially when He takes from us one of our dear ones. Again, the contemplation of the sufferings of Mary should fortify us in patience, whenever God is pleased to visit us with a light and small cross of affliction, or even with a sorrow that causes our heart to bleed. It should inspire us with a filial confidence in Mary, who thus suffered for us and gave her divine Son for our salvation. We can and ought to prove our love for her, not by sentimental feelings of affection, but by a sincere hatred of sin and great fervor in the service of her divine Son.

PRAYER OF THE CHURCH (p. 93).

Litany of Loreto (p. 301).

PRAYER

J COMPASSIONATE thee, sorrowing Mary, for the anguish felt by thy loving heart when Jesus' body was laid in the sepulchre. Dear Mother, by all the bitterness of desolation thou didst know, obtain for me the virtue of diligence and the gift of wisdom.

Hail Mary, etc.

EJACULATION (p. 94).

❧ NINTH DAY ❧

Reasons Why Mary Had to Suffer

PREPARATORY PRAYER (p. 91).

MEDITATION

*T*HE reasons why God permitted Mary to suffer so much may be briefly stated as follows: He did so from His love for Mary and from His love for us. He did so from His love for Mary, because by suffering she merited greater glory in heaven. As Mother of the Crucified she persevered beneath the cross, and now she thrones in heaven as the glorious Mother of the risen Redeemer. Because she shared in His suffering, she now shares His glory. Again, God permitted Mary to suffer because He loved us. If she had not experienced such bitter sorrow, we would not have recourse to her, for whosoever has not suffered himself can not have sympathy with the sufferings of others. Mary knows the pangs of sorrow by experience, and therefore knows also how to console and help us.

PRACTICE

*B*ECAUSE she herself drained the most bitter cup of sorrow, Mary is always willing to help those who invoke her aid. But above all she is inclined to help repentant sinners, because she knows how great the price of their redemption was, paid by the blood of her divine

Son. She is able to help us, because, after God, she is most powerful; she is most willing to help us, because she loves us, whom God so has loved "as to give His only-begotten Son" (John 3:16). Let us, therefore, have recourse to her in all our needs, and we shall experience the power of her help in life and death.

PRAYER OF THE CHURCH (p. 93).

Litany of Loreto (p. 301).

PRAYER

I COMPASSIONATE thee, sorrowing Mary, for all thy sorrows. I beseech thee, dear Mother, by thy heart pierced through by them, obtain for me full abandonment to the will of God in everything and perseverance to the end.

Hail Mary, etc.

EJACULATION (p. 94).

V

Novena for the Feast of the Assumption of the Blessed Virgin Mary

⟞ FIRST DAY ⟝

Mary's Death was without Pain

PREPARATORY PRAYER

O MARY, Virgin most blessed and Mother of Our Lord and Redeemer Jesus Christ, through thy mercy I beseech thee to come to my aid, and to inspire me with such confidence in thy power, that I may have recourse to thee, pray to thee, and implore thy aid in all needs of soul and body.

MEDITATION

MARY, the virgin Mother of God, was conceived without original sin. She never dimmed the luster of sanctifying grace which beautified her soul by actual sin. Nevertheless she had to pass through the dark portal of death before she was assumed, body and soul, into heaven. She had not been endowed with the privilege of immortality with which God had invested our first parents in paradise. It was meet that she should be like unto her divine Son in everything, even in death. But as she had drained the bitter cup of suffering during her whole life, and especially when standing beneath the cross, her death was to be free from pain and suffering. She quietly passed away, yielding up her spirit in a yearning desire to be united forever with her divine Son in heaven.

PRACTICE

*I*F YOU have dispossessed your heart of all unruly attachment to the goods and enjoyments of this earth, you, too, may hope for a happy and tranquil transition from this land of exile to your home in heaven. Therefore, if you are still attached to the transitory things of this life, disengage your heart from them now. The voluntary renouncement of earthly goods alone is meritorious before God. The separation from them enforced by the strong hand of death is of no supernatural value.

PRAYER OF THE CHURCH

*W*E BESEECH Thee, O Lord, pardon the shortcomings of Thy servants; that we who, by our own works, are not able to please Thee, may be saved by the intercession of the Mother of Thy Son, Our Lord Jesus Christ. Amen.

Litany of Loreto (p. 301).

PRAYER

O MOST benign Mother Mary! I rejoice that by thy happy and tranquil death the yearning of thy heart was appeased, and thy life, so rich in merit and sacrifice, received its crown. I rejoice that after passing from this life, thou, O most loving Mother, wast made the glorious and powerful queen of heaven and dost exercise thy influence as such for the benefit of thy frail, exiled children on earth. Obtain for me, I beseech thee, a happy death, that I may praise and glorify thy might and kindness forever in heaven.

Hail Mary, etc.

EJACULATION

Sweet heart of Mary be my salvation!

Indulgence. (1) 100 days, every time. (2) A plenary indulgence, once a month, on any day, to all who shall have said it every day for a month, under the usual conditions.

⇜ SECOND DAY ⇝

At Mary's Tomb

PREPARATORY PRAYER (p. 109).

MEDITATION

A N ANCIENT legend relates that, led by Heaven, all the Apostles, except St. Thomas, assembled at the Blessed Virgin's death-bed. After she had breathed forth her pure spirit, her sacred remains were prepared for the grave by wrapping the body in new white linen and decking it with flowers. Meanwhile the apostles, assembled in another room, sang psalms and hymns in praise of their departed Mother. The apostles, all the disciples, and the faithful dwelling in Jerusalem followed the blessed remains to the grave chanting psalms and hymns. Arrived in the valley of Josaphat, the body was gently placed in a sepulcher of stone not far from the Garden of Olives. After the entombment the apostles and crowds of the faithful lingered near the sacred spot in prayer, meditation, and chanting of psalms in which angels' voices were heard to mingle.

PRACTICE

*J*OIN in spirit with the apostles and faithful in their prayer and meditation at the grave of our blessed Mother. Contemplate and review her whole life. Could a course like hers have terminated more appropriately than with so beautiful, painless, and tranquil a passing away? Prepare yourself even now for your departure from this life. Do not postpone the settlement of your affairs, spiritual and temporal, until the last uncertain hours. Above all, remove now, or as soon as possible, all doubts, anxieties, and irregularities of conscience, because delay is dangerous and leads to impenitence, and because in the last hours the powers of hell usually assail the departing soul with all their might.

PRAYER OF THE CHURCH (p. 110).

Litany of Loreto (p. 301).

PRAYER

*G*LORIOUS Virgin, who for thy consolation didst deserve to die comforted by the sight of thy dear Son Jesus, and in the company of the apostles and angels; pray for us, that at that awful moment we, too, may be comforted by receiving Jesus in the most holy Eucharist, and may feel thee nigh when we breathe forth our soul.

Hail Mary, etc.

EJACULATION (p. 111).

◄ THIRD DAY ►

The Empty Tomb

PREPARATORY PRAYER (p. 109).

MEDITATION

*S*T. JOHN DAMASCENE writes: "St. Thomas was not with the other apostles when the Blessed Virgin died, but arrived in Jerusalem on the third day after that event. Ardently desiring to see once more and to venerate the sacred body which had given flesh and blood to his beloved Master, the grave was opened for this purpose. The body could nowhere be seen, and a delicious perfume filled the empty tomb. The apostles then became convinced that as God had preserved the body of Mary free from sin before, in, and after the birth of His Son, He was pleased likewise, after her death, to preserve that same body from corruption, and to glorify it in heaven."

A council held in Jerusalem in the year 1672 declared: "It is beyond all doubt that the Blessed Virgin is not only a great and miraculous sign on earth, because she bore God in the flesh and yet remained a virgin, but she is also a great and miraculous sign in heaven, because she was taken up thither with soul and body. For although her sinless body was enclosed in the tomb, yet, like the body of Our Lord, it arose on the third day and was carried up to heaven."

Although the doctrine of the bodily assumption of Mary into heaven was not defined by the Church as an article of faith in the strict sense, yet the learned Pope Benedict XIV remarks, "It would be presumptuous and blameworthy in any one to call into doubt or to question this beautiful and consoling belief of ages."

PRACTICE

*L*ET us rejoice at the thought of the glorious resurrection of our dear Mother. Let us unite ourselves in spirit with the apostles in heaven and with Holy Church to congratulate her on this extraordinary privilege. But let us also rejoice at the thought of our own resurrection. True, it shall not take place immediately after death, but it is therefore not the less certain, and it depends on us to make it glorious and blessed.

PRAYER OF THE CHURCH (p. 110).

Litany of Loreto (p. 301).

PRAYER

O GLORIOUS Virgin and Mother of God, Mary! As thy sacred body after death was preserved from corruption, and united with thy sinless soul was borne to heaven by the angels; obtain for me the grace that my life and death be holy, so that on the Day of Judgment I may arise to glory everlasting.

Hail Mary, etc.

EJACULATION (p. 111).

✎ FOURTH DAY ❧

Reasons for the Bodily Assumption of Mary into Heaven

PREPARATORY PRAYER (p. 109).

MEDITATION

1. *T*HE wages of sin is death. Now, as the Blessed Virgin from the first moment of her existence was preserved from all sin, and even from original sin, it necessarily follows that death could have no permanent dominion over her, and that her body would not be permitted to see corruption.

2. This sinless body had been the medium by which the body of Our Lord Jesus Christ, who was the conqueror of death, had been formed. How, then, could such a highly privileged body, a pure and virginal body, be permitted to pass through corruption and decay?

3. As Mary had yielded up her sacred person to be a dwelling-place for the Lord of heaven, it seems fitting that this same Lord, in His turn, should give the kingdom of heaven to her as her resting-place. St. Bernard expresses this sentiment as follows: "When Our Lord came into this world, Mary furnished Him with the noblest dwelling on earth, the temple of her virginal womb. In return, the Lord on this day raises her up to the highest throne in heaven."

PRACTICE

*I*F YOU desire to look forward to death without fear, and to expect your dissolution with confidence, follow the Apostle's injunction, "Therefore, whilst we have time, let us work good" (Gal. 6:10). Avoid sin, perform good works, be patient in affliction, and strive to expiate the punishment due to your sins by voluntary acts of penance, thus reducing your inclination to sin. Therefore offer up to God every morning, in a spirit of penitence, all your labors, trials, and sufferings.

PRAYER OF THE CHURCH (p. 110).

Litany of Loreto (p. 301).

PRAYER

O GLORIOUS Virgin and Mother of God, Mary! I beseech thee through the ineffable glory thou didst make for thy departure from this world by a life of retirement, full of merits and virtue, dedicated to God alone; obtain for me the grace that, following thy example, I may detach my heart from this world, and patiently bear affliction and adversity, carefully avoid sin, and always strive to advance in the love of God.

Hail Mary, etc.

EJACULATION (p. 111).

⫷ FIFTH DAY ⫸

Mary's Glorious Entrance into Heaven

PREPARATORY PRAYER (p. 109).

MEDITATION

A JOY greater than human heart can conceive fills the heavenly spirits when a soul enters heaven to receive her reward. What jubilant transports, then, must those have been with which they hailed the entrance into heavenly bliss of the most pure and holy Virgin, the Mother of the Son of God, body and soul, transfigured in glory!

And she is, and shall be, for all eternity, their mistress and queen! What an ineffable joy, too, for the Blessed Virgin, to behold the countless numbers of angels, to admire their beauty, their purity, their intense love of God! But as the feeble light of a candle disappears before the splendor of the sun's rays, thus are these choirs of angels obscured by the ineffable glory of her divine Son coming to welcome His Mother. Who can describe this affecting meeting? What a superabundant reward for affliction and suffering! What an ocean of joy and bliss, when the Son of God presented His Mother before the throne of His heavenly Father, who greeted her as His beloved Daughter! What a joy to behold the Holy Ghost, whose pure Spouse she had been even on earth! These transports of bliss baffle all attempts at description.

PRACTICE

*T*HOUGH we are unable to have an adequate perception of Mary's glory in heaven, by which she is raised above all angels and saints, yet it is in our power to do one thing; we can rejoice at the glory of our blessed Mother, and join the heavenly spirits and the saints in paying homage to her. Let us resolve to do this, and never to forget that Mary attained to the largest share of her divine Son's glory because she was foremost in sharing His sufferings. Let this encourage us to bear our cross, to bear it with our Saviour even to the height of Calvary, there to die with Him.

PRAYER OF THE CHURCH (p. 110).

Litany of Loreto (p. 301).

PRAYER

O GLORIOUS Virgin and Mother of God, Mary! I beseech thee through the preparation with which thou wast glorified by God—by the Father as His most beloved Daughter, by the Son as His immaculate Mother, and by the Holy Ghost as His most pure Spouse—in heaven; obtain for me the grace to share to some extent this thy glory, and therefore to live so that I may deserve it.

Hail Mary, etc.

EJACULATION (p. 111).

⮞ SIXTH DAY ⮜

Mary Crowned in Heaven

PREPARATORY PRAYER (p. 109).

MEDITATION

M ARY'S glory received its culmination by her coronation as queen of heaven and earth. It was meet that in her should be fulfilled the words of Holy Scripture: "Come from Libanus, my Spouse, come, thou shalt be crowned" (Cant. 4:8), and that her own prophetic words, "He hath put down the mighty from their seat, and hath exalted the humble" (Luke 1:52), should be exemplified in her. For it was reasonable and becoming that she, who once with Jesus wore the crown of shame and contempt, should now share with Him the crown of immortal glory. It was but fair and just that the immaculate being who was chosen, above all inhabitants of heaven and earth, to be the true and worthy Mother of God, should now be solemnly installed over all creatures in heaven and on earth as the queen of angels and men, and that to her should be offered homage, praise, and honor by the blessed spirits and by the souls of the saints. But the crown which she received is not one made of gold and precious stones; it is composed of the virtues with which Mary, in faithful co-operation with divine grace, embellished herself; it consists, too, of all the homage and glory which she receives as queen of heaven. The most precious gem in this crown is the filial love and gratitude Jesus shows toward His Mother in heaven.

PRACTICE

INDEED, "eye hath not seen, ear hath not heard, neither has it entered into the heart of man," what the heavenly Father has prepared in the mansions of eternal bliss for His beloved Daughter, the Son for His Blessed Mother, and the Holy Ghost for His chosen Spouse. She is now queen of heaven and earth; of heaven, for she is the queen of all angels and saints; of earth, for as Mother of God she is the Mother of all mankind, the mediatrix between the Redeemer and the redeemed.

You, too, may contribute a gem toward the crown of your heavenly Mother by paying her filial homage, imitating her virtues, and preserving, for the love of her, your innocence and purity of heart.

PRAYER OF THE CHURCH (p. 110).

Litany of Loreto (p. 301).

PRAYER

O GLORIOUS Virgin and Mother of God, Mary! I beseech thee through the everlasting crown of glory with which God has crowned thee queen of heaven and earth; obtain for me through thy mighty intercession the grace to persevere in virtue to the end, so that finally I may attain the crown of bliss prepared by God for those that love Him.

Hail Mary, etc.

EJACULATION (p. 111).

❧ SEVENTH DAY ☙

Mary's Bliss in Heaven

PREPARATORY PRAYER (p. 109).

MEDITATION

A CCORDING to Holy Scripture and the doctrine of the Church, there are in heaven various grades of glory and bliss, according to the rank and merit of the saints. They probably attain this higher grade of glory and bliss by the increase of their ability to enjoy the happiness of heaven. Their intellect is enabled to contemplate more profoundly the incomprehensible essence of God; their power of perception is augmented so that they may more readily recognize and admire the splendor of the angels, saints, and heavenly mansions; their will is enabled to be united, in a higher degree, with God. From this we may conclude that Mary's bliss in heaven transcends all human conception. Her heavenly glory and reward consists in the perfect adaptation of her whole being to the enjoyment of God and of eternal bliss.

PRACTICE

*L*OOK up, Christian soul, to this great and brilliant queen of heaven. She is your gentle Mother and assures you of her help, and the diadem she wears upon her brow is a proof that she has the power to help you. Do not, therefore, refuse the hand of this mighty friend in heaven, for she will lift you from the depths of your misery, from the rocky shoals of temptation, and lead you strong and victorious into the presence of her divine Son. Thus you will enter into a new and supernatural life in Christ, to share in the grace-laden mysteries of His life, passion, and triumph.

PRAYER OF THE CHURCH (p. 110).

Litany of Loreto (p. 301).

PRAYER

O GREAT and glorious queen of heaven, Mary! I beseech thee by that exalted throne upon which God has raised thee above all angels and saints; let me one day appear amongst them to join them in their praise of thee. Obtain for me the grace that I may never cease to honor thee as thou dost deserve to be honored, and thereby to become worthy of thy mighty protection in life and death.

Hail Mary, etc.

EJACULATION (p. 111).

✎ EIGHTH DAY ✎

Mary, the Queen of Mercy

PREPARATORY PRAYER (p. 109).

MEDITATION

M ARY is, then, a queen, but—what a consolation to know it!—a queen always mild and gentle, always willing to confer benefits upon us. Hence the Church teaches us to call her the Mother of mercy. The pious and learned author Gerson says: "God's dominion comprises justice and mercy. He divided it, retaining the administration of justice for Himself, and relinquishing, in a certain sense, the dispensation of mercy to Mary, by conferring through her hands all graces He grants to mankind." How consoling, then, the assurance that our merciful Mother is so mighty and so loving a queen!

PRACTICE

SO GREAT is the tenderness of Mary's maternal heart "that never was it heard that any one who fled to her protection, implored her help, and sought her intercession was left unaided." How many prayers, petitions, and thanksgivings ascend daily to the throne of this our exalted and merciful protectress! There is not a cry of an afflicted, struggling, and suffering soul that she does not graciously hear. Join, therefore, confidently in the prayer of Holy Church, "Hail, holy queen, Mother of mercy!" Approach her with filial trust. Neglect not to honor her yourself, and do all in your power to lead others to do her honor.

PRAYER OF THE CHURCH (p. 110).

Litany of Loreto (p. 301).

PRAYER

O GLORIOUS Virgin and Mother of God, Mary! Holy Church teaches me that despite the glory to which thou wast exalted, thou didst not forget thy miserable clients, and that in heaven thy mercy is still greater than it was during thy life on earth. Therefore I come to thee and trustingly lay at thy feet all my needs, miseries, and petitions. My queen, my Mother, turn not thy gracious eyes from me. Remember me with thy divine Son; cease not to pray for me and take me under thy protection, so that I may finally have the happiness to see and praise thee in thy glory for ever and ever.

Hail Mary, etc.

EJACULATION (p. 111).

✎ NINTH DAY ✎

Mary in Heaven, the Help of Christians on Earth

PREPARATORY PRAYER (p. 109).

MEDITATION

MARY'S help as Mother of mercy is not confined to individuals. She is the protectress and helper of the whole Church. All over the earth, wherever we cast our glance, in the records of the history of times long past and those of recent occurrence, we find testimony of the graces and benefits obtained through her intercession. The feasts celebrated by the Church throughout the year, what are they but evidences of gratitude offered to the queen of heaven for the oftentimes miraculous delivery from war, pestilence, and other great afflictions? Hence she is rightly invoked as the "Help of Christians."

PRACTICE

*I*N OUR days, too, storms and dangers threaten the Church. Let us, therefore, by calling on Mary for help, do our part toward shortening the days of visitation and trial. Let us not confine our petitions to her within the narrow limits of our own personal needs, but let us join in the cry for help ascending to the Mother of mercy throughout all Christendom. Let us daily, for Holy Church, send up our petition to Mary's heavenly throne: "Help of Christians, pray for us!"

PRAYER OF THE CHURCH (p. 110).

Litany of Loreto (p. 301).

PRAYER

O GLORIOUS Virgin and Mother of God, Mary, queen of heaven! Forget us not. Thou art the help of Christians; lighten our tribulations, and help us with motherly intercession at the throne of thy divine Son. With Holy Church I join in the petition to thee: "Holy Mary, aid the miserable, assist the desponding, strengthen the weak, pray for the people, plead for the clergy, intercede for the devout female sex. Let all who have recourse to thee

experience the efficacy of thy help!"
Hail Mary, etc.

EJACULATION (p. 111).

PART III

The Fourteen Holy Helpers

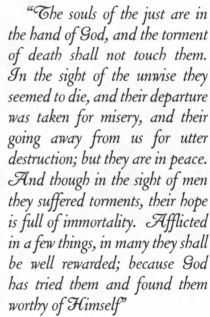

"The souls of the just are in the hand of God, and the torment of death shall not touch them. In the sight of the unwise they seemed to die, and their departure was taken for misery, and their going away from us for utter destruction; but they are in peace. And though in the sight of men they suffered torments, their hope is full of immortality. Afflicted in a few things, in many they shall be well rewarded; because God has tried them and found them worthy of Himself"

(Wis. 3:1-5.)

Fourteen Holy Helpers, pray for us.

CHAPTER I

The Fourteen Holy Helpers

AMONG the saints who in Catholic devotion are invoked with special confidence, because they have proved themselves efficacious helpers in adversity and difficulties, there is a group venerated under the collective name of Holy Helpers. They are:

1. St. George, Martyr.
2. St. Blase, Bishop and Martyr.
3. St. Pantaleon, Martyr.
4. St. Vitus, Martyr.
5. St. Erasmus, Bishop and Martyr.
6. St. Christophorus, Martyr.
7. St. Dionysius, Bishop and Martyr.
8. St. Cyriacus, Martyr.
9. St. Achatius, Martyr.
10. St. Eustachius, Martyr.
11. St. Giles, Abbot.
12. St. Catherine, Virgin and Martyr.
13. St. Margaret, Virgin and Martyr.
14. St. Barbara, Virgin and Martyr.

The reason why these saints are invoked as a group is said to have been an epidemic which devastated Europe from 1346 to 1349. It was called the Plague, or "Black Death," and among its symptoms were the turning black of the tongue, parching of the throat, violent headache, fever, and boils on the abdomen. The malady attacked its victims suddenly, bereft them of reason, and caused death in a few hours, so that many died without the last sacraments. Fear caused many attacks and disrupted social and family ties. To all appearances, the disease was incurable.

During this period of general affliction the people in pious confidence turned toward Heaven, and had recourse to the intercession of the saints, praying to be spared an attack, or to be cured when stricken. Among the saints invoked since the earliest times of the Church as special patrons in certain diseases were: St. Christopher and St. Giles against the plague, St. Dionysius against headache, St. Blase against ills of the throat, St. Catherine against those of the tongue, St. Erasmus against those of the abdomen, St. Barbara against fever, St. Vitus against epilepsy. St. Pantaleon was the patron of physicians, St. Cyriacus was had recourse to in temptations, especially in those at the hour of death; St. Achatius was invoked in death agony; Sts. Christopher, Barbara, and Catherine were appealed to for protection against a sudden and unprovided death; the aid of St. Giles was implored for making a good confession; St. Eustachius was patron in all kinds of difficulties, and, because peculiar circumstances separated him for a time from his family, he was invoked also in family troubles. Domestic animals, too, being attacked by the plague, Sts. George, Erasmus, Pantaleon, and Vitus were invoked for their protection. It appears from the invocation of these saints, so widespread in olden times during the plague and other epidemics, that their being grouped as the Fourteen Holy Helpers originated in a like visitation.

The fourteen saints venerated as the Holy Helpers are represented with the symbols of their martyrdom, or with the insignia of their state of life; also, as a group of children. The latter representation is accounted for as follows:

The abbey of Langheim, in the diocese of Bamberg, Bavaria, owned a farm on which the monks kept their flocks. The sheep were tended by shepherds, who led them along the hillsides, where they grazed quietly during the day, and were driven home in the evening.

On the evening of September 22, 1445, a young shepherd, Herman Leicht, who was gathering his flock for the homeward drive, heard what seemed to him to be the cry of a child, and looking about, saw a child sitting in a field near by. Surprised, and wondering how the child came there, he was about to approach, when it disappeared. Feeling rather disturbed, the boy returned to his flock. After reaching it, he turned to look back to the place where he had seen the apparition. There the child sat again, this time in a circle of light, and between two burning candles. Terrified at this second apparition, he made the sign of the cross. The child smiled, as if to encourage him, and he was about to approach it again, when it vanished a second time. Greatly perplexed, he drove his flock home and informed his parents of the occurrence. But they called the apparition a delusion and told him not to mention it to any one.

Nevertheless, feeling uneasy, and desiring an explanation, he went to the monastery and related his experience to one of the Fathers, who advised him to ask the child, if it ever should appear to him again, what it wanted.

Nearly a year later, June 28, 1446, the eve of the feast of Sts. Peter and Paul, the child again appeared to the boy in the same place as before and about sunset; but this time it was surrounded by thirteen other children, all in a halo of glory. He boldly approached the group and asked the child he had formerly seen in the name of the Father, and of the Son, and the Holy Ghost, what it desired. The child replied: "We are the Fourteen Helpers, and desire that a chapel be built for us. Be thou our servant, and we shall serve thee." Then the group of children disappeared, and the shepherd boy was filled with heavenly consolation.

The following Sunday, after he had driven his flock to the pasture, it seemed to him that he saw two lighted candles descending from the sky to the place where he had seen the apparition. A woman who was passing at the time declared that she also saw them. The boy hastened to the monastery and told about the two apparitions. The abbot, Frederic IV, and the rest of the community, were not inclined to believe in the apparition, and ascribed it to the boy's visionary fancy. But when, in the course of time, several extraordinary favors were granted to people who prayed at the place of the apparition, the monks built a chapel there. It was begun in 1447, and finished and dedicated next year under the invocation of the Blessed Virgin Mary and the Fourteen Holy Helpers. The bishop granted an indulgence for the day of the anniversary of the dedication, the Papal Nuncio, Cardinal Joannes, granted another, and Pope Nicholas V a third. These indulgences, and a number of other spiritual privileges granted to the chapel, attracted a great many visitors, so that it became a place of pious pilgrimage. Elector Frederic III, in fulfilment of a vow made when beset with difficulties, visited the chapel in 1485. Emperor Ferdinand also visited it and left, as a votive offering, his gold pectoral chain on the altar.

Devotion to the Fourteen Holy Helpers continued to spread. In 1743, a magnificent church, to replace the old chapel, was begun, and completed in 1772. Churches and altars in honor of these saints are found in Italy, Austria, Tyrol, Hungary, Bohemia, Switzerland, and other countries of Europe. In the United States of America two churches are dedicated under the invocation of the Holy Helpers: one in Baltimore, Md., the other in Gardenville, N. Y. Wherever and whenever invoked, these saints have proved themselves willing helpers in all difficulties, vicissitudes, and trials of their faithful clients.

CHAPTER II

Legends

*B*EFORE proceeding to relate the lives of the Fourteen Holy Helpers, we deem it opportune to define the term usually applied to the narrative of the lives of the saints.

The histories of the saints are called Legends. This word is derived from the Latin, and signifies something that is to be read; a passage, the reading of which is prescribed. The legends of the saints are the lives of the holy martyrs and confessors of the Faith. Some of them occur in the Roman Breviary, which the Catholic clergy is obliged to read every day.

Joseph von Goerres, an illustrious champion of the Church during the first half of the nineteenth century, writes as follows concerning legends:

"The histories of the lives of the saints were gathered from the earliest times. A collection of such histories is found in 'The Golden Legend.' The Passionales, too, containing the life of a saint for every day in the year, belong to this sort of literature. In Germany these histories were at first translations from the Latin; later, they were written in the native idiom, and, in style, were of a charming simplicity. At that time, when the upper classes did not yet judge themselves too highly cultivated to share in the Faith, and not too privileged to join in the sentiments and affections of the people, and were therefore more in harmony with the lower ranks of society, these legends were in general circulation among all classes: among the wealthy in manuscript, among the poor orally and in the form in which they had become acquainted with them in church and elsewhere.

"In early times the science of criticism was unknown; therefore little care was exercised in separating the poetic additions from the authentic legends, especially as the Church had not yet spoken on the subject. Faith was yet of that robust sort which is not affected by miraculous occurrences. Nearly all Europe then still accepted the adage now current only in Spain, 'It is better sometimes to believe what can not be established as truth, than to lose a single truth by want of faith.' But later the science of criticism came into its rights. The Church established canonical rules, according to which a strict investigation of all the facts submitted to her judgment was to be made, and rejected everything that could not stand the most rigid examination.

"Then Art devoted itself to that legendary lore which the Church, declaring it outside of her domain, permitted to be embellished at will. Thus poetic legends were multiplied, their authors being more or less convinced that the reader would be able to distinguish truth from poetical embellishment. The common people continued to make little distinction and did not permit criticism to influence their ancient beliefs. They regarded these legends as they regard the pictures of the saints; not as portraits of the persons depicted—for in the very next church the same saint might be represented in a quite different manner—but as illustrations, more or less apt, whose object was to attract the attention by their artistic character and thus to draw the mind to the contemplation of their original, and by it to God, and thereby serve the purpose of edification."

If we are not devoid of all sentiments of piety, the history of the combats and victories of the saints and martyrs, and the narrative of the miracles wrought through their intercession before and after their death, will always be a source of joy and consolation to us, and will tend to animate us with similar fortitude and love of virtue.

The legends of the Fourteen Holy Helpers are replete with the most glorious examples of heroic firmness and invincible courage in the profession of the Faith, which ought to incite us to imitate their fidelity in the performance of the Christian and social duties. If they, with the aid of God's grace, achieved such victories, why should not we, by the same aid, be able to accomplish the little desired of us? God rewarded His victorious champions with eternal bliss; the same crown is prepared for us, if we but render ourselves worthy of it. God placed the seal of miracles on the intrepid confession of His servants; and a mind imbued with the spirit of faith sees nothing extraordinary therein, because our divine Saviour Himself said, "Amen, amen I say to you, he that believeth in Me, the works that I do, he also shall do, and greater than these shall he do" (John 14:12). In all the miraculous events wrought in and by the saints appears only the victorious omnipotent power of Jesus Christ, and the living faith in which His servants operated in virtue of this power. To obliterate the miracles that appear in the lives of the saints, or even to enfeeble their import by the manner of relating them, would rob these legends of their intrinsic value. If our age is no longer robust enough to acknowledge the effects of divine omnipotence and grace, it does not follow that they must be disavowed or denied.

The Legends of the Fourteen Holy Helpers

I.

St. George, Martyr

LEGEND

S T. GEORGE is honored throughout Christendom as one of the most illustrious martyrs of Jesus Christ. In the reign of the first Christian emperors numerous churches were erected in his honor, and his tomb in Palestine became a celebrated place of pilgrimage. But his history is involved in great obscurity, as no early records of his life and martyrdom are at present in existence. The following are the traditions concerning him which have been handed down to us by the Greek historians, and which are celebrated in verse by that illustrious saint and poet of the eighth century, St. John Damascene.

St. George is said to have been born in Cappadocia of noble Christian parents. After the death of his father, he traveled with his mother into Palestine, of which she was a native. There she possessed a considerable estate, which fell to him upon her death. Being strong and robust in body, he embraced the profession of a soldier, and was made a tribune, or colonel, in the army. His courage and fidelity attracted the attention of Emperor Diocletian, who bestowed upon him marks of special favor. When that prince declared war against the Christian religion, St. George laid aside the signs of his rank, threw up his commission, and rebuked the emperor for the severity of his bloody edicts. He was immediately cast into prison, and alternate threats and promises were employed to induce him to apostatize. As he continued firm, he was put to the torture and tormented with great cruelty. "I despise your promises," he said to the judge, "and do not fear your threats. The emperor's power is of short duration, and his reign will soon end. It were better for you, to acknowledge the true God and to seek His kingdom." Thereupon a great block of stone was placed on the breast of the brave young officer, and thus he was left in prison.

Next day he was bound upon a wheel set with sharp knives, and it was put in motion to cut him to pieces. Whilst suffering this cruel torture, he saw a heavenly vision, which consoled and encouraged him, saying, "George, fear not; I am with thee." His patience and fortitude under the torments inflicted on him so affected the numerous pagan spectators that many of them were converted to the Faith and suffered martyrdom for it. On the next day, April 23, 303, St. George was led through the city and beheaded. This took place at Lydda, the city in which, as we read in the Acts of the Apostles (chapter 9), St. Peter healed a man sick with the palsy.

St. George is usually represented as a knight tilting against a dragon; but this is only emblematical of the glorious combat in which he encountered and overthrew the devil, winning for himself thereby a martyr's crown.

LESSON

WE TOO, like St. George, often have opportunity to confess our faith in Christ. We confess it by patiently bearing adversity, by suppressing our evil inclinations, by suffering injustice without retaliating evil for evil, by using every opportunity of performing deeds of charity, by devoting ourselves unremittingly to our daily duties, by carefully guarding our tongue, etc. Examine yourself whether you have not often denied your Faith, if not in words, through your works.

PRAYER OF THE CHURCH

O GOD, who dost rejoice us by the merits and intercession of Thy blessed martyr George; graciously grant that we, who through him implore Thee for Thy bounty, may receive thereby the gift of Thy grace. Through Christ our Lord. Amen.

II

St. Blase, Bishop and Martyr

LEGEND

S T. BLASE was born at Sebaste, Armenia. He became a physician, but at the same time devoted himself zealously to the practice of his Christian duties. His virtuous conduct gained for him the esteem of the Christian clergy and people to such a degree, that he was elected bishop of his native city. Henceforth he devoted himself to ward off the dangers of soul from the faithful, as he had hitherto been intent on healing their bodily ills. To all, he was a shining example of virtue.

During the reign of Emperor Licinius a cruel persecution of Christians broke out. The persecutors directed their fury principally against the bishops, well knowing that when the shepherd is stricken the flock is dispersed. Listening to the entreaties of the faithful, and mindful of the words of Our Lord, "When they shall persecute you in this city, flee into another" (Matt. 10:23), St. Blase hid himself in a cave. But one day the prefect Agricola instituted a chase, and his party discovered the holy bishop and brought him before their master.

St. Blase remained steadfast in the Faith, and by its able confession and defense attracted the attention of the attendants at his trial. The cruel tyrant had him bound and tortured with iron combs. After suffering these torments with great patience and meekness, the saint was cast into prison. He was kept there a long time, because the prefect hoped to exhaust his powers of endurance, and to bring him to sacrifice to the idols. His jailer permitted the holy bishop to receive visitors in his prison, and many sick and suffering availed themselves of this privilege. He cured some of them and gave good advice to others.

One day a mother brought to him her boy, who, while eating, had swallowed a fishbone, which remained in his throat, and, causing great pain, threatened suffocation. St. Blase prayed and made the sign of the cross over the boy, and behold, he was cured. For this reason the saint is invoked in throat troubles.

At length the holy bishop was again brought before the judge and commanded to sacrifice to the idols. But he said: "Thou art blind, because thou art not illuminated by the true light. How can a man sacrifice to idols, when he adores the true God alone? I do not fear thy threats. Do with me according to thy pleasure. My body is in thy power, but God alone has power over my soul. Thou seekest salvation with the idols; I hope and trust to receive it from the only true and living God whom I adore."

Then the prefect sentenced him to death. St. Blase was beheaded, suffering death for the Faith February 3, 316.

LESSON

S T. BLASE gave us a glorious example of fortitude in the confession of the Faith. According to the teaching of St. Paul, confession of the Faith is necessary for our salvation. He says, "For if thou confess with thy mouth the Lord Jesus, and believe in thy heart that God hath raised Him up from the dead, thou shalt be saved. For with the heart we believe unto justice, but with the mouth confession is made unto salvation" (Rom. 10:9, 10). We are, therefore, not permitted to be silent, much less to agree, when our Faith, and whatever is connected therewith, as the sacraments, ceremonies, priests, etc., are ridiculed and reviled. Parents especially must be most careful in speaking of these subjects before their children and servants, and do so only with due reverence.

On the contrary, we must confess our Faith, and if necessary, defend it against all attacks. Often one serious word will suffice to silence a calumniator of the Faith and cause him to blush. We must confess our Faith not only in the bosom of our family, but also in public. We must let our fellow-men know that we are true Catholics, who adhere to our Faith from conviction, without regard to what others say of us, or how they judge us, remembering the words of Our Lord, "Every one, therefore, that shall confess me before men, I will also confess him before my Father who is in heaven" (Matt. 10:32).

It was remarked above that St. Blase is the patron invoked in throat troubles. Therefore the Church, on his feast, February 3, gives a special blessing, at which she prays over those receiving it: "By the intercession of St. Blase, bishop and martyr, may God deliver thee from all ills of the throat and from all other ills; in the name of the Father, and of the Son, and of the Holy Ghost. Amen." Do not neglect to receive this blessing, if you have the opportunity. The blessings of the Church are powerful and effective, for she is God's representative on earth. Therefore her blessing is God's blessing, and is always effective, except we ourselves place an obstacle in its way.

PRAYER OF THE CHURCH

O GOD, who dost rejoice us through the memory of Thy blessed bishop and martyr Blase: graciously grant us, that we, who honor his memory, may experience his protection. Through Christ our Lord. Amen.

III

St. Erasmus, Bishop and Martyr

LEGEND

*T*HE pious historians of the early Christian times state, as a rule, only what the saints did and suffered for the Faith, and how they died. They deemed the martyrs' glorious combat and their victorious entrance into heaven more instructive, and therefore more important, than a lengthy description of their lives.

Hence we know little of the native place and the youth of St. Erasmus, except that at the beginning of the fourth century of the Christian era he was bishop of Antioch in Asia Minor, the city where the name of "Christian" first came into use. When a long and cruel persecution broke out under the Emperor Diocletian, St. Erasmus hid himself in the mountains of the Libanon, and led there, for some years, an austere life of penance and fasting. Finally he was discovered and dragged before the judge.

At first, persuasions and kindness were employed to induce him to deny the Faith, but when these efforts failed recourse was had to the most cruel torments. He was scourged, and finally cast into a caldron filled with boiling oil, sulphur, and pitch. In this seething mass God preserved him from harm, and by this miracle many spectators were converted to the Faith. Still more enraged thereat, the judge ordered the holy bishop to be thrown into prison and kept there in chains till he died of starvation. But God delivered him, as He had once delivered St. Peter. One night an angel appeared to him and said: "Erasmus, follow me! Thou shalt convert a great many." Thus far he had led numbers to the Faith by suffering, now he was to convert multitudes as a missionary.

Delivered from prison by the power of God, he went forth into many lands and preached the Faith. Mighty in word and deed, he wrought many miracles and converted great numbers of heathens. At length he came to Italy, where Emperor Maximin persecuted the Christians as fiercely as did Diocletian in the East. As soon as Maximin heard of Erasmus and the conversions effected by his preaching and miracles, he ordered the slaughter of three hundred of the converts. Erasmus himself was most cruelly tortured, but to no purpose. He remained firm. Then cast into prison, he was again liberated by an angel.

At last the hour of deliverance came to this valiant and apostolic confessor and martyr of Christ. He heard a heavenly voice, saying: "Erasmus, come now to the heavenly city and rest in the place which God has prepared for thee with the holy martyrs and prophets. Enjoy now the fruit of thy labor. By thee I was honored in heaven and on earth." Erasmus, looking toward heaven, saw a splendid crown, and the apostles and prophets welcoming him. He bowed his head, saying: "Receive, O Lord, the soul of thy servant!" and peacefully breathed forth his spirit on June 2, 308.

LESSON

*T*HE tortures which St. Erasmus suffered for the Faith seem almost incredible, and the events related of him are truly wonderful. Martyrdom and miracles illustrated the doctrine he preached; he converted multitudes and gained the crown of heaven.

Perhaps you say that in our times there are no longer any martyrs, at least not in civilized countries. Are you quite sure of it? St. Augustine writes: "Peace also has its martyrs." It is certainly not easy to suffer torments like the martyrs and to receive finally the death-dealing blow of the sword. But is it not also a martyrdom to suffer for years the pains of a lingering illness? Again, how difficult the combat with the world, the flesh, and the powers of hell! How carefully must we watch and pray to gain the victory! This is our martyrdom. Let us imitate the example of the holy martyrs in bearing the trials and sufferings of life, and we shall receive, as they did, the crown of heaven.

PRAYER OF THE CHURCH

O GOD, who dost give us joy through the memory of Thy holy martyrs, graciously grant that we may be inflamed by their example, in whose merits we rejoice. Through Christ our Lord. Amen.

IV

St. Pantaleon, Physician and Martyr

ST. PANTALEON was physician to Emperor Maximin and a Christian, but he fell through a temptation which is sometimes more dangerous than the most severe trials by the fiercest torments. This temptation was the bad example of the impious, idolatrous courtiers with whom the young physician associated. He was seduced by them and abandoned the Faith. But the grace of God called him, and he obeyed.

Hermolaus, a zealous priest, by prudent exhortation awakened Pantaleon's conscience to a sense of his guilt, and brought him back into the fold of the Church. Henceforth he devoted himself ardently to the advancement of the spiritual and temporal welfare of his fellow-citizens. First of all he sought to convert his father, who was still a heathen, and had the consolation to see him die a Christian. He divided the ample fortune which he inherited amongst the poor and the sick. As a physician, he was intent on healing his patients both by physical and by spiritual means. Christians he confirmed in the practice and confession of the Faith, and the heathens he sought to convert. Many suffering from incurable diseases were restored to health by his prayer and the invocation of the holy name of Jesus. His presence was everywhere fraught with blessings and consolation.

St. Pantaleon yearned to prove his fidelity to the Faith by shedding his blood for it, and the opportunity came to him when his heathen associates in the healing art denounced him to the emperor as a zealous propagator of Christianity. He was brought up before the emperor's tribunal and ordered to sacrifice to the idols. He replied: "The God whom I adore is Jesus Christ. He created heaven and earth, He raised the dead to life, made the blind see and healed the sick, all through the power of His word. Your idols are dead, they can not do anything. Order a sick person to be brought here, one declared incurable. Your priests shall invoke their idols for him and I shall call on the only true God, and we shall see who is able to help him." The proposal was accepted. A man sick with the palsy was brought, who could neither walk nor stand without help. The heathen priests prayed for him, but in vain. Then Pantaleon prayed, took the sick man by the hand, and said: "In the name of Jesus, the Son of God, I command thee to rise and be well." And the palsied man rose, restored to perfect health.

By this miracle a great number of those present were converted. But the emperor and the idolatrous priests were all the more enraged. Maximin now attempted to gain Pantaleon by blandishments and promises to deny the

Faith, but without success. Then he had recourse to threats, and as they too availed nothing, he proceeded to have them put into execution. The brave confessor of the Faith was tortured in every conceivable manner. Finally he was nailed to a tree, and then beheaded. The priest Hermolaus and the brothers Hermippos and Hermocrates suffered death with him, in the year 308.

LESSON

*H*APPY are they who, whatever may be their station or calling in life, are intent on bringing those with whom they come into contact under the influence of religion. But, alas, too many do just the reverse. They permit themselves to be led astray by bad example, and set aside the claims of the Church as too severe and exacting. How do you act in this regard? Do you shun the company of the wicked? A proverb says: "Tell me in whose company you are found, and I will tell you who you are." Bad company insensibly undermines faith and morals, overcomes the fear of evil and the aversion to it and weakens the will. "He that loveth danger shall perish in it" (Ecclus. 3:27).

As soon as St. Pantaleon came to a sense of his apostasy, he repented and returned to the practice of the Faith. He did this despite the knowledge that he thereby incurred hatred and persecution. The true Christian will ever follow the dictates of conscience and please God, whether he thereby incur the displeasure of men or not. If, to please men, we become remiss in the service of God, we show that we fear and love Him less than men. What a lamentable folly! Of whom have we to expect greater benefits or to fear greater evils—from God or man? Do not act thus unwisely; rather imitate St. Pantaleon, and live for God and His service.

PRAYER OF THE CHURCH

*A*LMIGHTY God, grant us through the intercession of Thy blessed martyr Pantaleon to be delivered and preserved from all ills of the body, and from evil thoughts and influences in spirit. Through Christ our Lord. Amen.

V

St Vitus, Martyr

LEGEND

ST. VITUS belonged to a noble pagan family of Sicily, and was born about the year 291, at Mazurra. His father, Hylas, placed him in early childhood in charge of a Christian couple named Modestus and Crescentia, who raised him in the Christian faith, and had him baptized. He grew in years and in virtue, till, at the age of twelve, he was claimed by his father, who, to his great anger, found him a fervent Christian. Convinced, after many unsuccessful attempts, that stripes and other chastisements would not induce him to renounce the Faith, his father delivered the brave boy up to Valerian, the governor, who in vain employed every artifice to shake his constancy. Finally he commanded Vitus to be scourged, but when two soldiers were about to execute this order their hands and those of Valerian were suddenly lamed. The governor ascribed this to sorcery, yet he invoked Vitus' help, and behold, when the Christian boy made the sign of the cross over the lamed members, they were healed. Then Valerian sent him back to his father, telling him to leave no means untried to induce his son to sacrifice to the idols.

Hylas now tried blandishments, pleasures, and amusements to influence the brave boy. He even sent a corrupt woman to tempt him, and for that purpose locked them both together in one room. But Vitus, who had remained firm amid tortures, resisted also the allurements of sensuality. Closing his eyes, he knelt in prayer, and behold, an angel appeared, filling the room with heavenly splendor, and stood at the youth's side. Terrified, the woman fled. But even this miracle did not change the obstinate father.

Finally Vitus escaped, and with Modestus and Crescentia fled to Italy. They landed safe in Naples, and there proclaimed Christ wherever they had an opportunity. Their fervor and many miracles which they wrought attracted the attention of Emperor Diocletian to them. He ordered them to be brought before his tribunal, which being done, he at first treated them kindly, employing blandishments and making promises to induce them to renounce Christ. When this had no effect, they were cruelly tormented, but with no other result than confirming them in their constancy. Enraged, the emperor condemned them to be thrown to the wild beasts. But the lions and tigers forgot their ferocity and cowered at their feet. Now Diocletian, whose fury knew no bounds, ordered them to be cast into a caldron of molten lead and boiling pitch. They prayed, "O God, deliver us through the power of Thy name!" and behold, they remained unharmed. Then the emperor condemned them to the rack, on which they expired, in the year 303.

LESSON

*T*HE heroic spirit of martyrdom exhibited by St. Vitus was owing to the early impressions of piety which he received through the teaching and example of his virtuous foster-parents. The choice of teachers, nurses, and servants who have the care of children is of the greatest importance on account of the influence they exert on them. The pagan Romans were most solicitous that no slave whose speech was not perfectly elegant and graceful should have access to children. Shall a Christian be less careful as to their virtue? It is a fatal mistake to imagine that children are too young to be infected with the contagion of vice. No age is more impressionable than childhood; no one observes more closely than the young, and nothing is so easily acquired by them as a spirit of vanity, pride, revenge, obstinacy, sloth, etc., and nothing is harder to overcome. What a happiness for a child to be formed to virtue from infancy, and to be instilled from a tender age with the spirit of piety, simplicity, meekness, and mercy! Such a foundation being well laid, the soul will easily, and sometimes without experiencing severe conflicts, rise to the height of Christian perfection.

PRAYER OF THE CHURCH

*W*E BESEECH Thee, O Lord, to graciously grant us through the intercession of Thy blessed martyrs Vitus, Modestus, and Crescentia, that we may not proudly exalt ourselves, but serve Thee in humility and simplicity, so as to avoid evil and to do right for Thy sake. Through Christ our Lord. Amen.

VI

St. Christophorus, Martyr

*A*N ANCIENT tradition concerning St. Christophorus relates: He was born in the land of Canaan, and was named Reprobus, that is Reprobate, for he was a barbarous heathen. In stature and strength he was a giant. Thinking no one his like in bodily vigor, he resolved to go forth in search of the mightiest master and serve him. In his wanderings, he met with a king who was praised as the most valorous man on earth. To him he offered his services and was accepted. The king was proud of his giant and kept him near his person. One day a minstrel visited the king's castle, and among the ballads he sung before the court was one on the power of Satan. At the mention of this name the king blessed himself, making the sign of the cross. Reprobus, wondering, asked him why he did that. The king replied: "When I make this sign, Satan has no power over me." Reprobus rejoined: "So thou fearest the power of Satan? Then he is mightier than thou, and I shall seek and serve him."

Setting forth to seek Satan, he came into a wilderness. One dark night he met a band of wild fellows riding through the forest. It was Satan and his escort. Reprobus bravely accosted him, saying he wished to serve him. He was accepted. But soon he was convinced that his new master was not the mightiest on earth. For one day, whilst approaching a crucifix by the wayside, Satan quickly took to flight, and Reprobus asked him for the reason. Satan replied: "That is the image of my greatest enemy, who conquered me on the cross. From him I always flee." When Reprobus heard this, he left the devil, and went in search of Christ.

In his wanderings, he one day came to a hut hidden in the forest. At its door sat a venerable old man. Reprobus addressed him, and in the course of the conversation that ensued the old man told him that he was a hermit, and had left the world to serve Christ, the Lord of heaven and earth. "Thou art my man," cried Reprobus; "Christ is He whom I seek, for He is the strongest and the mightiest. Tell me where I can find Him."

The hermit then began instructing the giant about God and the Redeemer, and concluded by saying: "He who would serve Christ must offer himself entirely to Him, and do and suffer everything for His sake. His reward for this will be immense and will last forever." Reprobus now asked the hermit to allow him to remain, and to continue to instruct him. The hermit consented. When Reprobus was fully instructed, he baptized him. After his baptism, a great change came over the giant. No longer proud of his great size and strength, he became meek and humble, and asked the hermit to assign to him some task by which he might serve God, his master. "For," said he, "I can not pray and fast; therefore I must serve God in some other way." The hermit led him to a broad and swift river nearby, and said: "Here build thyself a hut, and when wanderers wish to cross the river, carry them over for the love of Christ." For there was no bridge across the river.

Henceforth, day and night, whenever he was called, Reprobus faithfully performed the task assigned to him. One night he heard a child calling to be carried across the river. Quickly he rose, placed the child on his stout shoulder, took his staff and walked into the mighty current. Arrived in midstream, the water rose higher and higher, and the child became heavier and heavier. "O child," he cried, "how heavy thou art! It seems I bear the weight of the world on my shoulder." And the child replied, "Right thou art. Thou bearest not only the world, but the Creator of heaven and earth. I am Jesus Christ, thy King and Lord, and henceforth thou shalt be called Christophorus, that is, Christ-bearer. Arrived on yonder shore, plant thy staff in the ground, and in token of my power and might tomorrow it shall bear leaves and blossoms."

And the child disappeared. On reaching the other shore, Christophorus stuck his staff into the ground, and behold, it budded forth leaves and blossoms. Then, kneeling, he promised the Lord to serve Him ever faithfully. He kept his promise, and thenceforth became a zealous preacher of the Gospel, converting many to the Faith. On his missionary peregrinations he came also to Lycia, where, after his first sermon, eighteen thousand heathens requested baptism. When Emperor Decius heard of this, he sent a company of four hundred soldiers to capture Christophorus. To these he preached so convincingly, that they all asked for baptism. Decius became enraged thereat and had him cast into prison. There he first treated him with great kindness, and surrounded him with every luxury to tempt him to sin, but in vain. Then he ordered him to be tortured in the most cruel manner, until he should deny the Faith. He was scourged, placed on plates of hot iron, boiling oil was poured over and fire was lighted under him. When all these torments did not accomplish their purpose, the soldiers were ordered to shoot him with arrows. This, too, having no effect, he was beheaded, on July 25, 254.

Two great saints refer to the wonderful achievements of St. Christophorus. St. Ambrose mentions that this saint converted forty-eight thousand souls to Christ. St. Vincent Ferrer declares, that when the plague devastated Valencia, its destructive course was stayed through the intercession of St. Christophorus.

LESSON

*T*HE legend of St. Christophorus conveys a wholesome truth. We ought all to be Christ-bearers, by preserving in our hearts faith, hope, and charity, and by receiving Our Lord worthily in holy communion. He alone is worthy of our service. In the service that we owe to men, we ought to serve God by doing His will.

We can not divide our heart, for Our Lord Himself says, "No man can serve two masters" (Matt 6:24). If you serve the world, it deceives you, for it can not give you what it promises. If you serve sin, Satan is your master. He, too, deceives his servants, and leads them to perdition. Christ on the cross conquered these two tyrants, and with His help you can also vanquish them. Therefore, give yourself to Him with all your heart, and you shall find peace in this world, and eternal bliss in the next. St. Augustine learned this truth by sad experience, and therefore exclaims: "Thou hast created us for Thee, O Lord, and our heart is restless till it rests in Thee."

PRAYER OF THE CHURCH

*G*RANT us, almighty God, that whilst we celebrate the memory of Thy blessed martyr St. Christophorus, through his intercession the love of Thy name may be increased in us. Through Christ our Lord. Amen.

VII

St. Dionysius, Bishop and Martyr

LEGEND

WHEN St. Paul the Apostle, in the year of Our Lord 51, came to Athens to preach the Gospel, he was summoned to the Areopagus, the great council which determined all religious matters. Among the members of this illustrious assembly was Dionysius. His mind had already been prepared to receive the good tidings of the Gospel by the miraculous darkness which overspread the earth at the moment of Our Lord's death on the cross. He was at that time at Heliopolis, in Egypt. On beholding the sun obscured in the midst of its course, and this without apparent cause, he is said to have exclaimed: "Either the God of nature is suffering, or the world is about to be dissolved." When St. Paul preached before the Areopagus in Athens, Dionysius easily recognized the truth and readily embraced it.

The Apostle received him among his disciples, and appointed him bishop of the infant Church of Athens. As such he devoted himself with great zeal to the propagation of the Gospel. He made a journey to Jerusalem to visit the places hallowed by the footsteps and sufferings of our Redeemer, and there met the Apostles St. Peter and St. James, the evangelist St. Luke, and other holy apostolic men. He also had the happiness to see and converse with the Blessed Virgin Mary, and was so overwhelmed by her presence that he declared, that if he knew not Jesus to be God, he would consider her divine.

The idolatrous priests of Athens were greatly alarmed at the many conversions resulting from the eloquent preaching of Dionysius, and instigated a revolt against him. The holy bishop left Athens, and, going to Rome, visited the Pope, St. Clement. He sent him with some other holy men to Gaul. Some of his companions remained to evangelize the cities in the south, while Dionysius, with the priest Rusticus and the deacon Eleutherius continued their journey northward as far as Lutetia, the modern Paris, where the Gospel had not yet been announced. Here for many years he and his companions labored with signal success, and finally obtained the crown of martyrdom on Oct. 9, 119. Dionysius was beheaded at the advanced age of 110 years.

The spot where the three martyrs Dionysius, Rusticus, and Eleutherius suffered martyrdom, is the well-known hill of Montmartre. An ancient tradition relates that St. Dionysius, after his head was severed from his body, took it up with his own hands and carried it two thousand paces to the place where, later, a church was built in his honor. The bodies of the martyrs were thrown into the river Seine, but taken up and honorably interred by a Christian lady named Catulla not far from the place where they had been beheaded. The Christians soon built a chapel on their tomb.

St. Dionysius was not only a great missionary and bishop, but also one of the most illustrious writers of the early Church. Some of his works, which are full of Catholic doctrine and Christian wisdom, are still extant, and well worthy of a convert and disciple of St. Paul, whose spirit they breathe.

LESSON

*T*HE apostolic men like St. Dionysius, who converted so many to Christ, were filled with His spirit, and acted and lived for Him alone. They gave their lives to spread His religion, convinced that the welfare of individuals and nations depends upon it.

On religion depends the security and stability of all government and of society. Human laws are too weak to restrain those who disregard and despise the law of God. Unless a man's conscience is enlightened by religion and bound by its precepts, his passions will so far enslave him, that the impulse of evil inclinations will prompt him to every villainy of which he hopes to derive an advantage, if he can but accomplish his purpose secretly and with impunity.

True religion, on the contrary, insures comfort, peace, and happiness amid the sharpest trials, safety in death itself, and after death the most glorious and eternal reward in God. How grateful, therefore, must we be to the men who preached the true religion amid so many difficulties, trials, and persecutions; and also to those who preach it now, animated by the same spirit. And how carefully should we avoid all persons, books, and periodicals that revile and calumniate our holy Faith, and attempt its subversion!

PRAYER OF THE CHURCH

O GOD, who didst confer on Thy blessed servant Dionysius the virtue of fortitude in suffering, and didst join with him Rusticus and Eleutherius, to announce Thy glory to the heathens, grant, we beseech Thee, that following them, we may despise, for the love of Thee, the pleasures of this world, and that we do not recoil from its adversities. Through Christ our Lord. Amen.

VIII

St. Cyriacus, Deacon and Martyr

LEGEND

*E*MPEROR MAXIMIN in token of his gratitude to Diocletian, who had ceded the western half of his empire to him, ordered the building of that magnificent structure in Rome, whose ruins are still known as the "Baths of Diocletian." The Christians imprisoned for the Faith were compelled to labor under cruel overseers at this building. A zealous Christian Roman, touched with pity at this moving spectacle, resolved to employ his means in improving the condition of these poor victims of persecution.

Among the deacons of the Roman Church at that time was one by the name of Cyriacus, who was distinguished by his zeal in the performance of all good works. Him, with two companions, Largus and Smaragdus, the pious Roman selected for the execution of his plan. Cyriacus devoted himself to the work with great ardor. One day, whilst visiting the laborers to distribute food amongst them, he observed a decrepit old man, who was so feeble that he was unable to perform his severe task. Filled with pity, Cyriacus offered to take his place. The aged prisoner consenting, the merciful deacon thenceforth worked hard at the building. But after some time he was discovered, and cast into prison. There he again found opportunity to exercise his zeal. Some blind men who had great confidence in the power of his prayer, came to ask him for help in their affliction, and he restored their sight. He and his companions spent three years in prison, and during that time he healed many sick and converted a great number of heathens from the darkness of paganism.

Then Emperor Diocletian's little daughter became possessed by an evil spirit, and no one was able to deliver her from it. To the idolatrous priests who were called, the evil spirit declared that he would leave the girl only when commanded to do so by Cyriacus, the deacon. He was hastily summoned, and prayed and made the sign of the cross over the girl, and the evil spirit departed. The emperor loved his daughter, therefore he was grateful to the holy deacon, and presented him with a house, where he and his companions might serve their God unmolested by their enemies.

About this time the daughter of the Persian King Sapor was attacked by a similar malady, and when he heard what Cyriacus had done for Diocletian's daughter, he wrote to the emperor, asking him to send the Christian deacon. It was done, and Cyriacus, on foot, set out for Persia. Arrived at his destination, he prayed over the girl and the evil spirit left her. On hearing of this miracle, four hundred and twenty heathens were converted to the Faith. These the saint instructed and baptized, and then set out on his homeward journey.

Returned to Rome, he continued his life of prayer and good works. But when Diocletian soon afterward left for the East, his co-emperor Maximin seized the opportunity to give vent to his hatred for the Christians, and renewed their persecution. One of the first victims was Cyriacus. He was loaded with chains and brought before the judge, who first tried blandishments and promises to induce him to renounce Christ and to sacrifice to the idols, but in vain. Then the confessor of Christ was stretched on the rack, his limbs torn from their sockets, and he was beaten with clubs. His companions shared the same tortures. Finally, when the emperor and the judge were convinced that nothing would shake the constancy of the holy martyrs, they were beheaded. They gained the crown of glory on March 16, 303.

LESSON

*I*N THE life of St. Cyriacus two virtues shine forth in a special manner; his love of God and his charity toward his fellow-men. His love of God impelled him to sacrifice all, even his life, for His sake, thereby fulfilling the commandment: "Thou shalt love the Lord thy God with thy whole heart, and with thy whole soul, and with thy whole mind" (Matt. 22:37). A greater love of God no man can have than giving his life for Him.

St. Cyriacus also fulfilled the other commandment, of which Our Lord declared, "And the second is like to this: Thou shalt love thy neighbor as thyself" (Matt. 22:39). He helped his fellow-Christians to bear their burdens, relieved them in their sufferings, assisted and encouraged them by word and deed, and edified them by his example. His sole aim was to do good to all men, mindful of the words of the Royal Prophet: "Blessed is he that understandeth concerning the needy and the poor" (Ps. 40:2). He was so imbued with the virtue of charity, that he was disposed even to sacrifice his life for the relief and assistance of others.

How shall we justify our unfeeling hardness of heart, by which we seek every trifling pretense to exempt us from the duty of aiding the unfortunate? Remember the threat of the apostle, "Judgment without mercy to him that hath not done mercy" (James 2:13).

PRAYER OF THE CHURCH

O GOD, who rejoicest us by the remembrance of Thy blessed martyrs Cyriacus, Largus, and Smaragdus; grant, we beseech Thee, that we, by celebrating their memory, may imitate their fortitude in suffering. Through Christ our Lord. Amen.

IX

St. Achatius, Martyr

*O*F THE saints named Achatius, that one is reckoned among the Holy Helpers who, as a Roman soldier, died for Christ.

Achatius was a native of Cappadocia and as a youth joined the Roman army during the reign of Emperor Hadrian, attaining the rank of captain. One day, when leading his company against the enemy, he heard a voice saying to him, "Call on the God of Christians!" He obeyed, was instructed, and received Baptism. Filled with zeal, he henceforth sought to convert also the pagan soldiers of the army. When the emperor heard of this, Achatius was thrown into prison, then placed on the rack, bound to a post and scourged, because he refused to offer sacrifice to the idols. When all these tortures availed nothing, he was brought before the tribune Bibianus.

Asked by him what was his name and country, Achatius replied, "My name is Christian, because I am a follower of Christ; men call me Achatius. My country is Cappadocia. There my parents lived; there I was converted to the Christian faith, and was so inspired by the combats and sufferings of the Christian martyrs that I am resolved to shed my blood for Christ to attain heaven." Then Bibianus ordered him to be beaten with leaden clubs, after which he was loaded with chains and returned to the prison.

After Achatius had been in prison seven days, Bibianus was called to Byzantium, and ordered all prisoners to be transported there. On the journey Achatius suffered greatly, for his entire body was covered with wounds, his chains were galling, the guards were cruel and the roads were bad. He thought himself dying. Praying to God, a voice from the clouds answered him, "Achatius, be firm!" The soldiers of the guard were terrified and asked each other, "What is this? How can the clouds have a voice?" Many prisoners were converted. Next day some of the converts saw a number of men in shining armor speaking to Achatius, washing his wounds and healing them, so that not even a scar remained.

Arrived in Byzantium the saint was again cast into prison, and after seven days dragged before the judge. When neither promises nor the most cruel torments shook the constancy of the brave confessor of the Faith, the judge sent him to Flaccius, the proconsul of Thracia, who imprisoned him for five days, and meanwhile read the records of his former trials. Then he ordered him to be beheaded. Achatius suffered death for Christ on May 8, 311.

LESSON

*A*CHATIUS manfully and without fear confessed the Faith amid persecutions and sufferings. We, too, are often placed in circumstances where the profession of our Faith and the practice of the virtues inculcated by it cause us trials. But so deplorable are the effects of sensuality, avarice, and ambition, and such is the laxity and spiritual callousness of many Christians, that there is real cause for every one to be filled with alarm for the safety of his soul. It is not the crowd we are to follow, but the precepts of the Gospel. Therefore we ought to strive to give a good example by our faithful compliance with the demands of religion. For Our Lord Himself exhorts us: "So let your light shine before men, that they may see your good works, and glorify your Father, who is in heaven" (Matt. 5:16).

PRAYER OF THE CHURCH

O GOD, who dost give us joy through the remembrance of Thy blessed martyrs, Achatius and his companions; grant, we beseech Thee, that we may be inflamed by the example of those for whose merits we rejoice. Through Christ our Lord. Amen.

X

St. Eustachius, Martyr

LEGEND

AT THE beginning of the second century, during the reign of Emperor Trajan, there lived in Rome a famous general by the name of Placidus, who was distinguished among his fellow-citizens for his wealth and military prowess. It happened one day, that while following the chase he became separated from his companions, and was pursuing with eagerness a stag of extraordinary size, when suddenly it turned toward him, and he beheld raised aloft between its antlers the image of Jesus Christ suspended on the cross. At the same time our blessed Saviour addressed him in loving words, inviting him henceforth to follow Him by embracing the Christian faith, and to make eternal life in future the object of his pursuit.

Faithful to the grace which he had received, Placidus on his return home communicated the heavenly vision to his wife Tatiana, who informed him that she too had been favored with a heavenly apparition. Together they went immediately to the Pope, related their experience, and after due instruction received Baptism.

At the sacred font Placidus received the name of Eustachius, and his wife was called Theopista, while his sons were baptized by the names of Agapitus and Theopistus.

Upon returning to the spot where he first received the call, Eustachius was favored with another communication from Our Lord, announcing to him that he was destined to endure many and great afflictions for the sake of Christ. It was not long before his faith and patience were put to a severe trial. Stripped of all his possessions and forced to flee from the fury of the persecution, he was reduced to extreme distress, and in the course of his wanderings was by a series of calamitous events separated from his wife and children, of whom he lost all trace. For many years he dwelt in a remote spot, following the occupation of a farm laborer, until he was found by the messengers of the emperor, who was sadly in need of the skill of his former general, because a fierce war had broken out, in which the Romans sustained severe losses.

Being again invested with the command of the imperial troops, Eustachius set out for the seat of war, and achieved a decisive victory. In the course of his march he had the happiness, by a singular providence of God, to recover his wife and children, with whom he returned to Rome. His entrance into the city was attended with great rejoicings, and many were the congratulations which he received on his extraordinary good fortune. But soon afterward a solemn sacrifice of thanksgiving to the pagan deities was proclaimed, in which he was ordered by the emperor to take a part. Upon his refusal, after every effort had been made to shake his constancy, he was condemned to be exposed to the lions in the public amphitheater along with his wife and children. Finally, as the savage animals, laying aside their natural ferocity, refused to injure the confessors of Christ, Eustachius and his family were by order of the emperor enclosed in the body of an immense brazen bull, which was heated by means of a great fire enkindled beneath. The last moments of these heroic martyrs was spent in chanting the divine praises, in the midst of which their happy souls passed to the enjoyment of everlasting bliss. Their bodies, miraculously preserved uninjured, were buried with great devotion by the faithful Christians, and were afterward transferred to a magnificent church erected in their honor.

LESSON

*H*OW inspiring, to see a great man preferring justice, truth, and religion to the favor of the mighty, readily quitting estate, friends, country, and even sacrificing life, rather than consent to do violence to his conscience; and to see him, at the same time, meek, humble, patient in suffering, forgiving sincerely and loving his unjust and treacherous persecutors! Passion and revenge often beget anger and triumph over virtue and integrity. Ambition and the desire of wealth may, for a time, urge men on to brave danger, but finally they reduce them to the most abject slavery, and result in grievous crimes and misery. Religion alone is the source of charity, magnanimity, and true courage. It so enlightens the mind, as to place a man above the vicissitudes of the world; it renders him steadfast and calm in adversity, preserves him from error, teaches him to bear injustice and calumny in a tranquil spirit, and gives him that ineffable peace and joy which springs from the conviction that God's will is always most just and holy and that He protects, aids, and rewards His servants.

Does religion exert this powerful influence on us? Do we show it in our actions and conduct? Our courage and constancy must be apparent not only when we encounter danger and opposition, but also when our evil propensity urges us to yield to temptations that present sin to us in the guise of pleasure.

PRAYER OF THE CHURCH

O GOD, who dost permit us to celebrate the remembrance of Thy blessed martyrs, Eustachius and companions, grant us, that we may enjoy their company in eternal bliss. Through Christ our Lord. Amen.

St. Giles, Hermit and Abbot

ATHENS, in Greece, was the native city of St. Giles. He was of noble parentage, and devoted himself from early youth to piety and learning. After the death of his parents he distributed his rich inheritance to the poor, and to escape the applause of men for his charity left his country to bury himself in obscurity.

He sailed for France, and on his arrival there retired to a deserted country near the mouth of the river Rhone. Later he made his abode near the river Gard, and finally buried himself in a forest in the diocese of Nimes. In this solitude he passed many years, living on wild herbs and roots, with water for his drink. It is related that for some time a hind came daily to be milked by him, thus furnishing him additional sustenance. Here he lived, disengaged from earthly cares, conversing only with God, and engaged in the contemplation of heavenly things.

One day the king instituted a great hunt in the forest where Giles lived, and encountered the hind. Giving chase, the royal hunter was led to the saint's hut, where the panting animal had sought refuge. The king inquired who he was, and was greatly edified at the holiness of his life. The fame of the saintly hermit now spread far and wide, and was much increased by the many miracles wrought through his intercession. The king tried to persuade him to leave his solitude, but prevailed upon him only in so far, that Giles accepted several disciples and founded a monastery in which the rule of St. Benedict was observed, and of which he was chosen the abbot. He governed his community wisely and well, and at the earnest solicitation of his monks was ordained priest.

The fame of St. Giles' sanctity induced the Frankish King, Charles Martel to call him to his court to relieve him of a great trouble of conscience. The saint made the journey, and told the king that he would find relief and comfort only by the sincere confession of a sin which he had hitherto concealed. The king followed his advice, found interior peace and dismissed Giles with many tokens of gratitude. On his homeward journey the saint raised the recently deceased son of a nobleman to life.

After a short stay in his monastery St. Giles went to Rome, to obtain from the Pope the confirmation of some privileges and the apostolic blessing for his community. The Pope granted his wishes, and presented him, besides, with two grand and beautifully carved doors of cedar wood for his church.

St. Giles died at a ripe old age on September 1, 725. Many miracles were wrought at his tomb.

LESSON

*S*T. GILES left his native country and retired into solitude to escape the notice and applause of the world, and served God as a recluse. To lead such a life, there must be a special call from God. It is not suited to all, and even inconsistent with the duties of most men. But all are capable of disengaging their affections from the inordinate attachment to creatures, and of attaining to a pure and holy love of God. By making the service of God the motive of their thoughts and actions, they will sanctify their whole life.

In whatever conditions of life we may be placed, we have opportunities of subduing our evil inclinations and mortifying ourselves by frequent self-denials, of watching over our hearts and purifying our senses by recollection and prayer. Thus each one, in his station of life, may become a saint, by making his calling an exercise of virtue and his every act a step higher to perfection and eternal glory.

PRAYER OF THE CHURCH

O LORD, we beseech Thee to let us find grace through the intercession of thy blessed confessor Giles; that what we can not obtain through our merits be given us through his intercession. Through Christ our Lord. Amen.

XII

St. Margaret, Virgin and Martyr

S
T. MARGARET was the daughter of a pagan priest at Antioch. She lost her mother in infancy and was placed in the care of a nurse in the country, who was a Christian, and whose first care was to have her little charge baptized and to give the child a Christian education. Margaret grew up a modest, pious virgin, and when she returned to her father he was charmed with the grace and virtue of his daughter. He regretted only one thing; she took no part in the worship of the idols. When she told him the reason he was greatly displeased, for she stated that she was a Christian, and that nothing should separate her from the love of Christ.

Her father tried every means to change her mind, and when all his endeavors failed became enraged and drove her forth from his house. Margaret returned to her nurse and became her servant, doing all kinds of menial work, and at the same time perfecting herself in virtue.

About this time Emperor Diocletian began to persecute the Christians. One day Alybrius, the prefect of the city, saw Margaret, and fell in love with her. He sent a messenger to ask her in marriage. The pious virgin was filled with consternation at the proposal and replied to the messenger: "I can not be espoused to your master, because I am the spouse of Our Lord Jesus Christ. I am promised to Him, and to Him I wish to belong." When the prefect heard this, he became furious with rage, and gave orders to have the virgin brought to him by force. When she appeared before him he thus addressed her: "What is your name and condition?" She replied: "I am called Margaret, and belong to a noble family. I adore Christ and serve Him." The prefect now advised her to abandon the worship of a crucified God. Margaret asked him, "How do you know that we worship a crucified God?" The prefect replied: "From the books of the Christians." Margaret continued: "Why did you not read further on? The books of the Christians would have told you that the Crucified rose on the third day, and that He ascended into heaven. Is it love of truth to believe in the abasement of Christ and to reject His glorification, when both are related in the selfsame book?"

At this reproof the prefect became angry and ordered the tender virgin to be cruelly scourged, placed on the rack, and torn with iron combs. Then she was cast into prison. There Margaret fervently thanked God for the victory she had achieved and implored His help for the combat yet in store for her. Suddenly there appeared to her the arch-enemy of mankind in the shape of a furious dragon, threatening to swallow her. The brave virgin feared him not, but made the sign of the cross, and the monster vanished. Then her desolate prison cell became suffused with heavenly light, and her heart was filled with divine consolation. At the same time her terrible wounds were suddenly healed, and not the least scar was left.

Next day Margaret was again brought before the prefect. Surprised at her complete recovery from the effects of his cruelty, he remarked that no doubt it was due to the power of the pagan gods, and exhorted her to show her gratitude to them by sacrificing to the idols. Margaret maintained that she had been healed by the power of Christ alone and declared that she despised the heathen gods. At this, the rage of Alybrius knew no bounds. He ordered lighted torches to be applied to Margaret's body, and then had her cast into icy water to intensify her torture. But scarcely had this been done when a violent earthquake occurred. Her bonds were severed and she rose unscathed from the water, without a mark of the burns caused by the flaming torches. On witnessing this miracle, a great number of spectators were converted to the Faith.

Finally the prefect ordered Margaret to be beheaded. Her glorious martyrdom and death occurred about the year 275.

LESSON

*T*HE history of the virgin martyr St. Margaret teaches us that we can and ought to serve God even in youth. In the Old Law God commanded all the first-born and the first-fruits to be offered to Him. "Thou shalt not delay to pay thy tithes and first-fruits. Thou shalt give the first-born of thy sons to Me" (Ex. 22:29).

Certainly our whole life ought to be dedicated to the service of God; but from the above command we are to understand that God especially desires our service during the early years of our life. They are our first-fruits. St. Augustine calls the years of youth the blossoms, the most beautiful flowers of life, and St. Thomas Aquinas writes: "What the young give to God in their early years, they give of the bloom, of the full vigor and beauty of life."

Youth is the age beset with countless temptations. Safety is found only in the service of God, by obedience, humility, and docility. This is not so difficult as it appears, and Our Lord Himself invites you to His service, saying: "My son, give Me thy heart" (Prov. 23:26), and, "Taste and see that the Lord is sweet" (Ps. 33:9).

PRAYER OF THE CHURCH

WE BESEECH Thee, O Lord, grant us Thy favor through the intercession of Thy blessed virgin and martyr Margaret, who pleased Thee by the merit of her purity and by the confession of Thy might. Through Christ our Lord. Amen.

XIII

St Catherine, Virgin and Martyr

S T. CATHERINE was a native of Alexandria, Egypt, a city then famous for its schools of philosophy. She was a daughter of Costis, half-brother of Constantine, and of Sabinella, queen of Egypt. Her wisdom and acquirements were remarkable, the philosophy of Plato being her favorite study. While Catherine was yet young her father died, leaving her heiress to the kingdom. Her love of study and retirement displeased her subjects, who desired her to marry, asserting that her gifts of noble birth, wealth, beauty, and knowledge should be transmitted to her children.

The princess replied that the husband whom she would wed must be even more richly endowed than herself. His blood must be the noblest, his rank must surpass her own, his beauty without comparison, his benignity great enough to forgive all offences. The people of Alexandria were disheartened, for they knew of no such prince; but Catherine remained persistent in her determination to wed none other.

Now, it happened that a certain hermit who lived near Alexandria had a vision in which he saw the Blessed Virgin, who sent him to tell Catherine that her divine Son was the

Spouse whom she desired. He alone possessed all, and more, than the requirements she demanded. The holy man gave Catherine a picture of Jesus and Mary; and when the princess had gazed upon the face of Christ she loved Him so that she could think of naught else, and the studies in which she had been wont to take delight became distasteful to her.

One night Catherine dreamed that she accompanied the hermit to a sanctuary, whence angels came to meet her. She fell on her face before them, but one of the angelic band bade her, "Rise dear sister Catherine, for the King of glory delighteth to honor thee." She rose and followed the angels to the presence of the queen of heaven, who was surrounded by angels and saints and was beautiful beyond description. The queen welcomed her and led her to her divine Son, Our Lord. But He turned from her, saying: "She is not fair and beautiful enough for me."

Catherine awoke at these words and wept bitterly until morning. She then sent for the hermit and inquired what would make her worthy of the heavenly Bridegroom. The saintly recluse instructed her in the true Faith and, with her mother, she was baptized. That night, in a dream, the Blessed Virgin and her divine Son again appeared to her. Mary presented her to Jesus, saying: "Behold, she has been regenerated in the water of Baptism." Then Christ smiled on her and plighted His troth to her by putting a ring on her finger. When she awoke the ring was still there, and thenceforth Catherine despised all earthly things and longed only for the hour when she should go to her heavenly Bridegroom.

After the death of Sabinella, Emperor Maximin came to Alexandria and declared a persecution against the Christians. Catherine appeared in the temple and held an argument with the tyrant, utterly confounding him. The emperor ordained that fifty of the most learned men of the empire be brought to dispute with her; but, sustained by the power of God, Catherine not only vanquished them in argument, but converted them to the true Faith. In his fury Maximin commanded that the new Christians be burned; and Catherine comforted them, since they could not be baptized, by telling them that their blood should be their baptism and the flames their crown of glory.

The emperor then tried other means to overcome the virtue of the noble princess; but, failing to do this, he ordered her to be cast into a dungeon and starved to death. Twelve days later, when the dungeon was opened, a bright light and fragrant perfume filled it, and Catherine, who had been nourished by angels, came forth radiant and beautiful. On seeing this miracle, the empress and many noble Alexandrians declared themselves Christians, and suffered death at the command of the emperor.

Catherine was not spared, for Maximin made a further attempt to win her. He offered to make her mistress of the world if she would but listen to him, and when she still spurned his proposals, he ordered her to the torture. She was bound to four spiked wheels which revolved in different directions, that she might be torn into many pieces. But an angel consumed the wheels by fire, and the fragments flying around killed the executioners and many of the spectators. The tyrant then ordered her to be scourged and beheaded.

The sentence was carried into effect on November 25, 307.

A pious legend, recognized by the Church, says that angels bore Catherine's body to Mount Sinai, and buried it there.

LESSON

S T. CATHERINE, for her erudition and the spirit of piety by which she sanctified it, was chosen the model and patroness of Christian philosophers.

Learning, next to virtue, is the noblest quality and ornament of the human mind. Profane science teaches many useful truths, but when compared with the importance of the study of the science of the saints, they are of value only inasmuch as when made subservient to the latter. The study of the saints was to live in the spirit of Christ. This science is taught by the Church, and acquired by listening to her instructions, by pious reading and meditation.

Be intent on learning this science, and order your life according to its rules. It is the "one thing necessary," for it is the foundation of all wisdom and true happiness. "The fear of the Lord is the beginning of wisdom" (Ps. 110:10).

PRAYER OF THE CHURCH

O GOD, who didst give the law to Moses on the summit of Mount Sinai, and by the holy angels didst miraculously transfer there the body of blessed Catherine, virgin and martyr; grant us, we beseech Thee, to come, through her intercession, to the mountain which is Christ. Through the same Christ our Lord. Amen.

XIV

St. Barbara, Virgin and Martyr

*N*ICOMEDIA, a city in Asia Minor, was St. Barbara's birthplace. Her father Dioscurus was a pagan. Fearing that his only child might learn to know and love the doctrines of Christianity, he shut her up in a tower, apart from all intercourse with others. Nevertheless Barbara became a Christian. She passed her time in study, and from her lonely tower she used to watch the heavens in their wondrous beauty. She soon became convinced that the "heavens were telling the glory of God," a God greater than the idols she had been taught to worship. Her desire to know that God was in itself a prayer which He answered in His own wise way.

The fame of Origen, that famous Christian teacher in Alexandria, reached even the remote tower, and Barbara sent a trusty servant with the request that he would make known to her the truth. Origen sent her one of his disciples, disguised as a physician, who instructed and baptized her. She practised her new religion discreetly while waiting for a favorable opportunity of acquainting her father with her conversion.

This opportunity came in a short time. Some workmen were sent by Dioscurus to make another room in the tower, and when they had made two windows she directed them to make a third. When her father saw this additional window, he asked the reason for it. She replied, "Know, my father, that the soul receives light through three windows, the Father, the Son, and the Holy Ghost, and the three are one." The father became so angry at this discovery of her having become a Christian, that he would have killed his daughter with his sword, had she not fled to the top of the tower. He followed her, and finally had her in his power. First he wreaked his vengeance on her in blows, then clutching her by the hair he dragged her away and thrust her into a hut to prevent her escape. Next he tried every means to induce her to renounce her faith; threats, severe punishments, and starvation had no effect on the constancy of the Christian maiden.

Finding himself powerless to shake his daughter's constancy, Dioscurus delivered her to the proconsul Marcian, who had her scourged and tortured, but without causing her to deny the Faith. During her sufferings, her father stood by, exulting in the torments of his child. Next night, after she had been taken back to prison, Our Lord appeared to her and healed her wounds. When Barbara appeared again before him, Marcian was greatly astonished to find no trace of the cruelties that had been perpetrated on her body. Again she resisted his importunities to deny the Faith, and when he saw that all his efforts were in vain, he pronounced the sentence of death. Barbara was to be beheaded. Her unnatural father claimed the privilege to execute it with his own hands, and with one blow severed his daughter's head from her body, on December 4, 237.

At the moment of the saint's death a great tempest arose and Dioscurus was killed by lightning. Marcian, too, was overtaken by the same fate.

LESSON

SINCE early times St. Barbara is invoked as the patroness against lightning and explosions, and is called upon by those who desire the sacraments of the dying in their last illness, and many are the instances of the efficacy of her intercession.

We all wish for a happy and blessed death. To attain it, we must make the preparation for it the great object of our life; we must learn to die to the world and to ourselves, and strive after perfection in virtue. There is no greater comfort in adversity, no more powerful incentive to withdrawing our affections from this world, than to remember the blessing of a happy death. Well prepared, death may strike us in any form whatsoever, and however suddenly, it will find us ready.

We can be guilty of no greater folly than to delay our preparation for death, repentance, the reception of the sacraments, and the amendment of our life, from day to day, from the time of health to the time of illness, and in illness to the very last moments, thinking that even then we can obtain pardon. St. Augustine observes: "It is very dangerous to postpone the performance of a duty on which our whole eternity depends to the most inconvenient time, the last hour." And St. Bernard remarks: "In Holy Scripture we find one single instance of one who received pardon at the last moment. He was the thief crucified with Jesus. He is alone, that you despair not; he is alone, also, that you sin not by presumption on God's mercy." If you, therefore, wish for a happy death, prepare for it in time.

PRAYER OF THE CHURCH

O GOD, who among the wonders of Thy might didst grant the victory of martyrdom also to the weaker sex, graciously grant us that we, by recalling the memory of Thy blessed virgin and martyr Barbara, through her example may be led to Thee. Through Christ our Lord. Amen.

PART IV

Novenas to the Holy Helpers

✠

Prayers and Petitions

"In every thing by prayer and supplication with thanksgiving let your petitions be made known to God"

(Philipp. 4:6).

"God is wonderful in His saints. The God of Israel is He who will give power and strength to His people; blessed be God"

(Ps. 67:36).

Mary, conceived without sin, pray for us.

Novena to Each of the Holy Helpers

*A*LMIGHTY and eternal God! With lively faith and reverently worshiping Thy divine Majesty, I prostrate myself before Thee and invoke with filial trust Thy supreme bounty and mercy. Illumine the darkness of my intellect with a ray of Thy heavenly light and inflame my heart with the fire of Thy divine love, that I may contemplate the great virtues and merits of the saint in whose honor I make this novena, and following his example imitate, like him, the life of Thy divine Son.

Moreover, I beseech Thee to grant graciously, through the merits and intercession of this powerful Helper, the petition which through him I humbly place before Thee, devoutly saying, "Thy will be done on earth as it is in heaven." Vouchsafe graciously to hear it, if it redounds to Thy greater glory and to the salvation of my soul. Amen.

I

Novena in Honor of St. George

PREPARATORY PRAYER (p. 195).

PRAYER IN HONOR OF ST. GEORGE

O GOD, who didst grant to St. George strength and constancy in the various torments which he sustained for our holy faith; we beseech Thee to preserve, through his intercession, our faith from wavering and doubt, so that we may serve Thee with a sincere heart faithfully unto death. Through Christ our Lord. Amen.

INVOCATION OF ST. GEORGE

*F*AITHFUL servant of God and invincible martyr, St. George; favored by God with the gift of faith, and inflamed with an ardent love of Christ, thou didst fight valiantly against the dragon of pride, falsehood, and deceit. Neither pain nor torture, sword nor death could part thee from the love of Christ. I fervently implore thee for the sake of this love to help me by thy intercession to overcome the temptations that surround me, and to bear bravely the trials that oppress me, so that I may patiently carry the cross which is placed upon me; and let neither distress nor difficulties separate me from the love of Our Lord Jesus Christ. Valiant champion of the Faith, assist me in the combat against evil, that I may win the crown promised to them that persevere unto the end.

PRAYER

*M*Y LORD and my God! I offer up to Thee my petition in union with the bitter passion and death of Jesus Christ, Thy Son, together with the merits of His immaculate and blessed Mother, Mary ever virgin, and of all the saints, particularly with those of the holy Helper in whose honor I make this novena.

Look down upon me, merciful Lord! Grant me Thy grace and Thy love, and graciously hear my prayer. Amen.

II

Novena in Honor of St. Blase

PREPARATORY PRAYER (p. 195).

PRAYER IN HONOR OF ST. BLASE

O GOD, deliver us through the intercession of Thy holy bishop and martyr Blase, from all evil of soul and body, especially from all ills of the throat; and grant us the grace to make a good confession in the confident hope of obtaining Thy pardon, and ever to praise with worthy lips Thy most holy name. Through Christ our Lord. Amen.

INVOCATION OF ST. BLASE

S T. BLASE, gracious benefactor of mankind and faithful servant of God, who for the love of our Saviour didst suffer so many tortures with patience and resignation; I invoke thy powerful intercession. Preserve me from all evils of soul and body. Because of thy great merits God endowed thee with the special grace to help those that suffer from ills of the throat; relieve and preserve me from them, so that I may always be able to fulfil my duties, and with the aid of God's grace perform good works. I invoke thy help as special physician of souls, that I may confess my sins sincerely in the holy sacrament of Penance and obtain their forgiveness. I recommend to thy merciful intercession also those who unfortunately concealed a sin in confession. Obtain for them the grace to accuse themselves sincerely and contritely of the sin they concealed, of the sacrilegious confessions and communions they made, and of all the sins they committed since then, so that they may receive pardon, the grace of God, and the remission of the eternal punishment. Amen.

PRAYER (p. 197).

III

Novena in Honor of St Erasmus

PREPARATORY PRAYER (p. 195).

PRAYER IN HONOR OF ST. ERASMUS

O GOD, grant us through the intercession of Thy dauntless bishop and martyr Erasmus, who so valiantly confessed the Faith, that we may learn the doctrine of this faith, practise its precepts, and thereby be made worthy to attain its promises. Through Christ our Lord. Amen.

INVOCATION OF ST. ERASMUS

*H*OLY martyr Erasmus, who didst willingly and bravely bear the trials and sufferings of life, and by thy charity didst console many fellow-sufferers; I implore thee to remember me in my needs and to intercede for me with God. Staunch confessor of the Faith, victorious vanquisher of all tortures, pray to Jesus for me and ask Him to grant me the grace to live and die in the Faith through which thou didst obtain the crown of glory. Amen.

PRAYER (p. 197).

IV

Novena to St. Pantaleon

PREPARATORY PRAYER (p. 195).

PRAYER IN HONOR OF ST. PANTALEON

O GOD, who didst give to St. Pantaleon the grace of exercising charity toward his fellow-men by distributing his goods to the poor, and hast made him a special patron of the sick, grant, that we, too, show our charity by works of mercy; and through the intercession of this Thy servant preserve us from sickness. But if it be Thy will that illness should afflict us, give us the grace to bear it patiently, and let it promote our soul's salvation. Amen.

INVOCATION OF ST. PANTALEON

S T. PANTALEON, who during life didst have great pity for the sick and with the help of God didst often relieve and cure them; I invoke thy intercession with God, that I may obtain the grace to serve Him in good health by cheerfully fulfilling the duties of my state of life. But if it be His holy will to visit me with illness, pain, and suffering, do thou aid me with thy powerful prayer to submit humbly to His chastisements, to accept sickness in the spirit of penance and to bear it patiently according to His holy will. Amen.

PRAYER (p. 197).

V

Novena in Honor of St. Vitus

PREPARATORY PRAYER (p. 195).

PRAYER IN HONOR OF ST. VITUS

*G*RANT us, O God, through the intercession of St. Vitus, a due estimation of the value of our soul and of its redemption by the precious blood of Thy Son Jesus Christ; so that, for its salvation, we bear all trials with fortitude. Give this Thy youthful servant and heroic martyr as a guide and protector to Christian youths, that following his example they may after a victorious combat receive the crown of justice in heaven. Through Christ our Lord. Amen.

INVOCATION OF ST. VITUS

*S*T. VITUS, glorious martyr of Christ; in thy youth thou wast exposed to violent and dangerous temptations, but in the fear of God and for the love of Jesus thou didst victoriously overcome them. O amiable, holy youth, I implore thee by the love of Jesus, assist me with thy powerful intercession to overcome the temptations to evil, to avoid every occasion of sin, and thus to preserve spotless the robe of innocence and sanctifying grace, and to bring it unstained to the judgment-seat of Jesus Christ, that I may forever enjoy the beatific vision of God which is promised to the pure of heart. Amen.

PRAYER (p. 197).

VI

Novena in Honor of St. Christophorus

PREPARATORY PRAYER (p. 195).

PRAYER IN HONOR OF ST. CHRISTOPHORUS

O GOD, who didst make St. Christophorus a true Christ-bearer, who converted multitudes to the Christian faith, and who didst give him the grace to suffer for Thy sake the most cruel torments; through the intercession of this saint we implore Thee to protect us from sin, the only real evil. Preserve us, also, against harmful elementary forces, such as earthquake, lightning, fire, and flood. Amen.

INVOCATION OF ST. CHRISTOPHORUS

G REAT St. Christophorus, seeking the strongest and mightiest master thou didst find him in Jesus Christ, the almighty God of heaven and earth, and didst faithfully serve Him with all thy power to the end of thy life, gaining for Him countless souls and finally shedding thy blood for Him; obtain for me the grace to bear Christ always in my heart, as thou didst once bear Him on thy shoulder, so that I thereby may be strengthened to overcome victoriously all temptations and resist all enticements of the world, the devil, and the flesh, and that the powers of darkness may not prevail against me. Amen.

PRAYER (p. 197).

VII

Novena in Honor of St. Dionysius

PREPARATORY PRAYER (p. 195).

PRAYER IN HONOR OF ST. DIONYSIUS

O GOD, who didst confer Thy saving faith on the people of France through Thy holy bishop and martyr Dionysius, and didst glorify him before and after his martyrdom by many miracles; grant us through his intercession that the Faith practised and preached by him be our light on the way of life, so that we may be preserved from all anxieties of conscience, and if by human frailty we have sinned, we may return to Thee speedily by true penance. Through Christ our Lord. Amen.

INVOCATION OF ST. DIONYSIUS

G LORIOUS servant of God, St. Dionysius, with intense love thou didst devote thyself to Christ after learning to know Him through the apostle St. Paul, and didst preach His saving name to the nations, to bring whom to His knowledge and love thou didst not shrink from martyrdom; implore for me a continual growth in the knowledge and love of Jesus, so that my restless heart may experience that peace which He alone can give. Help me by thy powerful intercession with God to serve Him with a willing heart, to devote myself with abiding love to His service, and thereby to attain the eternal bliss of heaven. Amen.

PRAYER (p. 197).

VIII

Novena in Honor of St. Cyriacus

PREPARATORY PRAYER (p. 195).

PRAYER IN HONOR OF ST. CYRIACUS

O GOD, who didst grant to St. Cyriacus the grace of heroic charity and trustful resignation to Thy holy will; bestow upon us, through his intercession, the grace to walk before Thee in self-denying charity and to know and fulfil Thy will in all things. Through Christ our Lord. Amen.

INVOCATION OF ST. CYRIACUS

S T. CYRIACUS, great servant of God, loving Christ with all thy heart, thou didst for His sake also love thy fellow-men, and didst serve them even at the peril of thy life, for which charity God rewarded thee with the power to overcome Satan, the arch-enemy, and to deliver the poor obsessed from his dreadful tyranny; implore for me of God an effective, real, and true charity. Show thy power over Satan also in me; deliver me from his influence when he tries to tempt me. Help me to repel his assaults and to gain the victory over him in life and in death. Amen.

PRAYER (p. 197).

IX

Novena in Honor of St. Achatius

PREPARATORY PRAYER (p. 195).

PRAYER IN HONOR OF ST. ACHATIUS

O GOD, who didst fortify Thy holy martyr Achatius with constancy and trustful reliance on Thee in death; grant us through his intercession at the hour of our death to be free from all anxiety and victorious in our last combat with the enemy. Through Christ our Lord. Amen.

INVOCATION OF ST. ACHATIUS

*V*ALIANT martyr of Christ, St. Achatius, who preached Christ faithfully before kings and judges, and didst gain the victory over the enemies of God; help me through thy powerful intercession to resist and gain the victory over all the enemies of my salvation, over the world and its allurements, over the concupiscence of the flesh, and over the temptations of Satan. I implore thee particularly to assist me in my agony, when the powers of hell rise against me to rob my soul. Then do thou come to my aid and repel the assaults of the enemy, so that I surrender my soul into the hands of my Redeemer in faith, hope, and charity, and confiding in His infinite merits. Through the same Christ our Lord. Amen.

PRAYER (p. 197).

X

Novena in Honor of St. Eustachius

PREPARATORY PRAYER (p. 195).

PRAYER IN HONOR OF ST. EUSTACHIUS

O GOD, who didst lead Thy holy martyr Eustachius safely through many trials and dangers to the glorious crown of martyrdom; enlighten and strengthen us through his intercession, that we persevere in Thy love amid the trials of this life, and by resignation to Thy holy will come forth from the darkness of this earth into the light of Thy eternal glory. Amen.

INVOCATION OF ST. EUSTACHIUS

*H*EROIC servant of God, St. Eustachius, cast from the height of earthly glory and power into the deepest misery, thou wast engaged for a long time in the labor of a menial servant, eating the bitter bread of destitution; but never didst thou murmur against the severe probation to which God subjected thee. I implore thee to aid me with thy powerful intercession, that in all conditions I may resign myself to the holy will of God, and particularly that I may bear poverty and its consequences with patience, trusting in God's providence, completely resigned to the decrees of Him who humbles and exalts, chastises and heals, sends trials and consolations, and who has promised to those who follow Him in the spirit of poverty His beatific vision throughout all eternity. Amen.

PRAYER (p. 197).

XI

Novena in Honor of St. Giles

PREPARATORY PRAYER (p. 195).

PRAYER IN HONOR OF ST. GILES

O GOD, we beseech Thee to grant us through the merits and intercession of St. Giles to flee from the vanity and praise of this world, to avoid carefully all occasions of sin, to cleanse our hearts from all wickedness by a sincere confession, to leave this world in Thy love and rich in good works, and to find Thee gracious on the day of judgment. Through Christ our Lord. Amen.

INVOCATION OF ST. GILES

Z EALOUS follower of Christ, St. Giles; from early youth thou didst take to heart the words of our Saviour: "Learn of Me, because I am meek and humble of heart." Therefore thou didst flee from the praise and honors of the world, and wast rewarded with the grace to preserve thy heart from all sin and to persevere in a holy life to a ripe old age. I, on my part, through pride, self-confidence, and negligence, yielded to my evil inclinations, and thereby sinned grievously and often, offending my God and Lord, my Creator and Redeemer, my most loving Father. Therefore I implore thee to help me through thy mighty intercession to be enlightened by the Holy Ghost, that I may know the malice, grievousness, and multitude of my sins, confess them humbly, fully, and contritely, and receive pardon, tranquillity of heart, and peace of conscience from God. Amen.

PRAYER (p. 197).

XII

Novena in Honor of St. Margaret

PREPARATORY PRAYER (p. 195).

PRAYER IN HONOR OF ST. MARGARET

O GOD, grant us through the intercession of thy holy virgin and martyr Margaret, undauntedly to confess the Faith, carefully to observe the chastity of our state of life, and to overcome the temptations of the world, the devil, and the flesh, and thereby escape the punishments of eternal damnation. Amen.

INVOCATION OF ST. MARGARET

S T. MARGARET, holy virgin and martyr, thou didst faithfully preserve the robe of holy innocence and purity, valiantly resisting all the blandishments and allurements of the world for the love of thy divine Spouse, Jesus Christ; help me to overcome all temptations against the choicest of all virtues, holy purity, and to remain steadfast in the love of Christ, in order to preserve this great gift of God. Implore for me the grace of perseverance in prayer, distrust of myself, and flight from the occasions of sin, and finally the grace of a good death, so that in heaven I may "follow the Lamb whithersoever He goeth." Amen.

PRAYER (p. 197).

XIII

Novena in Honor of St. Catherine

PREPARATORY PRAYER (p. 195).

PRAYER IN HONOR OF ST. CATHERINE

O GOD, who didst distinguish Thy holy virgin and martyr Catherine by the gift of great wisdom and virtue, and a victorious combat with the enemies of the Faith; grant us, we beseech Thee, through her intercession, constancy in the Faith and the wisdom of the saints, that we may devote all the powers of our mind and heart to Thy service. Through Christ our Lord. Amen.

INVOCATION OF ST. CATHERINE

ST. CATHERINE, glorious virgin and martyr, resplendent in the luster of wisdom and purity; thy wisdom refuted the adversaries of divine truth and covered them with confusion; thy immaculate purity made thee a spouse of Christ, so that after thy glorious martyrdom angels carried thy body to Mount Sinai. Implore for me progress in the science of the saints and the virtue of holy purity, that vanquishing the enemies of my soul, I may be victorious in my last combat and after death be conducted by the angels into the eternal beatitude of heaven. Amen.

PRAYER (p. 197).

XIV

Novena in Honor of St. Barbara

PREPARATORY PRAYER (p. 195).

PRAYER IN HONOR OF ST. BARBARA

O GOD, who didst adorn Thy holy virgin and martyr Barbara with extraordinary fortitude in the confession of the Faith, and didst console her in the most atrocious torments; grant us through her intercession perseverance in the fulfilment of Thy law and the grace of being fortified before our end with the holy sacraments, and of a happy death. Through Christ our Lord. Amen.

INVOCATION OF ST. BARBARA

*I*NTREPID virgin and martyr, St. Barbara, through thy intercession come to my aid in all needs of my soul. Obtain for me the grace to be preserved from a sudden and unprovided death; assist me in my agony, when my senses are benumbed and I am in the throes of death. Then, O powerful patroness of the dying, come to my aid! Repel from me all the assaults and temptations of the evil one, and obtain for me the grace to receive before death the holy sacraments, that I breathe forth my soul confirmed in faith, hope, and charity, and be worthy to enter eternal glory. Amen.

> St. Barbara, at my last end
> > Obtain for me the Sacrament;
> Assist one in that direst need
> > When I my God and Judge must meet:
> That robed in sanctifying grace
> > My soul may stand before His face.

PRAYER (p. 197).

Novena to All the Fourteen Holy Helpers

PREPARATORY PRAYER

(By St Alphonsus Liguori.)

GREAT princes of heaven, Holy Helpers, who sacrificed to God all your earthly possessions, wealth, preferment, and even life, and who now are crowned in heaven in the secure enjoyment of eternal bliss and glory; have compassion on me, a poor sinner in this vale of tears, and obtain for me from God, for whom you gave up all things and who loves you as His servants, the strength to bear patiently all the trials of this life, to overcome all temptations, and to persevere in God's service to the end, that one day I too may be received into your company, to praise and glorify Him, the supreme Lord, whose beatific vision you enjoy, and whom you praise and glorify for ever. Amen.

❧ FIRST DAY ❧

The Devotion to the Fourteen Holy Helpers

PREPARATORY PRAYER (p. 212).

MEDITATION

*T*HE practice of honoring and invoking the saints to obtain, through their intercession, help in the various needs of body and soul, is as old as the Church. At what period, however, the custom of having recourse to the fourteen saints called Holy Helpers originated, is unknown. Nevertheless it is certain that each one of them was invoked for his intercession with God since his entrance into heaven. Prayer is the Christian's resource in every difficulty: and difficulties and trials are never wanting on earth.

Because the needs of mankind on earth are various, the faithful selected certain saints as intercessors in certain cases of distress, and obtained relief; hence these saints came to be regarded as special patrons in such trials, and were called Holy Helpers.

PRACTICE

*M*AKE this novena with full confidence in the power of the intercession of the Fourteen Holy Helpers. During their earthly life they devoted their whole

energy to the spreading of God's kingdom and the relief
and succor of their fellow-men. Much more efficiently can
they do so now when they are in the enjoyment of eternal
happiness, and can supplicate for us at the very throne of
God.

The saints *can* help us through their intercession. God
hears their prayers and He wrought miracles to confirm us
in this belief, even whilst His servants sojourned here on
earth. They *desire* and are willing to help us. St. Bernard
says: "In heaven hearts do not grow cold; they are rather
rendered more affectionate and tender. By receiving the
crown of justice the saints were not hardened against the
sufferings of their brethren on earth."

Therefore, in calling on them, have full confidence in
their power and ability to come to your aid.

PRAYER

*W*E BESEECH Thee, O Lord, to hear the
prayer which we send up to Thee in honor of
Thy glorified servants, the Fourteen Holy Helpers: and as
we can not rely upon our own justice, grant our petition
through the intercession of those whose merits have made
them especially dear to Thee. Through Christ our Lord.
Amen.

Litany of the Fourteen Holy Helpers

LORD, have mercy on us.

Christ, have mercy on us.

Lord, have mercy on us.

Christ, hear us.

Christ, graciously hear us.

God the Father of heaven, have mercy on us.

God the Son, Redeemer of the world, have mercy on us.

God the Holy Ghost, have mercy on us.

Holy Trinity, one God, have mercy on us.

Holy Mary, queen of martyrs,

St. Joseph, helper in all needs,

Fourteen Holy Helpers,

St. George, valiant martyr of Christ,

St. Blase, zealous bishop and benefactor of the poor,

St. Erasmus, mighty protector of the oppressed,

St. Pantaleon, miraculous exemplar of charity,

St. Vitus, special protector of chastity,

St. Christophorus, mighty intercessor in dangers,

St. Dionysius, shining mirror of faith and confidence,

St. Cyriacus, terror of hell,

St. Achatius, helpful advocate in death,

St. Eustachius, exemplar of patience in adversity,

St. Giles, despiser of the world,

St. Margaret, valiant champion of the Faith,

St. Catherine, victorious defender of the Faith and of purity,

Pray for us.

St. Barbara, mighty patroness of the dying,
All ye Holy Helpers,
All ye saints of God,
In temptations against faith,
In adversity and trials,
In anxiety and want,
In every combat,
In every temptation,
In sickness,
In all needs,
In fear and terror,
In dangers of salvation,
In dangers of honor,
In dangers of reputation,
In dangers of property,
In dangers by fire and water,

Pray for us.

Be merciful, spare us, O Lord!
Be merciful, graciously hear us, O Lord!

From all sin,
From Thy wrath,
From the scourge of earthquake,
From plague, famine, and war,
From lightning and storms,
From a sudden and unprovided death,
From eternal damnation,
Through the mystery of Thy holy incarnation,
Through Thy birth and Thy life,
Through Thy cross and passion,

deliver us, O Lord.

Through Thy death and burial,
Through the merits of Thy blessed Mother Mary,
Through the merits of the Fourteen Holy Helpers,
On the Day of Judgment,

We sinners, beseech Thee, hear us.

That Thou spare us,
That Thou pardon us,
That Thou convert us to true penance,
That Thou give and preserve the fruits of the earth,
That Thou protect and propagate Thy holy Church,
That Thou preserve peace and concord among the nations,
That Thou give eternal rest to the souls of the departed,
That Thou come to our aid through the intercession of the Holy Helpers,
That through the intercession of St. George Thou preserve us in the Faith,
That through the intercession of St. Blase Thou confirm us in hope,
That through the intercession of St. Erasmus Thou enkindle in us Thy holy love,
That through the intercession of St. Pantaleon Thou give us charity for our neighbor,
That through the intercession of St. Vitus Thou teach us the value of our soul,
That through the intercession of St. Christophorus Thou preserve us from sin,
That through the intercession of St. Dionysius Thou give us tranquillity of conscience,
That through the intercession of St. Cyriacus Thou grant us resignation to Thy holy will,

That through the intercession of St. Eustachius Thou give us patience in adversity,

That through the intercession of St. Achatius Thou grant us a happy death,

That through the intercession of St. Giles Thou grant us a merciful judgment,

That through the intercession of St. Margaret Thou preserve us from hell,

That through the intercession of St. Catherine Thou shorten our purgatory,

That through the intercession of St. Barbara Thou receive us in heaven,

That through the intercession of all the Holy Helpers Thou wilt grant our prayers,

we beseech Thee, hear us.

Lamb of God, who takest away the sins of the world, spare us, O Lord.

Lamb of God, who takest away the sins of the world, graciously hear us, O Lord.

Lamb of God, who takest away the sins of the world, have mercy on us, O Lord.

V. Pray for us, ye Fourteen Holy Helpers.

R. That we may be made worthy of the promise of Christ.

LET US PRAY:

ALMIGHTY and eternal God, who hast bestowed extraordinary graces and gifts on Thy saints George, Blase, Erasmus, Pantaleon, Vitus, Christophorus, Dionysius, Cyriacus, Eustachius, Achatius, Giles, Margaret, Catherine, and Barbara, and hast illustrated them by miracles;

we beseech Thee to graciously hear the petitions of all who invoke their intercession. Through Christ our Lord. Amen.

O God, who didst miraculously fortify the Fourteen Holy Helpers in the confession of the Faith; grant us, we beseech Thee, to imitate their fortitude in overcoming all temptations against it, and protect us through their intercession in all dangers of soul and body, so that we may serve Thee in purity of heart and chastity of body. Through Christ our Lord. Amen.

INVOCATION OF THE HOLY HELPERS

*F*OURTEEN Holy Helpers, who served God in humility and confidence on earth and are now in the enjoyment of His beatific vision in heaven; because you persevered till death you gained the crown of eternal life. Remember the dangers that surround us in this vale of tears, and intercede for us in all our needs and adversities. Amen.

Fourteen Holy Helpers, select friends of God, I honor you as mighty intercessors, and come with filial confidence to you in my needs, for the relief of which I have undertaken to make this novena. Help me by your intercession to placate God's wrath, which I have provoked by my sins, and aid me in amending my life and doing penance. Obtain for me the grace to serve God with a willing heart, to be resigned to His holy will, to be patient in adversity and to persevere unto the end, so that, having finished my earthly course, I may join you in heaven, there to praise for ever God, who is wonderful in His saints. Amen.

~ SECOND DAY ~

The Destiny of Man

PREPARATORY PRAYER (p. 212).

MEDITATION

THE Holy Helpers faithfully co-operated with God's designs concerning their eternal destiny. No obstacle could prevail on them to stray from the path of duty. Always and everywhere they fulfilled the will of God.

You, too, have an eternal destiny. You are not your own master, but belong to God, whose servant and property you are. Therefore you must obey Him, and not your own inclinations; you must do His will, and not your own. God had the right of requiring our submission to Him without giving us a reward, because He is Our Lord; nevertheless He promised to give us Himself in reward for our faithful service. Ought this not be sufficient inducement for us to serve Him zealously and gratefully?

Remember, moreover, that you shall be unhappy both in this and in the next world if you do not give yourself entirely to God, for whom you were created. St. Augustine says: "Thou hast created us for Thee, O Lord, and our heart remains restless till it rests in Thee."

PRACTICE

THANK God for the undeserved grace of creation and redemption. Make an act of contrition for having served Him so negligently. Promise amendment, and invoke the aid of God's grace through the intercession of the Holy Helpers.

PRAYER

O GOD, who according to the decrees of Thy providence hast created man for eternal bliss; grant, through the intercession of the Holy Helpers, that I may attain to my destiny by being united with Thee in this life and loving and praising Thee for ever in heaven. Amen.

LITANY AND PRAYERS (p. 215).

✺ THIRD DAY ✺

The Virtue of Faith

PREPARATORY PRAYER (p. 212).

MEDITATION

*T*HE Holy Helpers were so thoroughly imbued with the virtue of divine faith, that they believed its sacred truths with perfect abandonment of their intellect, will, liberty, and whole being. They wavered not amid the severest torments, but remained firm until death in the confession of Christ.

Our time is noted for assaults on the Faith and on the Church that teaches it. The Church, the depository of divine revelation, is blasphemed in her doctrine, in her precepts, in her sacraments, in her ministers, in her cult, in her entire essence. Were you never ashamed of your Catholic name? What cowardliness, what timidity, what downright malice!

PRACTICE

*R*EVIVE your faith by the consideration of the example of the Holy Helpers. Do not, from human respect, neglect the sanctification of the Lord's Day, the observance of days of fast and abstinence, the reception of the holy sacraments, the profession of your belief in the real presence of Our Lord in the Blessed Sacrament, etc. Meditate frequently on the words of Christ: "He that shall deny Me before men, I will also deny him before My Father who is in heaven" (Matt. 10:33).

PRAYER

O GOD, I beseech Thee, through the faith of the Holy Helpers, grant me the grace to treasure in my heart the doctrines of our holy faith, to believe them firmly, to confess them bravely, and to live according to their precepts, that through that same faith I may become worthy to be admitted to Thy beatific vision in heaven. Amen.

LITANY AND PRAYERS (p. 215).

◆ FOURTH DAY ◆

The Virtue of Hope

PREPARATORY PRAYER (p. 212).

MEDITATION

"HOPE confoundeth not" (Rom. 5:6). According to the commentators these words of Holy Scripture are to be understood in the sense that our works must be in conformity with that which is the object of our hope; that is, we must live in such a manner that we really merit the reward of heaven.

We sin against hope also by presumption in God's mercy, by despair, and by over-confidence in our own righteousness. According to Holy Scripture we can not, of our own efficacy, perform a good act, but can do all in Him that strengthens us.

All these truths are exemplified in the lives of the Holy Helpers. Their hope was based on the firm foundation of faith, and consequently, like it, firm, constant, and unwavering.

PRACTICE

LIKE the Holy Helpers, hope to obtain from God all things necessary to salvation, for "the Lord is good to them that hope in Him, to the soul that seeketh Him" (Lam. 3:25). Live so that He can fulfil His promises.

Place no obstacle to His bounty and might by a sinful life.

PRAYER

*E*TERNAL God of love and mercy, I thank Thee for all the benefits Thou hast conferred upon me, and hope to obtain, through the intercession of the Holy Helpers, all the graces necessary for my salvation. Through Christ our Lord. Amen.

LITANY AND PRAYERS (p. 215).

FIFTH DAY

The Love of God

PREPARATORY PRAYER (p. 212).

MEDITATION

*T*HE love of God which inflamed the Holy Helpers showed forth in their whole life, and particularly at their death. We, too, ought to be inflamed with such love, for without it faith, wisdom, the gift of tongues, and good works in general, avail nothing; for the love of God must inspire them all. "And we know that to them that love God, all things work together unto good" (Rom. 8:28). Such, and such alone, will receive the crown of life. Did not God love us first? To redeem us from sin and eternal death

He spared not His only begotten, divine Son. All goods of life and fortune are gifts of His love, evidences of His infinite love. And we find it difficult to return this love? How ungrateful not to love God with your whole heart!

PRACTICE

*I*MITATE the Holy Helpers in their ardent love of God. Implore their intercession to obtain it. Meditate often on God's love for you, and your heart will be enflamed with love for Him.

PRAYER

O GOD of mercy and love, I thank Thee from all my heart for the countless graces which Thy infinite love has bestowed on me. By the ardent love which the Holy Helpers had for Thee, I implore Thee to enkindle in my heart the flame of Thy love, so that I may remain in Thee and Thou in me. Amen.

LITANY AND PRAYERS (p. 215).

✺ SIXTH DAY ✺

The Virtue of Charity

PREPARATORY PRAYER (p. 212).

MEDITATION

CHARITY is one of the fundamental virtues of the Christian religion. The moral doctrine preached by Christ is comprised in the words: "Thou shalt love the Lord thy God with thy whole heart, and with thy whole soul, and with thy whole mind. This is the greatest and the first commandment. And the second is like to this: Thou shalt love thy neighbor as thyself. On these two commandments dependeth the whole law and the prophets" (Matt. 22:37-40).

As in everything else, the Holy Helpers are our exemplars also in charity. Charity consists in wishing well to our fellow-men, rejoicing with the glad and sympathizing with the sad, doing good to all, excusing their faults whenever possible, disclosing them only when necessary, being friendly, indulgent, meek, and helpful toward them. We love our neighbor if we succor the poor and distressed, if we harbor no envy for the rich, if we esteem the just for their virtue, and hate—not the sinner—but sin. We love our neighbor if we are not content with harboring these sentiments in our heart, but show them by our actions.

PRACTICE

ENDEAVOR to exercise this charity according to the spirit of Christ. The love of your neighbor must not be a sentimental affection; it must not originate in casual qualities of character or rank, in inclination, etc., but must have the love of God for its motive. We must exercise charity toward all because God wills it, and in the manner in which He wills it. "Thou shalt love thy neighbor as thyself."

PRAYER

O GOD of charity, who dost will that I love my neighbor for Thy sake, grant me the grace, through the intercession of the Holy Helpers, to be animated with that spirit of charity which embraces all and excludes none, which "is patient, kind, envieth not, dealeth not perversely, is not puffed up, is not ambitious, seeketh not her own, is not provoked to anger, thinketh no evil, rejoiceth not in iniquity, but rejoiceth with the truth, beareth all things, believeth all things, endureth all things, and never falleth away" (1 Cor. 13:4-8). Amen.

LITANY AND PRAYERS (p. 215).

✑ SEVENTH DAY ✑

Human Respect

PREPARATORY PRAYER (p. 212).

MEDITATION

*B*Y THE conscientious fulfilment of the duties of their state of life the Holy Helpers show us that the will of God alone was the motive of all their actions. Human respect, regard for the opinion of others, did not influence them.

The cowardly fear, "What will people say?" was the ruin of many a soul. The enemy of mankind is ever intent upon preventing us from doing good through human respect. He insinuates that virtue and piety are out of date and ridiculed. From human respect many a person boasts of that which ought to make him blush; he thinks it discreditable to be less remiss in his religious obligations than others. Ought the opinion and ridicule of the world influence us to prevent our pleasing God? St. Paul says: "If I yet pleased men, I should not be the servant of Christ" (Gal. 1:10). Our Lord Himself tells us, "He that shall deny Me before men, I will also deny him before My Father who is in heaven" (Matt. 10:33).

PRACTICE

OUR Lord says: "So let your light shine before men, that they may see your good works and glorify your Father who is in heaven" (Matt. 5:16). Do not stray from the path of duty on account of human respect; do not let yourself be influenced by the judgments of the world.

PRAYER

MERCIFUL God, who gavest the Holy Helpers the grace to fulfil Thy will regardless of human respect; grant that we may obtain through their intercession and merits the courage to despise the opinion of men, and ever serve Thee with a fearless heart. Amen.

LITANY AND PRAYERS (p. 215).

✦ EIGHTH DAY ✦

Prayer

PREPARATORY PRAYER (p. 212).

MEDITATION

*T*HE Holy Helpers, well knowing the efficacy of prayer, assiduously devoted themselves to it. From it they drew that wonderful strength which sustained them in their combat for the Faith.

Prayer is the elevation of the mind to God, intercourse with Him by acts of adoration, praise, thanksgiving, and petition. St. Chrysostom says of prayer: "Without prayer it is impossible to lead a good life; for no one can practise virtue except he humbly implores God for it, who alone can give him the necessary strength. Who ceases to love and practise prayer, no longer possesses the gifts of the Spirit. But he that perseveres in the service of God, and deems it an irreparable loss to miss constant prayer, possesses every virtue and is a friend of God."

PRACTICE

*O*FFER yourself at the beginning of each day to God, and thereby you will belong to Him throughout its whole course. Renew your consecration to Him frequently during the day by short acts of virtue and especially by a good intention, thus rendering all your work a prayer, and you will attain perfection.

PRAYER

O GOD, I implore Thee through the merits and intercession of the Holy Helpers, to grant me the spirit of prayer, that following their example I may walk in Thy presence and ever enjoy the consolation of intercourse with Thee. Through Christ our Lord. Amen.

LITANY AND PRAYERS (p. 215).

☙ NINTH DAY ❧

Perseverance

PREPARATORY PRAYER (p. 212).

MEDITATION

A VICTORIOUS death was the reward of the Holy Helpers' perseverance in the service of

God. During this novena you have, no doubt, formed many good resolutions, exclaiming with the Royal Prophet, "And I said, now I have begun" (Ps. 76:11). But it happens that many, despite their good will, become remiss in the pursuit of virtue. Satan is assiduously trying to accomplish their ruin, representing to them and exaggerating the difficulties to be encountered on the path of virtue. They hesitate, falter, and finally turn back. This is the most unfortunate happening that can occur. Of the condition of such a one Our Lord Himself says: "When the unclean spirit is gone out of a man, he walketh through places without water, seeking rest; and not finding, he saith: 'I will return into my house whence I came out.' And when he is come, he findeth it swept and garnished. Then he goeth and taketh with him seven spirits more wicked than himself, and entering in they dwell there. And the last state of that man becometh worse than the first" (Luke 11:24-26). Are these words not a sufficient warning to encourage us to persevere in our good resolves?

PRACTICE

*I*N concluding this novena, survey again the depth of that incomprehensible eternity which is awaiting you. Contemplate in spirit the endless chain of centuries following each other there in reward or in punishment. Does this thought not banish all the difficulties of perseverance?

PRAYER

O GOD, whose mercies are infinite and whose goodness is without limit, I beseech Thee through the merits and intercession of the Holy Helpers, grant me the grace of perseverance in Thy love and service to the end. Thou, who dost dispense so many favors through the Holy Helpers, despise not my prayer, but graciously hear and grant it. Amen.

LITANY AND PRAYERS (p. 215).

CONCLUDING PRAYER

O FAITHFUL servants of God and powerful protectors of man, Holy Helpers! Since Our Lord appointed you the heavenly advocates for our needs on earth, I confidently turn to you for help in my distress. Countless numbers praise you for aiding them with counsel in doubt, with consolation in anxiety, with health in illness, with safety in danger, with delivery from prison, and with help and assistance in all tribulations. Therefore I, too, have recourse to you, and implore you not to refuse me your aid.

Give thanks to God for me for all the graces He granted me during this novena. I ascribe them to your great merits and powerful intercession. I thank you all together, and each one in particular, for your interest in my favor before the throne of God. I commend myself to your continued protection, that I may one day be united with you in heaven, there to thank the Giver of all good things and to praise Him for all eternity. Amen.

Prayers of Petition and Intercession

I. THREE INVOCATIONS

*G*REAT friends of God, Holy Helpers, humbly saluting and venerating you, I implore your help and intercession. Bring my prayers before the throne of the Most Holy Trinity, so that I may experience in all the difficulties and trials of life the mercy of the eternal Father, the love of the incarnate divine Son, and the assistance of the Holy Ghost; that despondency may not depress me when God's wise decree imposes on my shoulders a heavy burden. Above all, I implore your assistance at the hour of death. Help me then to gain the victory over the temptations and assaults of Satan, and to leave this world hopefully trusting in God's mercy, to join you in heaven, there to praise Him for ever and ever. Amen.

*W*ITH confiding trust I turn to you, Holy Helpers, who were selected by God before many other saints to be the special intercessors and advocates of the distressed. Obtain for me strength and courage to struggle and suffer on earth for the glory of God, for the propagation of our holy faith, and for my own perfection.

You are fruitful branches of the true and living vine, Jesus Christ, for whom you heroically suffered hunger and thirst, persecution and ignominy, afflictions and adversity, tortures and death. Here on earth you were true disciples and dauntless martyrs of Christ. Assist me to follow your example and to suffer for His sake, so that I may not be parted from Him as a useless member, but persevere in His service despite all trials and tribulations of life. Knowing my inconstancy and weakness, I have recourse to you, O glorious members of the Church triumphant, and implore you to support my feeble prayers, and to bear them before the throne of the Almighty, who, for your sake, will hear them. Amen.

GREAT friends and servants of God, Holy Helpers! Humbly saluting and venerating you, I implore your help and intercession. God has promised and granted that whosoever invokes your aid shall be relieved in his needs and succored at the hour of death. Therefore I have recourse to you and confidently implore your aid. I am surrounded by difficulties and my soul is oppressed with grief. Burdened with sins, the fear of God's rigorous judgment appalls me, whilst Satan ceases not to exert all his power to accomplish my eternal ruin.

Therefore I implore your assistance, powerful Holy Helpers, in my dire distress. By the penitential life you led, by the cruel tortures you suffered, and by your holy death I entreat you to pray for me. Obtain for me the remission of my sins and perseverance to the end in God's grace. Assist me in my agony and protect me against the wily assaults of Satan, that through your help I may die a happy death and enter a blissful eternity. Amen.

II. PRAYER IN ILLNESS

COMPASSIONATE Holy Helpers, who restored health to so many through the power of the name of Jesus; behold me suffering from bodily illness and from wounds of the soul. Implore the kind, merciful Good Samaritan, your and my Lord Jesus Christ, to heal the wounds of my soul by washing them in His most precious blood, and to quicken my spirit by His sanctifying grace. If it, then, be God's holy will and for the welfare of my soul, let me experience the powerful effect of your intercession, that, restored to health, I may serve God with greater fervor, and promote your veneration together with so many who experienced your help in illness and suffering. Amen.

III. PRAYER FOR THE SICK

MERCIFUL Holy Helpers, look benignly upon me, who implore your intercession for a sick person. Our Lord and Redeemer Jesus Christ, who Himself went about healing and doing good, appointed you the special protectors and intercessors of the sick, and restored to bodily and spiritual health many for whom you prayed. Encouraged thereby to invoke you, I implore you to offer up to His sacred Heart all the pains and torments He suffered during His bitter passion. Offer up to Him also your own sufferings for God's glory, which you underwent during life, and in death; offer up to Him all the anguish and distress suffered by the sick person for whom I invoke your intercession. Ask Him to restore him to health of body, and to infuse into his soul the grace of salvation, so that he may devote his life with renewed vigor to the service of God and to the fulfilment of his duties, and thereby gather rich merits for eternity.

But if God, in the designs of His providence, should otherwise dispose, implore for the sick person patience in his illness, resignation to the divine will, and the grace of a happy death. Assist him in his agony, and conduct his soul to the throne of the Almighty. Amen.

IV. PRAYER OF PARENTS FOR THEIR CHILDREN

*H*OLY Helpers, assist me to give thanks to God for blessing me with children. Having received them from Him, it is my duty to train them for His service. Therefore I commend them to your special protection. Guard them from sin, help them to know and fulfil their duties, preserve them from all harm of body and soul; pray for them that they may be and remain children of God. For me, obtain the grace always to take good care of them, to edify them by good example, to punish their faults wisely, to preserve their innocence, and to instruct them unto piety, so that they and I may together enjoy the eternal happiness of heaven. Amen.

V. PRAYER OF CHILDREN FOR THEIR PARENTS

*H*OLY Helpers, mighty intercessors with God in all necessities; God strictly commanded that children should love, honor, and obey their parents. Our Lord and Saviour Jesus Christ Himself gave them the example of submission and obedience by being subject to His mother and foster-father. I commend myself to your powerful intercession and implore you to obtain for me the grace to follow His example. For my parents I implore protection from all evil of body and soul, a long and prosperous life, and a happy death. Reward them for all the care, anxiety, labor, and trouble which they underwent patiently for my sake with the eternal crown of heavenly glory. Amen.

VI. PRAYER OF MARRIED PEOPLE

*H*OLY Helpers, powerful intercessors at the throne of God, by whose providence we were indissolubly joined in holy wedlock through the sacramental bonds of matrimony; obtain for us, through your intercession, the grace to dwell together in mutual love and peace, and to fulfil faithfully the duties of our state of life; that following the example of the saints and elect who lived in wedlock, we may merit God's grace and blessing by a virtuous life here on earth, and united in heaven praise and bless Him for ever. Amen.

PART V

General Devotions

"*The Lord is nigh unto all them that call upon Him, to all that call upon Him in truth. He will do the will of them that fear Him, and He will bear their prayer and save them*"

(Ps. 144: 18, 19).

"*Rejoicing in hope, patient in tribulation, instant in prayer*"

(Rom. 12:12).

Hail Mary, full of grace, pray for us.

Morning Prayers

On awaking, sign yourself with the sign of the cross, saying:

*I*N THE name of the Father, ✠ and of the Son, and of the Holy Ghost. Amen.

I rise in the name of Our Lord Jesus Christ, who redeemed me by His precious blood. Bless, guide, and protect me from all evil, O Lord! Strengthen me to all good and lead me to eternal life. Amen.

After dressing, kneel and say:

My Lord and my God! I prostrate myself before the throne of Thy divine Majesty, and give Thee infinite thanks, O Lord, that I have passed this night safely and have not died in my sins, but was preserved by Thy bounty for Thy further service.

I offer up to Thee all that I shall do and suffer today, and unite it with the prayers, labors, and sufferings of Our Lord Jesus Christ and of His blessed Mother Mary.

OFFERING

*T*AKE, O Lord, and receive all my liberty, my memory, my understanding, and my whole will. Thou hast given me all that I am and all that I possess;

I surrender it all to Thee that Thou mayest dispose of it according to Thy will. Give me only Thy love and Thy grace; with these I will be rich enough, and will have no more to desire.

Indulgence. 300 days, once a day. (Leo XIII, May 26, 1883.)

Acts of Faith, Hope, and Charity

*M*Y LORD and God! I most firmly believe all that Thou hast revealed and all that Thy holy Church believes and teaches, because Thou, who art infallible Truth, hast so revealed and commanded.

My Lord and God! Because Thou art almighty, infinitely good and merciful, I hope that by the merits of the passion and death of Jesus Christ, our Saviour, Thou wilt grant me eternal life, which Thou hast promised to all who shall do the works of a good Christian, as I purpose to do by Thy help.

My Lord and God! Because Thou art the highest and most perfect good, I love Thee with my whole heart, and above all things; and rather than offend Thee, I am ready to lose all things else; and for Thy love, I love and desire to love my neighbor as myself.

Indulgence. (1) A plenary indulgence, once a month, for devoutly making these acts daily; under the usual conditions. (2) A plenary indulgence at the hour of death, under the same conditions. (3) Seven years and seven quarantines, every time. (Benedict XIV, January 28, 1728.) The same Pope declared that it is not necessary to use any set formula, but that any form of words may be used, provided it expresses the particular motive of each of the three theological virtues.

To the Blessed Virgin Mary

Hail Mary, etc.

*M*Y QUEEN, my Mother! I give myself entirely to thee; and to show my devotion to thee I consecrate to thee this day my eyes, my ears, my mouth, my heart, my whole being, without reserve. Wherefore, good Mother, as I am thine own, keep me, guard me, as thy property and possession.

Indulgence. (1) 100 days, once a day. (2) A plenary indulgence, once a month, for saying it every day; under the usual conditions. (Pius IX, Aug. 5, 1851.)

To the Angel Guardian

*A*NGEL of God, my guardian dear,
To whom His love committed me here,
Ever this day be at my side,
To light and guard, to rule and guide! Amen.

Indulgence. (1) 100 days, every time. (2) A plenary indulgence on the feast of the holy Guardian Angels, for saying it morning and evening throughout the year; under the usual conditions. (3) A plenary indulgence at the hour of death, for saying it often during life. (Pius VI, Oct 2, 1795, and June 11, 1796.) (4) A plenary indulgence, once a month, for saying it daily; under the usual conditions. (Pius VII, May 15, 1821.)

Evening Prayers

*E*TERNAL and merciful God! I adore Thee and give Thee thanks for all the graces and benefits which Thou hast conferred upon me during my whole life, and particularly during this day. May the saints and elect, especially the Holy Helpers, praise and thank Thee for me.

Enlighten me now through Thy holy Spirit, and let me know whether and how I have offended Thee today in thought, word, deed, and omission of duty.

Examine your conscience.

AN ACT OF CONTRITION

O MY God! I am deeply sorry for all my sins, forthose I committed to-day, and for those of my whole life, because thereby I offended Thy supreme and most loving goodness. Pardon me for the sake of Jesus, Thy Son, who shed His most precious blood on the cross for our sins. With the help of Thy grace, I firmly resolve to amend my life, and rather to die than again offend Thee by a mortal sin.

PETITION

*P*ROTECT me and mine and all men during this night, and through the intercession of the blessed Virgin Mary and of the Holy Helpers preserve us from all dangers of body and soul. Keep away from us sickness, fire, and calamities of every kind. Protect us against the assaults of the wicked and of Satan. Into Thy hands I commend my body and soul; let me rest in Thy most holy wounds.

Visit, we beseech Thee, O Lord, this habitation, and repel from it all the snares of the enemy; let Thy holy angels dwell herein to preserve us in peace, and may Thy blessings be upon us for ever. Through Christ our Lord. Amen.

To the Sacred Heart of Jesus

(Prayer of St Alphonsus.)

ADORABLE Heart of my Jesus, Heart created expressly for the love of men! Until now I have shown toward Thee only ingratitude. Pardon me, O my Jesus! Heart of my Jesus, abyss of love and of mercy, how is it possible that I do not die of sorrow when I reflect on Thy goodness to me and my ingratitude to Thee? Thou, my Creator, after having created me, hast given Thy blood and Thy life for me; and, not content with this, Thou hast invented a means of offering Thyself up every day for me in the Holy Eucharist, exposing Thyself to a thousand insults and outrages. O Jesus, do Thou wound my heart with a great contrition for my sins, and a lively love for Thee. Through Thy tears and Thy blood give me the grace of perseverance in Thy fervent love until I breathe my last sigh. Amen.

To the Blessed Virgin Mary

REMEMBER, O most gracious Virgin Mary, that never was it known that any one who fled to thy protection, implored thy help, and sought thy intercession, was left unaided. Inspired with this confidence, I fly unto thee, O Virgin of virgins, my Mother! To thee I come; before thee I stand, sinful and sorrowful. O Mother of the Word incarnate, despise not my petitions, but in thy mercy hear and answer me. Amen.

Indulgence. (1) 300 days, every time, (2) A plenary indulgence, once a month, for having said it daily; under the usual conditions. (Pius IX, December 11, 1846.)

Litany of Loreto (p. 322).

To St. Joseph

GUARDIAN of virgins and father, holy Joseph, to whose faithful care Christ Jesus, very innocence, and Mary, Virgin of virgins, were committed; I pray and beg of thee by these dear pledges, Jesus and Mary, free me from all uncleanness, and make me with spotless mind, pure heart, and chaste body, ever most chastely to serve Jesus and Mary all the days of my life. Amen.

Indulgence. 100 days, once a day. (Pius IX, Feb. 4, 1877.)

Before Retiring

(Prayer of St. Alphonsus.)

*M*Y LORD and God Jesus Christ! I adore Thee and give Thee thanks for all the graces which Thou hast granted me to-day. I offer up to Thee my rest and every moment of this night, and implore Thee to preserve me from all sin. Therefore I place myself into the wound of Thy sacred side, and beneath the protecting mantle of my Mother Mary. May Thy holy angels assist me and watch over my peace, and may Thy holy blessing remain with me.

Indulgence. 60 days, once a day, also for the souls in purgatory. (Leo XIII, June 30, 1898.)

INVOCATION

*J*ESUS, Mary, and Joseph, I give you my heart and my soul.

Jesus, Mary, and Joseph, assist me in my last agony.

Jesus, Mary, and Joseph, may I breathe forth my soul in peace with you.

Indulgence. 100 days for the recital of any one of these invocations, 300 days for all three. (Pius VII, Aug. 26, 1814.)

Prayers at Holy Mass

PREPARATORY PRAYER

ALMIGHTY and eternal God! I appear in Thy presence to assist at the most holy sacrifice of the body and blood of Jesus Christ, Thy Son, my Redeemer, and to offer it up jointly with the priest and the faithful here present, in grateful remembrance of His passion and death, for the promotion of Thy glory, and for my salvation. Together with all the holy Masses that are celebrated throughout the world, I offer up this august sacrifice for the following intentions: To adore Thee, O my God, as Thou dost deserve to be adored; to give Thee due thanks for the innumerable benefits which I owe to Thy bounty; to make reparation for the many offenses I have committed; to appease Thy just anger, and to invoke Thy infinite mercy for me, for Thy holy Church, for the whole world, and for the souls in purgatory. Amen.

AT THE BEGINNING OF MASS

O HEAVENLY Father! Hear the prayer of Thy holy Church invoking Thy divine Majesty in the name of Our Lord Jesus Christ, to come to the aid of Thy children in all their needs. Turn not from us Thy gracious eyes, but deliver us from all evil, so that we may live to please Thee, die in Thy love, and enter the kingdom of glory. Amen.

AT THE GOSPEL

ALMIGHTY God, Thou source of all truth, holiness, and justice; having spoken in the Old Law by the mouth of Thy prophets, Thou spokest in the fulness of time through Thy divine Son Jesus Christ, and speakest now through Thy holy Church, appointed by Thee the Teacher of truth. We thank Thee for the saving doctrines entrusted to her for our good, and implore Thy grace to practise them and to please Thee by all our actions.

AT THE CREDO

Say the Apostles' Creed.

AT THE OFFERING

ALMIGHTY and eternal God! Look graciously on the forms of bread and wine offered up to Thee on the altar by the priest, imploring Thee to bless and sanctify them for the eucharistic sacrifice of the New Law. With this sacrifice, O my God, I offer up to Thee my heart with all its affections, desires, and inclinations. Sanctify my thoughts, words, and deeds, that they may become a sacrifice acceptable and pleasing to Thee.

AT THE PREFACE

*T*O THEE, O Lord, I raise my heart in gratitude for all Thy mercies. For truly meet and just, right and salutary is it for us to give Thee always and everywhere praise and thanks, O holy Lord, almighty Father and eternal God, through Christ our Lord; through whom the angels and archangels, the cherubs and the seraphs praise Thy majesty and adore Thy might. With them I unite my voice, joining in their hymns of praise, and saying:

AT THE SANCTUS

*H*OLY, holy, holy, Lord, God of hosts. Heaven and earth are filled with Thy glory. Hosanna in the highest. Blessed is He that cometh in the name of the Lord. Hosanna in the highest.

AT THE CANON

O GOD! Let my prayer be acceptable to Thee, and graciously hear the intercession which I make confiding in the virtue of this holy sacrifice. I commend to Thy mercy our holy Father, N., our bishop, N., and all bishops and priests of Thy holy Church. Let Thy kingdom be spread more and more all over the earth; grant peace and concord to the nations; protect our country; preserve peace and love in all families. Remember graciously my parents, brothers, sisters, and relatives, my benefactors, my enemies, and all for whom I am in justice or charity bound to pray.

AT THE ELEVATION

*H*AIL, thou body of my Saviour, conceived by the Holy Ghost, born of Mary the immaculate Virgin! With profound humility I adore Thee. Lord, have mercy on me!

Eternal Father, I offer Thee the precious blood of Jesus, in satisfaction for my sins, and for the wants of holy Church.

Indulgence. 100 days, every time. (Pius VII, Sept. 22, 1817.)

AFTER THE ELEVATION

*M*OST amiable Jesus! Thou art now present on the altar, God and man, really, truly, and essentially. Divine victim for our sins, have mercy on us! Be our mediator with Thy Father; avert from us the punishment we have deserved for our sins, deliver us from all dangers that threaten us, and from all evil. Promote the welfare of Thy Church, and remember in Thy mercy those who have gone before us with the sign of faith and rest in peace. (*Remember the departed for whom you intend to pray.*)

To these, O Lord, and to all that sleep in Christ, grant, we beseech Thee, a place of refreshment, light, and peace.

Also to us sinners, Thy servants, confiding in the multitude of Thy mercies, grant some part and fellowship with Thy saints, through whose intercession we invoke Thy favor, and into whose company we beseech Thee to admit us, not in consideration of our merit, but of Thy own pardon. Through Christ our Lord. Amen.

AT THE PATER NOSTER

*I*NSTRUCTED by Thy saving precepts and
following Thy divine directions, we presume to say:
Our Father, etc.

AT THE AGNUS DEI

*L*AMB of God, who takest away the sins of the world,
have mercy on us.

Lamb of God, who takest away the sins of the world,
have mercy on us.

Lamb of God, who takest away the sins of the world,
give us peace.

AT COMMUNION

*L*ORD, I am not worthy that Thou shouldst enter
under my roof; say but the word, and my soul shall
be healed. (*Three times.*)

SPIRITUAL COMMUNION

O JESUS, I firmly believe that Thou art truly present
in the Blessed Sacrament. I see Thee therein full of
love, willing to pardon us, anxious to be united with us. I
wish most earnestly to respond to this Thy desire and love.
I detest all the sins by which I have ever displeased Thee.
Pardon me, O Lord! I desire to receive Thee into my heart,
and since I now can not receive Thee sacramentally, come
at least spiritually to me.

I embrace Thee, I unite myself with Thee as if Thou wert really present in my heart. With all my love I cling to Thee. Preserve me from sin, that I may never be separated from Thee, but remain united with Thee for ever.

Indulgence. 60 days, once a day. Also for the suffering souls. (Leo XIII, June 30, 1893.)

AT THE BLESSING

*B*LESS me, O Lord, by the hand of Thy priest, and let the power of this blessing remain upon me for ever. In the name of the Father, and of the Son, and of the Holy Ghost. Amen.

AT THE LAST GOSPEL

O JESUS, incarnate Word of the eternal Father, Thou true light which enlightens the world! I give thanks to Thee at all times for having dwelt among us, the only-begotten Son of the Father, full of grace and truth. Amen.

Prayers after Mass

Hail Mary, etc. (*Three times.*)

SALVE REGINA

*H*AIL, holy queen, Mother of mercy, our life, our sweetness, and our hope! To thee do we cry, poor banished children of Eve; to thee do we send up our sighs, mourning and weeping in this vale of tears. Turn then, most gracious advocate, thine eyes of mercy toward us, and after this our exile show unto us the blessed fruit of thy womb, Jesus. O clement, O loving, O sweet Virgin Mary!

V. Pray for us, O holy Mother of God.

R. That we may be made worthy of the promises of Christ.

Let Us Pray.

O GOD, our refuge and our strength! Look down with favor upon Thy people crying to Thee; and through the intercession of the glorious and immaculate Virgin Mary, Mother of God, of her spouse, blessed Joseph, of thy holy apostles Peter and Paul, and all Thy saints, mercifully and graciously hear the prayers which we pour forth to Thee for the conversion of sinners and for the liberty and exaltation of holy mother Church. Through Christ our Lord. Amen.

S T. MICHAEL the archangel, defend us in battle; be our protection against the malice and snares of the devil. Command him, O God, we humbly beseech Thee, and do thou, O prince of the heavenly hosts, by the divine power, cast into hell Satan and the other evil spirits who roam through the world seeking the ruin of souls. Amen.

Indulgence. 300 days. (Leo XIII, September 25, 1888.)

Prayers for Confession

BEFORE CONFESSION

MERCIFUL God! I give infinite thanks to Thee for the many and great graces Thou hast bestowed upon me during my whole life. Would that I had never been ungrateful to Thee, that I never had offended Thee. But I have sinned exceedingly and often, and have done so again since my last confession. Therefore I come to Thee, imploring Thee in profoundest humility to give me Thy light and Thy grace, that I may know and acknowledge all my sins, faults, and transgressions, be truly sorry for them, sincerely confess them, do penance, and amend my life; for Thy greater glory and for the salvation of my soul.

Examine your conscience.

SUPREME God and Lord! A poor sinner, I cast myself at the throne of Thy divine Majesty, and contritely confess that I have sinned in thought, word, and deed, and through the omission of my duties. I am heartily sorry that I was ungrateful to Thee and have deserved to be punished in this life and in the life to come. Above all I am sorry because by my sins I have offended Thee, my supreme and infinite God, who art worthy to be loved and honored above all else for Thy supreme goodness and mercy. I detest and abhor my sins above all other evils, and wish I had never committed them. Humbly I implore Thy pardon, and confidently hope to obtain it through the merits of the blood of Jesus Christ shed for us poor sinners, and through those of the Blessed Virgin Mary, of the Holy Helpers, and of all the saints.

I firmly purpose to amend my life, to avoid all occasions of sin, to use the means for conquering my passions, and to practise virtue by ordering my life according to Thy divine will and pleasure, and rather to die than to offend Thee again, my God and Lord. I am now ready to make reparation to Thy divine Justice for all the offenses of which I have been guilty against Thee, as far as is in my power. Therefore I will confess my sins sincerely, contritely, fully, and perform the penance imposed upon me.

Before entering the confessional:

The Lord be in my heart and on my lips that I may worthily and competently confess my sins.

AFTER CONFESSION

O GOD of infinite mercy! I give Thee due thanks, and praise Thee for having admitted me to the confession of my sins and for having, through Thy minister, granted me absolution for them. I implore Thee by the merits of Jesus Christ, Thy Son, of Mary, His most blessed

Mother, of the Holy Helpers, and of all the saints, to accept my confession, and in Thy infinite mercy to condone and amend all the defects and faults I committed in making it, and to ratify in heaven the absolution I received on earth.

O my Jesus! How blind I was in not knowing Thee and preferring transitory beauty and earthly attractions to Thy grace and love, and thereby offending Thee! Now I acknowledge my fault, and am convinced that it is my duty and privilege to love Thee above all things. Too late I have learned it, but I shall zealously strive to make reparation for my past neglect. Therefore I renounce the pleasures, vanities, and joys of this deceitful world, and abhor sin and all that leads to it. In the future nothing shall ever part me from Thy love. From this moment on I am resolved nevermore to offend Thee. Confirm, O Jesus, this my resolution, and with Thy almighty power strengthen my frailty. Seal my purpose of amendment with the bestowal of Thy grace, and preserve me in Thy grace and love unto the end. Amen.

Prayers for Holy Communion

BEFORE COMMUNION

AN ACT OF FAITH

*M*Y LORD and Saviour Jesus Christ! I firmly believe that Thou art really present in the Blessed Sacrament. I believe it contains Thy body and blood, Thy soul and divinity. I acknowledge these truths, I believe these wonders. I adore Thy power which has wrought them; I praise Thy infinite goodness which has prepared them for me. "I will praise Thee, my God, with my whole heart, and will recount all Thy admirable works; I will rejoice in Thee, and bless Thy holy name" (Ps. 9:2, 3). In this faith, and with this acknowledgment, I presume to approach this adorable banquet, wherein Thou bestowest on me the divine food of Thy body and blood to nourish my soul. Grant, O Jesus, that I may approach Thee with such a sense of reverence and humility as is due to Thy divine Majesty. Who am I, O God, that Thou shouldst work such wonders for my sake? Grant, O Lord, that I be not altogether unworthy of them, and that I may now receive Thee with a pure heart, a clean conscience, and a sincere and lively faith. Pardon my sins, which have rendered me most unworthy to approach Thee. I detest them from the bottom of my heart, because they are displeasing to Thee, my God. I renounce them for ever, and promise to be faithful to Thee.

AN ACT OF HOPE

*I*N THEE, sweet Jesus, I place all my hope, because Thou alone art my salvation, my strength, my refuge, and the foundation of all my happiness. Were it not for the confidence I place in Thy merits, and in the precious blood Thou didst shed for my redemption, I would not presume to partake of this banquet. Encouraged, therefore, by Thy goodness, I come to Thee as one sick to his physician, as a condemned criminal to his powerful intercessor. Heal me as my physician, and as my powerful advocate deliver me from the sentence of sin and death. It is in Thy mercy that I put all my trust. Have pity, therefore, O Jesus, on me, and save me, for Thou forsakest none that place their hope in Thee.

AN ACT OF LOVE

O DIVINE Redeemer, how strong was the force of Thy love, that, being about to depart from this world to Thy eternal Father, Thou didst provide for us this divine banquet, enriched with all heavenly sweetness! It was through an excess of Thy love that Thou hast left us Thy body and blood for the food and nourishment of our souls; that, as Thou didst unite Thyself to our humanity, so we might be partakers of Thy divinity. I desire to love Thee, my Jesus, who art my only comfort in this place of banishment, the only hope of my infirm soul, my happiness above all I can enjoy in this life. I love Thee, my God, with my whole heart, with my whole soul, and with all my mind and strength. I wish that, as every moment is an increase of my life, so it may also be of my love toward Thee. I desire, with all the affections and powers of my soul, that, as the inmost thanks are due to Thee, so they may be returned to Thee by all the faithful, for this divine food, which is our refreshment, support, strength, armor, and defense in all our miseries; and that my love may never cease, inflame my heart with the fire of heaven, that it may continue burning till, nature and corruption being consumed, I may at length be transformed into Thee. Come, O Lord, hasten to release me from the bonds of sin, and prepare me for the blessing Thou art now about to bestow on me.

AN ACT OF DESIRE

MY LORD and Saviour, Jesus Christ! "As the heart panteth after the fountains of waters so my soul panteth after Thee, O God!" (Ps. 41:1). Tired with my own evil ways, I now return to Thee, to taste Thy banquet, that my soul may be refreshed. I henceforth despise all human consolations, that I may be comforted by Thee, my only good, my God and Saviour, whom I love above all things and desire to entertain within my heart with as much devotion and affection as is conceived by Thy chosen servants, who now sit at Thy table in celestial bliss. And however I may have been wanting hitherto in my duty, I now for ever renounce my folly and weakness, and from my heart request that for the future my joy, my relief, my treasure, and rest may be entirely centered in Thee. May I never desire anything besides Thee, and may all things seem contemptible and as nothing without Thee, O my God!

AN ACT OF FEAR

O MY God and Saviour, it is with fear and trembling that I approach Thy banquet, having nothing to confide in but Thy goodness and mercy, being of myself a sinner, destitute of all virtue. My soul and body are defiled with many crimes, my thoughts and tongue have been under no restraint. I have frequently resolved to amend, and yet where do I remain but in the midst of sin and vice? How little pains do I take to recover from this misery and return to Thee, to whom I have repeatedly promised to be faithful! These thoughts cause me to fear that what Thou hast mercifully ordained for my salvation, I should now receive to my judgment and condemnation. In this wretched condition I hasten to Thee; to Thee I expose all my wounds, to Thee I disclose my depravity. Look, therefore, on me with the eyes of compassion, and have mercy on me, O Lord and Saviour!

AN ACT OF HUMILITY

O IMMENSE, almighty, and incomprehensible God, who am I, that Thou shouldst vouchsafe to come to be my food, and to take Thy habitation within my soul? The consideration of Thy greatness and my unworthiness penetrates me with awe and confusion. With the utmost sincerity I can only declare the extent of my misery, and admire that infinite goodness which induces Thee to visit personally the lowest and basest of Thy creatures. Receive, then, Thy unworthy servant into the compassionate arms of Thy mercy. Cast all my sins out of Thy sight, and with the tenderness of a loving father extend Thy arms to receive me; and let me effectually experience the truth of Thy prophet's words: "A sacrifice to God is an afflicted spirit; a contrite and humble heart, O God, Thou wilt not despise" (Ps. 50:19).

IMMEDIATELY BEFORE COMMUNION

L ORD, I am not worthy that Thou shouldst enter under my roof: say but the word, and my soul shall be healed.

The body of Our Lord Jesus Christ preserve my soul to life everlasting.

AFTER COMMUNION

AN ACT OF THANKSGIVING

O JESUS, my God and Saviour! I return Thee thanks for having, out of Thy pure mercy, without any desert of mine, been pleased to feed my soul with Thine own most sacred body and blood. Suffer me sooner to be forgetful of myself than to be ever unmindful of this great favor. Although I have hitherto been ungrateful, with the help of Thy grace I shall be so no more. But what return can I make Thee, being of myself insolvent, indigent, and miserable? The sacrifice of all that I am or have is not worthy to be presented to Thee; but, behold I offer Thee Thyself, and consider all my debts as abundantly discharged. May Thy infinite mercy be for ever exalted for having given me such an excellent means of repaying Thee to the full. O that I could ever remember Thee, think of Thee, ever love Thee alone! Imprint the memory of what Thou didst for me so deeply in my heart, that I spend my whole life in thanking Thee for all Thy benefits, but especially for this banquet of Thy love. Amen.

AN ACT OF ADORATION

U NDER the sacred veil of Thy eucharistic presence, where Thy love of man conceals the splendor of Thy majesty, I most humbly adore Thee, O almighty God! The grandeur of the heavens is as nothing in Thy sight; they shall perish, but Thou shalt remain for ever. The earth Thou hast poised in Thy hand. The ocean is before Thee but as a drop of water. All nature bows and trembles in Thy presence. How, then, shall I extol Thee, immortal King of glory? What homage can I give in proportion to Thy greatness? Thou art the perfect image of Thy Father's substance. Thou art the splendor of His glory. Thou art His almighty Word, supporting all things. Thee He has seated at His right hand. Thy throne, O God, is for ever and ever; a scepter of justice is the scepter of Thy reign. I bow before Thy sacred Majesty. I acknowledge with the sincerest gratitude that Thou art my redeemer, my creator, the supreme arbiter of my eternal destiny. I desire to humble myself as profoundly for Thy sake as Thou art humbled for my love in the center of my soul, and to consecrate to the glory of Thy name the whole extent of my being. Amen.

AN ACT OF OBLATION

O MY Saviour! What pledge can I give as an earnest of the gratitude I owe to Thee? I have nothing worthy of Thee, and if I had, I have nothing but what is Thine on several accounts. But such is Thy goodness as to be content to accept from us what is already Thine. Wherefore, behold, I offer to Thee my body and soul, which are both now sanctified by the honor of Thy divine presence. I consecrate them to Thee for ever, since Thou hast chosen them for Thy temple; my body to be continually employed in Thy service, and nevermore to become an instrument of sin; my soul to know Thee, to love Thee and be evermore faithful to Thee. And as I am now resolved to serve Thee with body and soul, I will take pains to correct their evil inclinations. I will declare war against myself, renounce my wonted pleasures, my delights, my passions, my anger, my self-love, my pride, my own will, and, in fine, whatever may offend Thee.

OFFERING AND PETITION

*A*LMIGHTY God, I offer Thee this holy communion in union with the superabundant merits of Jesus Christ, Thy beloved Son, and the infinite love of His adorable Heart; in union with the Blessed Virgin and the ardent love of her immaculate heart; in union with the Holy Helpers and all the happy souls who enjoy Thy glorious vision in heaven, and with all the just on earth. O my God and Saviour, Jesus Christ, present in me in the eucharistic species; fill me with that lively faith, profound humility, tender confidence, pure conscience, and ardent love, with which so many happy souls are inflamed in partaking of this sacred banquet, and supply by Thy mercy all my deficiencies. I offer my communion to render Thee the honor and glory which are due to Thy infinite majesty; to satisfy Thy justice, which I have provoked by my sins; to thank Thee for the innumerable benefits which I have received from Thy bounty; and to obtain from Thy infinite mercy the graces necessary for me; particularly the grace to subdue my predominant passion and to acquire the virtue in which I am most deficient; but especially the grace of a happy death.

I likewise offer my communion, O merciful Father, in memory of the passion and death of Thy dear Son, my divine Redeemer, to love Him with more ardor and perfection; to participate in the merits of His labors and sufferings; to acquire His spirit; to imitate His virtues; to model my life on His, and to make His adorable Heart a public reparation for all the sacrilegious communions, irreverences, and profanations which are committed against Him in this sacrament of His love. I offer it to thank Thee, O God, for all the graces Thou hast bestowed on mankind, particularly for all those Thou hast conferred on Thy blessed Mother, on all the angels and saints, especially on my guardian angel, on my holy patron, and on the Holy Helpers. I offer it, likewise, for the triumph of our holy religion, for the exaltation of the Catholic Church, for the conversion of infidels, heretics, schismatics, and all those who are in the unhappy state of sin. Also for the needs of my relatives, friends, benefactors, and enemies; for the perseverance of the just, the comfort of the afflicted, and the deliverance of the souls in purgatory; in a word, for all those for whom I am bound to pray; and I desire to enter into the intentions requisite for gaining the indulgences granted by the Church to-day for worthy communicants.

INVOCATIONS

SOUL of Christ, sanctify me!
Body of Christ, save me!
Blood of Christ, inebriate me!
Water from the side of Christ, wash me!

Passion of Christ, strengthen me!

O good Jesus, hear me!

Within Thy wounds, hide me!

Permit me not to be separated from Thee!

From the malignant enemy defend me!

In the hour of my death call me!

And bid me come to Thee,

That, with Thy saints, I may praise Thee

For ever and ever. Amen.

Indulgence, (1) 300 days, every time. (2) 7 years, once a day, after receiving communion. (3) A plenary indulgence, once a month, to all who have the pious custom of saying it at least once a day for a month; under the usual conditions. (Pius IX, January 9, 1854.)

PRAYER TO JESUS CRUCIFIED

*L*OOK down upon me, good and gentle Jesus, while before Thy face I humbly kneel, and with burning soul pray and beseech Thee to fix deep in my heart lively sentiments of faith, hope, and charity, true contrition for my sins, and a firm purpose of amendment; while I contemplate with great love and tender pity Thy five wounds, pondering over them within me, and calling to mind the words which David Thy prophet said of Thee, my Jesus: "They pierced my hands and my feet; they numbered all my bones" (Ps. 21:17, 18).

Indulgence. A plenary indulgence, under the usual conditions, if said before an image or picture of the crucified Redeemer, after holy communion. (Pius IX, July 31, 1858.)

Visit to the Blessed Sacrament

(Prayer of St. Alphonsus.)

LORD Jesus Christ, who through the love which Thou bearest to man, dost remain with them day and night in this sacrament, full of mercy and love, expecting, inviting, and receiving all who come to visit Thee; I believe that Thou art present in the Sacrament of the Altar. From the abyss of my nothingness I adore Thee, and I thank Thee for all the favors which Thou hast bestowed upon me, particularly for having given me Thyself in this sacrament, for having given me for my advocate Thy most holy Mother Mary, and for having called me to visit Thee in this church.

I this day salute Thy most loving Heart, and I wish to salute it for three ends: first, in thanksgiving for this great gift; second, in compensation for all the injuries Thou hast received from Thy enemies in this sacrament; third, I wish by this visit to adore Thee in all places in which Thou art least honored and most abandoned in this holy sacrament. My Jesus, I love Thee with my whole heart. I am sorry for having hitherto offended Thy infinite goodness. I purpose, with the assistance of Thy grace, nevermore to offend Thee; and at this moment, miserable as I am, I consecrate my whole being to Thee. I give Thee my entire will, all my affections and desires, and all that I have. From this day forward, do what Thou wilt with me and with whatsoever belongs to me. I ask and desire only Thy holy love, the gift of final perseverance, and the perfect accomplishment of Thy will. I recommend to Thee the souls in purgatory, particularly those who were most devoted to the Blessed Sacrament and to most holy Mary; and I also recommend to Thee all poor sinners. Finally, my dear Saviour, I unite all my affections with the affections of Thy most loving Heart; and thus united I offer them to Thy eternal Father, and I entreat Him, in Thy name and for Thy sake, to accept them.

Indulgence. (1) 300 days, every time this prayer is said before the Blessed Sacrament. (2) A plenary indulgence, once a month, for saying it every day for a month; under the usual conditions. (Pius IX, Sept. 7, 1854.)

AN ACT OF OBLATION TO THE SACRED HEART

*D*IVINE Heart of my Jesus! I adore Thee with all the powers of my soul, which I consecrate to Thee for ever, with my thoughts, my words, my works, and my whole self. I purpose to offer to Thee, as far as I can, acts of adoration, love, and glory, like unto those which Thou offerest to Thy eternal Father. Be Thou, I beseech Thee, the repairer of my transgressions, the protector of my life, my refuge and asylum in the hour of death. By Thy sighs, and by that sea of bitterness in which Thou wast plunged for me throughout Thy whole mortal life, grant me true contrition for my sins, contempt of earthly things, a burning desire of eternal glory, trust in Thy infinite merits, and final perseverance in Thy grace.

Heart of Jesus, all love! I offer Thee these humble prayers for myself and for all who unite with me in spirit to adore Thee. Vouchsafe out of Thy great goodness to hear and answer them, chiefly for that one among us who will first end this mortal life. Sweet Heart of Jesus! pour into his heart, in his death agony, Thine inward consolations; receive him within Thy sacred wound; cleanse him from all stains in that furnace of love, so that Thou mayest soon open to him the gates of Thy eternal glory, there to intercede with Thee for all those who tarry yet in this land of exile.

Most holy Heart of my most loving Jesus! For myself, a wretched sinner, and for all who unite with me in adoring Thee, I purpose to renew and offer to Thee these acts of adoration and these prayers at every moment and to the last instant of my life. I recommend to Thee, my Jesus, our holy Church, Thy well-beloved spouse and our true mother; the souls who are following the path of justice, poor sinners, the afflicted, the dying, all men on the face of the entire earth. Let not Thy blood be shed in vain for them; and vouchsafe, lastly, to apply it for the relief of the souls in purgatory, and above all, for those who in life were foremost in their devotion to Thee.

Most loving heart of Mary, which, amongst the hearts of all God's creatures, is at once the purest and the most inflamed with love for Jesus, and the most compassionate toward us poor sinners, obtain for us from the Heart of Jesus, our Redeemer, all graces which we ask of thee.

Mother of mercies, one throb, a single beat of thy burning heart, offered by thee to the Heart of Jesus, has power to console us to the full. Grant us, then, this favor. And then the Heart of Jesus, through the filial love He had for thee, and will ever have, will not fail to hear and answer our request. Amen.

DAILY OFFERING

O LORD Jesus Christ! In union with that divine intention, with which Thou, whilst on earth, didst give praise to God through Thy most sacred Heart, and which Thou dost still everywhere offer to Him in the Holy Eucharist, even to the consummation of the world; I, in imitation of the most sacred heart of the ever-immaculate Virgin Mary, do most cheerfully offer to Thee, during this entire day, all my thoughts and intentions, all my affections and desires, my words and all my works.

Indulgence. 100 days, once a day. (Leo XIII, Dec. 19, 1885.)

EJACULATION

J esus, meek and humble of heart, make my heart like unto Thine!

Indulgence. 300 days, once a day. (Pius IX, January 25, 1858.)

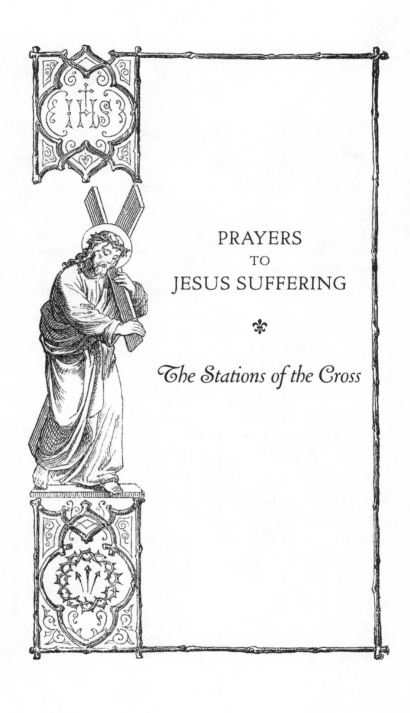

PRASYERS
TO
JESUS SUFFERING

❧

The Stations of the Cross

PREPARATORY PRAYER

*M*OST merciful Jesus! With a contrite heart and penitent spirit I bow down in profound humility before Thy divine majesty. I adore Thee as my supreme Lord and master; I believe in Thee, I hope in Thee, I love Thee above all things. I am heartily sorry for having offended Thee, my supreme and only good. I resolve to amend my life; and though I am unworthy to obtain mercy, yet the sight of Thy holy cross, on which Thou didst die, inspires me with hope and consolation. I will therefore meditate on Thy sufferings, and visit the stations of Thy passion in company with Thy sorrowful Mother and my guardian angel, with the intention of promoting Thy glory and saving my soul.

I desire to gain all the indulgences granted for this exercise, for myself and for the suffering souls in purgatory. O merciful Redeemer, who hast said; "And I, if I be lifted up from the earth, will draw all things to myself," draw my heart and my love to Thee, that I may perform this devotion as perfectly as possible, and that I may live and die in union with Thee. Amen.

FIRST STATION

Jesus is Condemned to Death

We adore Thee, O Christ, and praise Thee:
Because by Thy holy cross Thou hast redeemed the world.

JESUS, most innocent, who neither did nor could commit sin, was condemned to death, and, moreover, to the ignominious death of the cross. To remain a friend of Caesar, Pilate delivered Him to His enemies. A fearful crime—to condemn innocence to death, and to offend God, in order not to displease men.

PRAYER

O INNOCENT Jesus, having sinned I am guilty of eternal death, but Thou dost willingly accept the unjust sentence of death, that I might live. For whom, then, shall I henceforth live, if not for Thee, my Lord? Should I desire to please men, I could not be Thy servant. Let me, therefore, rather displease men and all the world than not please Thee, O Jesus.

Our Father, etc. Hail Mary, etc.

Lord Jesus, crucified: Have mercy on us.

SECOND STATION

Jesus Carries His Cross

We adore Thee, O Christ, and praise Thee:
Because by Thy holy cross Thou hast redeemed the world.

ON BEHOLDING the cross, our divine Saviour most willingly stretched out His bleeding arms, lovingly embraced it, tenderly kissed it, and placing it on His bruised shoulder, despite His exhaustion joyfully carried it.

PRAYER

O MY Jesus, I can not be Thy friend and follower if I refuse to carry the cross. O dearly beloved cross, I embrace thee, I kiss thee, I rejoice to receive thee from the hands of God. Far be it from me to glory in anything save in the cross of my Lord and Redeemer. By it the world shall be crucified to me, and I to the world, that I may be Thine for ever.

Our Father, etc. Hail Mary, etc.

Lord Jesus, crucified: Have mercy on us.

THIRD STATION

Jesus Falls the First Time

We adore Thee, O Christ, and praise Thee:
Because by Thy holy cross Thou hast redeemed the world.

OUR dear Saviour carrying the cross was so weakened by its heavy weight as to fall exhausted to the ground. Our sins and misdeeds were the heavy burden which oppressed Him; the cross was to Him light and sweet, but our sins were galling and insupportable.

PRAYER

O MY Jesus! Thou didst bear my burden and the heavy weight of my sins. Should I, then, not bear in union with Thee my easy burden of suffering and accept the sweet yoke of Thy commandments? Thy yoke is sweet and Thy burden light; I therefore willingly accept it. I will take up Thy cross and follow Thee.

Our Father, etc. Hail Mary, etc.

Lord Jesus, crucified: Have mercy on us.

FOURTH STATION

Jesus Meets His Afflicted Mother

We adore Thee, O Christ, and praise Thee:
Because by Thy holy cross Thou hast redeemed the world.

HOW painful and how sad it must have been for Mary, the sorrowful Mother, to behold her beloved Son laden with the burden of the cross! What unspeakable pangs her most tender heart experienced! How earnestly she yearned to die instead of, or at least with, Jesus! Implore this sorrowful Mother that she assist you in the hour of your death.

PRAYER

O JESUS, O Mary! I am the cause of the great and manifold pains which pierce your loving hearts. O that my heart also would feel and experience at least some of your sufferings! O Mother of sorrows, let me participate in the sufferings which thou and thy Son endured for me, and let me experience thy sorrow, that, afflicted with thee, I may enjoy thy assistance in the hour of my death.

Our Father, etc. Hail Mary, etc.

Lord Jesus, crucified: Have mercy on us.

FIFTH STATION

Simon of Cyrene Helps Jesus to Carry the Cross

We adore Thee, O Christ, and praise Thee:
Because by Thy holy cross Thou hast redeemed the world.

SIMON of Cyrene was compelled to help Jesus carry His cross, and Jesus accepted His assistance. How willingly He would permit you also to carry the cross! He calls you, but you hear Him not; He invites you, but you decline. What a reproach, to bear the cross reluctantly!

PRAYER

O JESUS! Whosoever does not take up His cross and follow Thee is not worthy of Thee. Behold, I join Thee in the way of Thy cross; I will be Thy assistant, following Thy footsteps, that I may come to Thee in eternal life.

Our Father, etc. Hail Mary, etc.

Lord Jesus, crucified: Have mercy on us.

SIXTH STATION

Veronica Wipes the Face of Jesus

We adore Thee, O Christ, and praise Thee:
Because by Thy holy cross Thou hast redeemed the world.

*I*MPELLED by devotion and compassion, Veronica presents her veil to Jesus to wipe His disfigured face. And Jesus imprints on it His holy countenance; a great recompense for so slight a service. What return do you make to your Saviour for His great and manifold benefits?

PRAYER

*M*OST merciful Jesus! What return shall I make for all the benefits Thou didst bestow on me? Behold, I consecrate myself entirely to Thy service. I offer and consecrate to Thee my heart. Imprint upon it Thy sacred image, never to be effaced again by sin.

Our Father, etc. Hail Mary, etc.

Lord Jesus, crucified: Have mercy on us.

SEVENTH STATION

Jesus Falls the Second Time

We adore Thee, O Christ, and praise Thee:
Because by Thy holy cross Thou hast redeemed the world.

*J*ESUS, suffering under the weight of His cross, again falls to the ground; but His cruel executioners do not permit Him to rest a moment. Pushing and striking Him, they urge Him onward. It is the frequent repetition of our sins which oppresses Jesus. Witnessing this, how can I continue to sin?

PRAYER

O JESUS, son of David, have mercy on me! Offer me Thy helping hand, and aid me that I may not fall again into my former sins. From this very moment I will earnestly strive to reform; nevermore will I sin. Do Thou, O sole support of the weak, by Thy grace, without which I can do nothing, strengthen me to carry out faithfully this my resolution.

Our Father, etc. Hail Mary, etc.

Lord Jesus, crucified: Have mercy on us.

EIGHTH STATION

The Daughters of Jerusalem Weep over Jesus

We adore Thee, O Christ, and praise Thee:
Because by Thy holy cross Thou hast redeemed the world.

THESE devoted women, moved by compassion, weep over the suffering Saviour. But He turns to them, saying, "Weep not for Me, who am innocent, but weep for yourselves and for your children." Weep thou also; for there is nothing more pleasing to Our Lord, and nothing more profitable for thyself, than tears shed from contrition for thy sins.

PRAYER

O JESUS, who shall give to my eyes a torrent of tears, that day and night I may weep for my sins? I beseech Thee through Thy bloody tears to move my heart by Thy divine grace, so that from my eyes tears may flow abundantly, and I may weep all days over Thy sufferings, and still more over their cause, my sins.

Our Father, etc. Hail Mary, etc.

Lord Jesus, crucified: Have mercy on us.

NINTH STATION

Jesus Falls the Third Time

We adore Thee, O Christ, and praise Thee:
Because by Thy holy cross Thou hast redeemed the world.

*J*ESUS, arriving exhausted at the foot of Calvary, falls for the third time to the ground. His love for us is not exhausted, not diminished. What a fearfully oppressive burden our sins must be to cause Jesus to fall so often! Had He, however, not taken them upon Himself, they would have plunged us into the abyss of hell.

PRAYER

*M*OST merciful Jesus! I return Thee infinite thanks for not permitting me to continue in sin, and to fall, as I have so often deserved, into the depths of hell. Enkindle in me an earnest desire of amendment. Let me never again relapse, but vouchsafe me Thy grace to persevere to the end of my life.

Our Father, etc. Hail Mary, etc.

Lord Jesus, crucified: Have mercy on us.

TENTH STATION

Jesus is Stripped of His Garments

We adore Thee, O Christ, and praise Thee:
Because by Thy holy cross Thou hast redeemed the world.

AFTER arriving on Calvary, our Saviour was cruelly despoiled of His garments. How painful must this have been, because they adhered to His wounded and torn body, and with them parts of His bloody skin were removed! All the wounds of Jesus are renewed. He is despoiled of His garments that He might die possessed of nothing. How happy shall I die after laying aside my former self with all evil inclinations and desires!

PRAYER

INDUCE me, O Jesus! to lay aside my former self, and to be renewed according to Thy will and desire. I will not spare myself, however painful this should be for me; despoiled of things temporal, of my own will, I desire to die, in order to live for Thee for ever.

Our Father, etc. Hail Mary, etc.

Lord Jesus, crucified: Have mercy on us.

ELEVENTH STATION

Jesus is Nailed to the Cross

We adore Thee, O Christ, and praise Thee:
Because by Thy holy cross Thou hast redeemed the world.

*J*ESUS, being stripped of His garments, was violently thrown upon the cross, and His hands and feet were most cruelly nailed thereto. In such excruciating torments He remained silent, because it thus pleased His heavenly Father. He suffered patiently because He suffered for us. How do I act in suffering and affliction? How fretful and impatient, how full of complaints I am!

PRAYER

O JESUS, gracious Lamb of God! I renounce for ever my impatience. Crucify, O Lord, my flesh and its concupiscences. Scorch, scathe, and punish me in this world; do but spare me in the next! I commit my destiny to Thee, resigning myself to Thy holy will; may it be done in all things.

Our Father, etc. Hail Mary, etc.

Lord Jesus, crucified: Have mercy on us.

TWELFTH STATION

Jesus is Raised upon the Cross, and Dies

We adore Thee, O Christ, and praise Thee:
Because by Thy holy cross Thou hast redeemed the world.

*B*EHOLD Jesus crucified! Behold the wounds He received for the love of you! His whole appearance betokens love. His head is bent to kiss you; His arms are extended to embrace you; His Heart is open to receive you. O superabundance of love! Jesus, the Son of God, dies that man may live and be delivered from everlasting death.

PRAYER

O MOST amiable Jesus! Who will grant me that I may die for love of Thee? I will at least endeavor to die to the world. How must I regard the world and its vanities, when I behold Thee hanging on the cross, covered with wounds? O Jesus, receive me into Thy wounded Heart; I belong entirely to Thee; for Thee alone do I desire to live and to die.

Our Father, etc. Hail Mary, etc.

Lord Jesus, crucified: Have mercy on us.

THIRTEENTH STATION

Jesus is Taken Down from the Cross

We adore Thee, O Christ, and praise Thee:
Because by Thy holy cross Thou hast redeemed the world.

*J*ESUS did not descend from the cross, but remained on it till after His death. And when taken down from it, He, in death as in life, rested on the bosom of His Mother. Persevere in your resolutions of reform, and do not part from the cross; he that persevereth to the end shall be saved. Consider, moreover, how pure the heart should be that receives the body and blood of Christ in the adorable Sacrament of the Altar.

PRAYER

O LORD Jesus! Thy lifeless body, mangled and torn, found a worthy resting-place on the bosom of Thy virgin Mother. Have I not compelled Thee often to dwell in my heart, full of sin and impurity as it was? Create in me a new heart, that I may worthily receive Thy most sacred body in holy communion, and that Thou mayest remain in me, and I in Thee, for all eternity.

Our Father, etc. Hail Mary, etc.

Lord Jesus, crucified: Have mercy on us.

FOURTEENTH STATION

Jesus is Laid in the Sepulcher

We adore Thee, O Christ, and praise Thee:
Because by Thy holy cross Thou hast redeemed the world.

*T*HE body of Jesus is laid in a stranger's tomb. He who in this world had not whereupon to rest His head, would not even have a grave of His own, because He was not of this world. You, who are so attached to the world, henceforth despise it, that you may not perish with it.

PRAYER

O JESUS, Thou hast set me apart from the world; what, then, shall I seek therein? Thou hast created me for heaven; what, then, have I to do with the world? Depart from me, deceitful world, with Thy vanities! Henceforth I will follow the way of the cross traced out for me by my Redeemer, and journey onward to my heavenly home, there to dwell for ever and ever.

Our Father, etc. Hail Mary, etc.

Lord Jesus, crucified: Have mercy on us.

CONCLUSION

*A*LMIGHTY and eternal God, merciful Father, who hast given to the human race Thy beloved Son as an example of humility, obedience, and patience, to precede us on the way of life, bearing the cross; graciously grant, that we, inflamed by His infinite love, may take up the sweet yoke of His Gospel, together with the mortification of the cross, following Him as His true disciples, so that we shall one day rise gloriously with Him, and joyfully hear the final sentence: "Come, ye blessed of my Father, and possess the kingdom which has been prepared for you from the beginning," where Thou reignest with the Father and the Holy Ghost, and where we hope to reign with Thee throughout all eternity. Amen.

PRAYER TO OUR SUFFERING REDEEMER

O MY Lord Jesus Christ! Who, to redeem the world, didst vouchsafe to be born amongst men, to be circumcised, to be rejected and persecuted by the Jews, to be betrayed by the traitor Judas with a kiss, and as a lamb, gentle and innocent, to be bound with cords and dragged, in scorn, before the tribunals of Annas, Caiphas, Pilate, and Herod; who didst suffer Thyself to be accused by false witnesses, to be torn by the scourge and overwhelmed with ignominy; to be spit upon, to be crowned with thorns, buffeted, struck with a reed, blindfolded, stripped of Thy garments; to be nailed to the cross and raised on it between two thieves; to be given gall and vinegar to drink, and to be pierced with a lance; do Thou, O Lord, by these Thy most sacred pains, which I, all unworthy, call to mind, and by Thy holy cross and death, save me from the pains of hell, and vouchsafe to bring me whither Thou didst bring the good thief who was crucified with Thee, who with the Father and the Holy Ghost, livest and reignest God, for ever and ever. Amen.

Our Father, Hail Mary, and Glory be to the Father, etc., five times.

Indulgence. (1) 300 days, once a day. (2) A plenary indulgence, under the usual conditions, on any one of the last three days of the month, after saying this prayer daily for a month. (Pius VII, August 25, 1820.)

PRAYER TO THE BLESSED VIRGIN MARY

(By St. Alphonsus.)

MOST holy and immaculate virgin, O my Mother, thou who art the Mother of my Lord, the queen of the world, the advocate, hope, and refuge of sinners! I, the most wretched among them, come now to thee. I venerate thee, great queen, and give thee thanks for the many favors thou hast bestowed on me in the past. Most of all do I thank thee for having saved me from hell, which I so often deserved. I love thee, Lady most worthy of love, and by the love which I bear thee I promise ever in the future to serve thee, and to do what in me lies to win others to thy love. In thee I put all my trust, all my hope of salvation. Receive me as thy servant, and cover me with the mantle of thy protection, thou who art the Mother of mercy! And since thou hast so much power with God, deliver me from all temptations, or at least obtain for me the grace ever to overcome them. From thee I ask a true love of Jesus Christ, and the grace of a happy death. O my Mother, by thy love for God I beseech thee to be at all times my helper, but above all at the last moment of my life. Leave me not until thou seest me safely in heaven, there for endless ages to bless thee and sing thy praises. Amen.

Indulgence, (1) 300 days, every time. (2) A plenary indulgence, once a month, for having said it daily during the month; under the usual conditions. (Pius IX, Sept. 7, 1854.)

PRAYER FOR ALL THINGS NECESSARY
FOR SALVATION

O MY God! I believe in Thee; do Thou strengthen my faith. All my hopes are in Thee; do Thou secure them. I love Thee with my whole heart; teach me to love Thee more and more. I am sorry that I have offended Thee; do Thou increase my sorrow. I adore Thee as my first beginning; I aspire after Thee as my last end. I give Thee thanks as my constant benefactor; I call upon Thee as my sovereign protector. Vouchsafe, O my God, to conduct me by Thy wisdom, to restrain me by Thy justice, to comfort me by Thy mercy, to defend me by Thy power.

To Thee I desire to consecrate all my thoughts, my actions, and my sufferings, that I henceforward may think only of Thee, speak only of Thee, and ever refer all my actions to Thy greater glory, and suffer willingly whatever Thou shalt appoint. O Lord, I desire that in all things Thy will be done, because it is Thy will, and in the manner that Thou willest. I beg of Thee to enlighten my understanding, to inflame my will, to purify my body, and to sanctify my soul. Give me strength, O my God, to expiate my offenses, to overcome my temptations, to subdue my passions, to acquire the virtues proper for my state. Fill my heart with tender affection for Thy goodness, a hatred of my faults, a love for my neighbor, and a contempt for the world. Let me always be submissive to my superiors, condescending to my inferiors, faithful to my friends, and charitable to my enemies. Assist me to overcome sensuality by mortification, avarice by almsdeeds, anger by meekness, and tepidity by zeal. O my God, make me prudent in my undertakings, courageous in dangers, patient in affliction, and humble in prosperity. Grant that I may be ever attentive at my prayers, temperate at my meals, diligent in my employments, and constant in my resolutions. Let my conscience be ever upright and pure, my exterior modest, my conversation edifying, my comportment regular. Assist me, that I may continually labor to overcome nature, correspond with Thy grace, keep Thy commandments, and work out my salvation. Discover to me, O my God, the nothingness of this world, the greatness of heaven, the shortness of time, the length of eternity. Grant that I may be prepared for death, fear Thy judgments, escape hell, and, in the end, obtain heaven.

All that I have asked for myself I confidently ask for others; for my family, my relations, my benefactors, my friends, and also for my enemies. I ask it for the whole Church, for all the orders of which it is composed; more especially for our Holy Father, the Pope; for our bishop, for our pastors, and for all who are in authority; also for all those for whom Thou desirest that I should pray. Give them, O Lord, all that Thou knowest to be conducive to Thy glory and necessary for their salvation. Strengthen the just in virtue, convert sinners, enlighten infidels, heretics, and schismatics; console the afflicted, give to the faithful departed rest and eternal life; that together we may praise, love, and bless Thee for all eternity. Amen.

The Four Approved Litanies

Litany of the Most Holy Name of Jesus

*L*ORD, have mercy on us.

Christ, have mercy on us.

Lord, have mercy on us.

Jesus, hear us.

Jesus, graciously hear us.

God the Father of heaven,

God the Son, Redeemer of the world,

God the Holy Ghost,

Holy Trinity, one God,

Jesus, Son of the living God,

Jesus, splendor of the Father,

Jesus, brightness of eternal light,

Jesus, king of glory,

Jesus, sun of justice,

Jesus, Son of the Virgin Mary,

Jesus amiable,

Jesus admirable,

Jesus, powerful God,

Jesus, Father of the world to come,

Jesus, angel of the great council,

Jesus most powerful,

Have mercy on us.

Jesus most patient,
Jesus most obedient,
Jesus meek and humble of heart,
Jesus, lover of chastity,
Jesus, lover of us,
Jesus, God of peace,
Jesus, author of life,
Jesus, model of all virtues,
Jesus, zealous for souls,
Jesus, our God,
Jesus, our refuge,
Jesus, father of the poor,
Jesus, treasure of the faithful,
Jesus, good shepherd,
Jesus, true light,
Jesus, eternal wisdom,
Jesus, infinite goodness,
Jesus, our way and our life,
Jesus, joy of angels,
Jesus, king of patriarchs,
Jesus, master of the apostles,
Jesus, teacher of the evangelists,
Jesus, strength of martyrs,
Jesus, light of confessors,
Jesus, purity of virgins,
Jesus, crown of all saints,

Have mercy on us.

Be merciful, spare us, O Jesus.
Be merciful, graciously hear us, O Jesus.

From all evil,

From all sin,

From Thy wrath,

From the snares of the devil,

From the spirit of fornication,

From eternal death,

From the neglect of Thy inspirations,

By the mystery of Thy holy incarnation,

By Thy nativity,

By Thy infancy,

By Thy most divine life,

By Thy labors,

By Thy agony and passion,

By Thy cross and dereliction,

By Thy languors,

By Thy death and burial,

By Thy resurrection,

By Thy ascension,

By Thy joys,

By Thy glory,

deliver us, O Jesus.

Lamb of God, who takest away the sins of the world:
    Spare us, O Jesus.

Lamb of God, who takest away the sins of the world:
    Graciously hear us, O Jesus.

Lamb of God, who takest away the sins of the world:
    Have mercy on us, O Jesus.

Jesus, hear us.

Jesus, graciously hear us.

Let us pray:

O LORD Jesus Christ, who hast said: Ask, and ye shall receive; seek, and ye shall find; knock, and it shall be opened unto you: mercifully attend to our supplications, and grant us the gift of Thy divine charity, that we may ever love Thee with our whole hearts, and never desist from Thy praise.

Give us, O Lord, a perpetual fear and love of Thy holy name, for Thou never ceasest to direct and govern by Thy grace those whom Thou instructest in the solidity of Thy love; who livest and reignest world without end. Amen.

Indulgence. 300 days, once a day. (Leo XIII, January 16, 1886.)

Litany of the Sacred Heart of Jesus

(Approved by Pope Leo XIII, April 2, 1899.)

*L*ORD, have mercy on us.
Christ, have mercy on us.
Lord, have mercy on us.
Christ, hear us.
Christ, graciously hear us.
God, the Father of heaven,
God the Son, Redeemer of the world,
God the Holy Ghost,
Holy Trinity, one God,
Heart of Jesus, Son of the eternal Father,
Heart of Jesus, formed by the Holy Ghost in the womb
   of the Virgin Mother,
Heart of Jesus, substantially united to the Word of God,
Heart of Jesus, of infinite majesty,
Heart of Jesus, sacred temple of God,
Heart of Jesus, tabernacle of the Most High,
Heart of Jesus, house of God and gate of heaven,
Heart of Jesus, burning furnace of charity,
Heart of Jesus, abode of justice and love,
Heart of Jesus, full of goodness and love,
Heart of Jesus, abyss of all virtues,

Have mercy on us.

Heart of Jesus, most worthy of all praise,

Heart of Jesus, king and center of all hearts,

Heart of Jesus, in whom are all the treasures of wisdom and knowledge,

Heart of Jesus, in whom dwells the fulness of divinity,

Heart of Jesus, in whom the Father was well pleased,

Heart of Jesus, of whose fulness we have all received,

Heart of Jesus, desire of the everlasting hills,

Heart of Jesus, patient and most merciful,

Heart of Jesus, enriching all who invoke Thee,

Heart of Jesus, fountain of life and holiness,

Heart of Jesus, propitiation for our sins,

Heart of Jesus, loaded down with opprobrium,

Heart of Jesus, bruised for our offences,

Heart of Jesus, obedient unto death,

Heart of Jesus, pierced with a lance,

Heart of Jesus, source of all consolation,

Heart of Jesus, our life and resurrection,

Heart of Jesus, our peace and reconciliation,

Heart of Jesus, victim for sin,

Heart of Jesus, salvation of those who trust in thee,

Heart of Jesus, hope of those who die in Thee,

Heart of Jesus, delight of all the saints,

Have mercy on us.

Lamb of God, who takest away the sins of the world:
Spare us, O Lord.

Lamb of God, who takest away the sins of the world:
Graciously hear us, O Lord.

Lamb of God, who takest away the sins of the world:
Have mercy on us, O Lord.

V. Jesus, meek and humble of Heart:

R. Make our hearts like unto Thine.

Let us pray:

O ALMIGHTY and eternal God! Look upon the
Heart of Thy dearly beloved Son, and upon the
praise and satisfaction He offers Thee in the name of sinners
and of those who seek Thy mercy; be Thou appeased, and
grant us pardon in the name of the same Jesus Christ, Thy
Son; who liveth and reigneth with Thee, in the unity of the
Holy Ghost, world without end. Amen.

Indulgence. 300 days. (Leo XIII, April 2, 1899.)

The Litany of Loreto

In Honor of the Blessed Virgin Mary

*L*ORD, have mercy on us,
  Christ, have mercy on us.
Lord, have mercy on us,
Christ, hear us.
Christ, graciously hear us.

God the Father of heaven, have mercy on us.
God the Son, Redeemer of the world, have mercy on us.
God the Holy Ghost, have mercy on us.
Holy Trinity, one God, have mercy on us.

Holy Mary,
Holy Mother of God,
Holy Virgin of virgins,
Mother of Christ,
Mother of divine grace,
Mother most pure,
Mother most chaste,
Mother inviolate,
Mother undefiled,
Mother most amiable,
Mother most admirable,

pray for us.

Mother of good counsel,
Mother of our Creator,
Mother of our Redeemer,
Virgin most prudent,
Virgin most venerable,
Virgin most renowned,
Virgin most powerful,
Virgin most merciful,
Virgin most faithful,
Mirror of justice,
Seat of wisdom,
Cause of our joy,
Spiritual vessel,
Vessel of honor,
Singular vessel of devotion,
Mystical rose,
Tower of David,
Tower of ivory,
House of gold,
Ark of the covenant,
Gate of heaven,
Morning star,
Health of the sick,
Refuge of sinners,
Comforter of the afflicted,
Help of Christians,
Queen of angels,
Queen of patriarchs,

pray for us.

Queen of prophets, pray for us.

Queen of apostles, pray for us.

Queen of martyrs, pray for us.

Queen of confessors, pray for us.

Queen of virgins, pray for us.

Queen of all saints, pray for us.

Queen conceived without original sin, pray for us.

Queen of the most holy rosary, pray for us.

pray for us.

Lamb of God, who takest away the sins of the world:
Spare us, O Lord.

Lamb of God, who takest away the sins of the world:
Graciously hear us, O Lord.

Lamb of God, who takest away the sins of the world:
Have mercy on us, O Lord.

V. Pray for us, O holy Mother of God:

R. That we may be made worthy of the promises of
Christ.

Let us pray:

POUR forth, we beseech Thee, O Lord, Thy grace
into our hearts, that we, to whom the incarnation
of Christ Thy Son was made known by the message of an
angel, may by His passion and cross be brought to the glory
of His resurrection. Through the same Christ our Lord.
Amen.

V. Pray for us, O holy Mother of God.

R. That we may be made worthy of the promises of
Christ.

Let us pray:

𝒱OUCHSAFE, O Lord, that we may be helped by the merits of Thy most holy Mother's spouse; that what of ourselves we can not obtain may be given us through his intercession. Who livest and reignest, world without end. Amen.

Indulgence. (1) 300 days, every time. (2) A plenary indulgence on the following five feasts of the Blessed Virgin: Immaculate Conception, Nativity, Purification, Annunciation, and Assumption; under the usual conditions, to all who shall have said it daily during the year. (Pius VII, September 30, 1817.) These indulgences are granted for the litany alone; hence the prayers following it may be omitted.

Litany of the Saints

LORD, have mercy on us.
Christ, have mercy on us.
Lord, have mercy on us.
Christ, hear us.
Christ, graciously hear us.

God the Father of heaven, have mercy on us.
God the Son, Redeemer of the world, have mercy on us.
God the Holy Ghost, have mercy on us.
Holy Trinity, one God, have mercy on us.

Holy Mary,
Holy Mother of God,
Holy Virgin of virgins,
St. Michael,
St. Gabriel,
St. Raphael,
All ye holy angels and archangels,
All ye holy orders of blessed spirits,
St. John Baptist,
St. Joseph,
All ye holy patriarchs and prophets,
St. Peter,

pray for us.

St. Paul,
St. Andrew,
St. James,
St. John,
St. Thomas,
St. James,
St. Philip,
St. Bartholomew,
St. Matthew,
St. Simon,
St. Thaddaeus,
St. Mathias,
St. Barnabas,
St. Luke,
St. Mark,
All ye holy apostles and evangelists,
All ye holy disciples of Our Lord,
All ye holy innocents,
St. Stephen,
St. Lawrence,
St. Vincent,
SS. Fabian and Sebastian,
SS. John and Paul,
SS. Cosmas and Damian,
SS. Gervaise and Protaise,
All ye holy martyrs,
St. Sylvester,

pray for us.

St. Gregory,
St. Ambrose,
St. Augustine,
St. Jerome,
St. Martin,
St. Nicholas,
All ye holy bishops and confessors,
All ye holy doctors,
St. Anthony,
St. Benedict,
St. Bernard,
St. Dominic,
St. Francis,
All ye holy priests and levites,
All ye holy monks and hermits,
St. Mary Magdalen,
St. Agatha,
St. Lucy,
St. Agnes,
St. Cecilia,
St. Catherine,
St. Anastasia,
All ye holy virgins and widows,

pray for us.

All ye men and women, saints of God:
    Make intercession for us.

Be merciful: Spare us, O Lord.
Be merciful: Graciously hear us, O Lord.

From all evil,
From all sin,
From a sudden and unprovided death,
From the snares of the devil,
From anger, hatred, and ill will,
From the spirit of fornication,
From lightning and tempest,
From the scourge of earthquake,
From pestilence, famine, and war,
From everlasting death,
Through the mystery of Thy holy incarnation,
Through Thy coming,
Through Thy nativity,
Through Thy baptism and holy fasting,
Through Thy cross and passion,
Through Thy death and burial,
Through Thy holy resurrection,
Through Thy admirable ascension,
Through the coming of the Holy Ghost, the Comforter,
In the Day of Judgment,

O Lord, deliver us.

We sinners, Beseech Thee, hear us.

That Thou spare us,
That Thou pardon us,
That Thou vouchsafe to bring us to true penance,
That Thou vouchsafe to govern and preserve Thy holy Church,
That Thou vouchsafe to preserve our apostolic prelate and all ecclesiastical orders in holy religion,

we beseech Thee, hear us.

That Thou vouchsafe to humble the enemies of Thy holy Church,

That Thou vouchsafe to give peace and true concord to Christian kings and princes,

That Thou vouchsafe to grant peace and unity to all Christian people,

That Thou vouchsafe to confirm and preserve us in Thy holy service,

That Thou lift up our minds to heavenly desires,

That Thou render eternal good things to all our benefactors,

That Thou deliver our souls and those of our brethren, kinsfolk, and benefactors from eternal damnation,

That Thou vouchsafe to give and preserve the fruits of the earth,

That Thou vouchsafe eternal rest to all the faithful departed,

That Thou vouchsafe graciously to hear us,

Son of God,

we beseech Thee, hear us.

Lamb of God, who takest away the sins of the world: Spare us, O Lord.

Lamb of God, who takest away the sins of the world: Graciously hear us, O Lord.

Lamb of God, who takest away the sins of the world: Have mercy on us, O Lord.

Christ, hear us.

Christ, graciously hear us.

Lord, have mercy on us.

Christ, have mercy on us.

Lord, have mercy on us.

Our Father, etc.

V. And lead us not into temptation.

R. But deliver us from evil.

PSALM LXIX

*I*NCLINE unto my aid, O God: O Lord, make haste to help me.

Let them be confounded and ashamed: that seek after my soul.

Let them be turned backward and blush for shame: that desire evils unto me.

Let them be presently turned away blushing for shame, that say to me: Tis well, 'tis well.

Let all that seek Thee rejoice and be glad in Thee: and let such as love Thy salvation say always, The Lord be magnified.

But I am needy and poor: O God, help Thou me.

Thou art my helper and my deliverer: O Lord, make no delay.

Glory be to the Father, etc.

V. Save Thy servants:

R. Trusting in Thee, O my God.

V. Be unto us, O God, a tower of strength:

R. From the face of the enemy.

V. Let not the enemy prevail against us:

R. Nor the son of iniquity have power to hurt us.

V. O Lord, deal not with us according to our sins:

R. Neither reward us according to our iniquities.

V. Let us pray for our chief bishop, N.

R. The Lord preserve him, and give him life, and make him blessed upon earth, and deliver him not up to the will of his enemies.

V. Let us pray for our benefactors:

R. Vouchsafe, O Lord, for Thy name's sake, to reward with eternal life all those who have done us good.

V. Let us pray for the faithful departed:

R. Eternal rest give to them, O Lord, and let perpetual light shine upon them.

V. May they rest in peace.

R. Amen.

V. For our absent brethren:

R. O my God, save Thy servants trusting in Thee.

V. Send them help, O Lord, from Thy holy place:

R. And from Sion protect them.

V. O Lord, hear my prayer:

R. And let my cry come unto Thee.

Let us pray:

O GOD, whose property it is always to have mercy and to spare, receive our petitions, that we, and all Thy servants who are bound by the chain of sin, may, in the compassion of Thy goodness, mercifully be absolved.

Hear, we beseech Thee, O Lord, the prayer of Thy suppliants, and pardon the sins of them that confess to Thee, that of Thy bounty Thou mayest grant us pardon and peace.

Out of Thy clemency, O Lord, show Thy unspeakable mercy to us, that so Thou mayest both acquit us of our sins and deliver us from the punishment we deserve for them.

O God, who by sin art offended and by penance pacified, mercifully regard the prayers of Thy people who make supplication to Thee, and turn away the scourges of Thy anger, which we deserve for our sins.

O almighty and eternal God, have mercy on Thy servant N., our chief bishop, and direct him, according to Thy clemency, in the way of everlasting salvation, that, by Thy grace, he may desire the things that are agreeable to Thy will, and perform them with all his strength.

O God, from whom all holy desires, righteous counsels, and just works do come, give to Thy servants that peace which the world can not give; that, our hearts being disposed to keep Thy commandments, and the fear of enemies being taken away, the times, by Thy protection, may be peaceable.

Inflame, O Lord, our reins and hearts with the fire of the Holy Spirit; to the end that we may serve Thee with a chaste body, and please Thee with a clean heart.

O God, the Creator and Redeemer of all the faithful, give to the souls of Thy servants departed the remission of all their sins, that by pious supplications they may obtain the pardon they have always desired.

Direct, we beseech Thee, O Lord, our actions by Thy holy inspirations, and carry them on by Thy gracious assistance; that every prayer and work of ours may always begin from Thee, and by Thee be happily ended.

Almighty and eternal God, who hast dominion over the living and the dead, and art merciful to all whom Thou foreknowest shall be Thine by faith and good works; we humbly beseech Thee that they for whom we have purposed to offer our prayers, whether this present world still detains them in the flesh, or the next world has already received them divested of their bodies, may, by the clemency of Thine own goodness and the intercession of Thy saints, obtain pardon and full remission of all their sins. Through Our Lord Jesus Christ, who liveth and reigneth with Thee in the unity of the Holy Ghost, world without end. Amen.

V. O Lord, hear my prayer.

R. And let my cry come unto Thee.

V. May the almighty and merciful Lord graciously hear us.

R. Amen.

V. May the souls of the faithful departed through the mercy of God rest in peace.

R. Amen.

PART VI

Thoughts and Counsels of the Saints for Every Day of the Year

"Every day will I bless Thee, and I will praise Thy name forever"
(Ps. 144:2).

Mary, Queen of Heaven, pray for us.

Thoughts and Counsels of the Saints
for Every Day in the Year

JANUARY

1 THERE are two guarantees of a wise rule of conduct: the thought before action, and self-command afterward.—St. IGNATIUS.

2 When we receive with an entire and perfect resignation the afflictions which God sends us they become for us favors and benefits; because conformity to the will of God is a gain far superior to all temporal advantages.—St. VINCENT DE PAUL.

3 All perfection consists in the love of God; and the perfection of divine love consists in the union of our will with that of God.—St. ALPHONSUS.

4 Leave to every one the care of what belongs to him, and disturb not thyself with what is said or done in the world.—St. THOMAS AQUINAS.

5 Place before your eyes as models for imitation, not the weak and cowardly, but the fervent and courageous.
—St. IGNATIUS.

6 Prayer is a pasturage, a field, wherein all the virtues find their nourishment, growth, and strength. —ST. CATHERINE OF SIENA.

7 A single act of resignation to the divine will in what it ordains contrary to our desires, is of more value than a hundred thousand successes conformable to our will and taste.—ST. VINCENT DE PAUL.

8 The shortest, yea, the only way to reach sanctity, is to conceive a horror for all that the world loves and values. —ST. IGNATIUS.

9 As long as we are in this mortal life, nothing is more necessary for us than humility.—ST. TERESA.

10 Learning without humility has always been pernicious to the Church; and as pride precipitated the rebellious angels from heaven, it frequently causes the loss of learned men.—ST. VINCENT DE PAUL.

11 Why remain sad and idle? Why exhaust thyself in the anguish of melancholy? Have courage, do violence to thyself; meditate on the passion of Jesus Christ, and thou shalt overcome thy sorrow.—BL. HENRY SUSO.

12 Here is the difference between the joys of the world and the cross of Jesus Christ: after having tasted the first, one is disgusted with them; and on the contrary, the more one partakes of the cross, the greater the thirst for it.—ST. IGNATIUS.

13 When the sky is free from clouds we can see more clearly the brightness of the sun. In like manner, when the soul is free from sin and the gloom of passion, it participates in the divine light.—VEN. LOUIS DE GRANADA.

14 Our works are of no value if they be not united to the merits of Jesus Christ.—ST. TERESA.

15 If we are very determined to mortify ourselves and not to be too much occupied with our corporal health, we will soon, by the grace of God, become masters of our bodies.—ST. TERESA.

16 In every creature, however small it be, we may see a striking image of divine wisdom, power, and goodness.—VEN. BARTHOLOMEW OF MARTYRS.

17 Time is but a period. It passes like the lightning flash. Suffering passes with time; suffering, then, is very short.—BL. HENRY SUSO.

18 In order to bear our afflictions with patience, it is very useful to read the lives and legends of the saints who endured great torments for Jesus Christ.—ST. TERESA.

19 Open thine ears to the voices of nature, and thou shalt hear them in concert inviting thee to the love of God.—VEN. LOUIS DE GRANADA.

20 On the feasts of the saints consider their virtues, and beseech God to deign to adorn you with them.—ST. TERESA.

21 When faith grows weak, all virtues are weakened. When faith is lost, all virtues are lost. —ST. ALPHONSUS.

22 A precious crown is reserved in heaven for those who perform all their actions with all the diligence of which they are capable; for it is not sufficient to do our part well; it must be done more than well.—ST. IGNATIUS.

23 Nothing created has ever been able to fill the heart of man. God alone can fill it infinitely. —ST. THOMAS AQUINAS.

24 We should only make use of life to grow in the love of God.—ST. ALPHONSUS.

25 In vain men try. They can never find in creatures sincere affection, perfect joy, or true peace. —BL. HENRY SUSO.

26 God is supreme strength, fortifying those who place their trust and confidence in Him. —ST. CATHERINE OF SIENA.

27 God gives each one of us sufficient grace ever to know His holy will, and to do it fully. —ST. IGNATIUS.

28 Shun useless conversation. We lose by it both time and the spirit of devotion.—ST. THOMAS AQUINAS.

29 The upright intention is the soul of our actions. It gives them life and makes them good. —St. Alphonsus.

30 The truth of faith alone, deeply graven in the soul, is sufficient to encourage us to very perfect works; for it strengthens man and increases his charity. —St. Teresa.

31 It is folly not to think of death. It is greater folly to think of it, and not prepare for it.—St. Alphonsus.

FEBRUARY

1 THE most perfect and meritorious intention is that by which, in all our actions, we have in view only the good pleasure of God and the accomplishment of His holy will.—St. Alphonsus.

2 Mary's sorrow was less when she saw her only Son crucified, than it is now at the sight of men offending Him by sin.—St. Ignatius.

3 There is nothing more unreasonable than to estimate our worth by the opinion of others. Today they laud us to the skies, tomorrow they will cover us with ignominy.— Ven. Louis de Granada.

4 Act as if every day were the last of your life, and each action the last you perform.—St. Alphonsus.

5 Perfection consists in renouncing ourselves, in carrying our cross, and in following Jesus Christ. Now, he who renounces himself most perfectly carries his cross the best and follows nearest to Jesus Christ is he who never does his own will, but always that of God.—ST. VINCENT DE PAUL.

6 That which would have easily been remedied at first, becomes incurable by time and habit—ST. IGNATIUS.

7 Among the gifts of grace which the soul receives in holy communion there is one that must be numbered among the highest. It is, that holy communion does not permit the soul to remain long in sin, nor to obstinately persevere in it.—ST. IGNATIUS.

8 Be assured that one great means to find favor when we appear before God is to have pardoned the injuries we have received here below.—VEN. LOUIS DE GRANADA.

9 Woe to him who neglects to recommend himself to Mary, and thus closes the channel of grace! —ST. ALPHONSUS.

10 It is folly to leave your goods where you can never return, and to send nothing to that place where you must remain for ever.—VEN. LOUIS DE GRANADA.

11 Discretion is necessary in spiritual life. It is its part to restrain the exercises in the way of perfection, so as to keep us between the two extremes.—ST. IGNATIUS.

12 By denying our self-love and our inclinations in little things, we gradually acquire mortification and victory over ourselves.—St. TERESA.

13 Should we fall a thousand times in a day, a thousand times we must rise again, always animated with unbounded confidence in the infinite goodness of God. —VEN. LOUIS DE GRANADA.

14 God's way in dealing with those whom He intends to admit soonest after this life into the possession of His everlasting glory, is to purify them in this world by the greatest afflictions and trials.—St. IGNATIUS.

15 After the flower comes the fruit: we receive, as the reward of our fatigues, an increase of grace in this world, and in the next the eternal vision of God. —BL. HENRY SUSO.

16 God refuses no one the gift of prayer. By it we obtain the help that we need to overcome disorderly desires and temptations of all kinds.—St. ALPHONSUS.

17 To establish ourselves in a virtue it is necessary to form good and practical resolutions to perform certain and determined acts of that virtue, and we must, moreover, be faithful in executing them.—St. VINCENT DE PAUL.

18 Love ought to consist of deeds more than of words.—St. IGNATIUS.

19 There are many things which seem to us misfortunes and which we call such; but if we understood the designs of God we would call them graces. —ST. ALPHONSUS.

20 Let us abandon everything to the merciful providence of God.—BL. ALBERT THE GREAT.

21 Jesus Christ, our great Model, suffered much for us; let us bear our afflictions cheerfully, seeing that through them we have the happiness of resembling Him. —BL. HENRY SUSO.

22 Remember that virtue is a very high and rugged mountain, difficult to ascend, and requiring much fatigue and exertion before we arrive at the summit to rest.—BL. HENRY SUSO.

23 Labor to conquer yourself. This victory will assure you a brighter crown in heaven than they gain whose disposition is more amiable.—ST. IGNATIUS.

24 We should not examine articles of faith with a curious and subtle spirit. It is sufficient for us to know that the Church proposes them. We can never be deceived in believing them.—ST. VINCENT DE PAUL.

25 We should guard against jealousy, and even the slightest sentiment thereof. This vice is absolutely opposed to a pure and sincere zeal for the glory of God, and is a certain proof of secret and subtle pride.—ST. VINCENT DE PAUL.

26 Charity requires us always to have compassion on human infirmity.—St. CATHERINE OF SIENA.

27 When one does not love prayer, it is morally impossible for him to resist his passions. —St. ALPHONSUS.

28 Docility and easy acquiescence with good advice are the signs of a humble heart.—VEN. JULIENNE MOREL.

29 There is nothing richer, nothing surer, nothing more agreeable than a good conscience.—VEN. BARTHOLOMEW OF MARTYRS.

MARCH

1 IT SEEMS as if God granted to other saints to free us from some particular needfulness; but I know by experience that the glorious St. Joseph assists us generally in all our necessities.—St. TERESA.

2 A most powerful and efficacious remedy for all evils, a means of correcting all imperfections, of triumphing over temptation, and preserving our hearts in an undisturbed peace, is conformity with the will of God.—St. VINCENT DE PAUL.

3 It often happens that when we take less care of our body, we have better health than when we bestow upon it too much care.—St. TERESA.

4 Do nothing, say nothing before considering if that which you are about to say or do is pleasing to God, profitable to yourself, and edifying to your neighbor. —St. Ignatius.

5 Sometimes God leaves us for a long time unable to effect any good, that we may learn to humble ourselves, and never to glory in our efforts.—St. Vincent Ferrer.

6 We easily lose peace of mind, because we make it depend, not on the testimony of a good conscience, but on the judgment of men.—Ven. Bartholomew of Martyrs.

7 You may fast regularly, give alms, and pray without ceasing, but as long as you hate your brother, you will not be numbered among the children of God. —Ven. Louis de Blois.

8 He who at the hour of death finds himself protected by St. Joseph, will certainly experience great consolation.—St. Teresa.

9 Take care that the worldling does not pursue with greater zeal and anxiety the perishable goods of this world than you do the eternal.—St. Ignatius.

10 We should consider our departed brethren as living members of Jesus Christ, animated by His grace, and certain of participating one day of His glory. We should therefore love, serve, and assist them as far as is in our power.—St. Vincent de Paul.

11 Control thy senses, guard thy mouth, bridle thy tongue, subjugate thy heart, bear all provocation with charity, and thou shalt perfectly fulfil the will of God.—Bl. Henry Suso.

12 Our perfection consists in uniting our will so intimately with God's will, that we will only desire what He wills. He who conforms most perfectly to the will of God will be the most perfect Christian.—St. Vincent de Paul.

13 Humility, modesty, sobriety, purity, piety, and prudence, with meekness, ornament the soul, and make us live on earth a truly angelic life.—Bl. Jordan of Saxony.

14 In recalling to mind the life and actions of the saints, walk in their footsteps as much as possible, and humble thyself if thou canst not attain to their perfection. —St. Thomas Aquinas.

15 When the devil again tempts you to sin, telling you that God is merciful, remember that the Lord showeth mercy to them that fear Him, but not to them who despise Him.—St. Alphonsus.

16 In prayer we should particularly combat our predominant passion or evil inclination. We should devote continual attention to it, because when it is once conquered we will easily obtain the victory over all our other faults.—St. Vincent de Paul.

17 I will carefully consider how, on the day of judgment, I would wish to have discharged my office or my duty; and the way I would wish to have done it then I shall do now.—ST. IGNATIUS.

18 It is well to deny ourselves that which is permitted, in order to avoid more easily that which is not. —ST. BENEDICT.

19 I have noticed that all persons who have true devotion to St. Joseph and tender him special honor, are very much advanced in virtue, for he takes great care of souls who recommend themselves to him; and I have never asked of him anything which he did not obtain for me.—ST. TERESA.

20 He who forgets himself in the service of God may be assured that God will not forget Him. —ST. IGNATIUS.

21 Let all our actions be directed to the end that God may be glorified in all things.—ST. BENEDICT.

22 He who suffers in patience, suffers less and saves his soul. He who suffers impatiently, suffers more and loses his soul.—ST. ALPHONSUS.

23 When we remember or hear that the enemies of the Church burn and destroy God's temples, we should grieve therefor; but we should also rejoice much when we see new ones built, and we should co-operate in their erection as much as we possibly can.—ST. TERESA.

24 We should carefully beware of giving ourselves so completely to any employment as to forget to have recourse to God from time to time.—St. Teresa.

25 Our Lady, deign to intercede for us sinners with thy divine Son, our Lord, and obtain of Him a blessing for us in our trials and tribulations!—St. Ignatius.

26 Whoever would follow Jesus Christ, must walk in His footsteps, if he would not go astray. —St. Teresa.

27 Let us thank God for having called us to His holy faith. It is a great gift, and the number of those who thank God for it is small.—St. Alphonsus.

28 The trials of life cease to oppress us if we accept them for the love of God.—Ven. Louis de Granada.

29 If you wish to take up your abode in the tabernacle of the heavenly kingdom, you must reach there through your good works, without which you can not hope to enter.—St. Benedict.

30 It is a great folly to be willing to violate the friendship of God, rather than the law of human friendship.—St. Teresa.

31 When the afflictions of this life overcome us, let us encourage ourselves to bear them patiently by the hope of heaven.—St. Alphonsus.

APRIL

1 TO PUT into practice the teachings of our holy faith, it is not enough to convince ourselves that they are true; we must love them. Love united to faith makes us practise our religion.—ST. ALPHONSUS.

2 Unite all your works to the merits of Jesus Christ, and then offer them up to the eternal Father if you desire to make them pleasing to Him.—ST. TERESA.

3 God pardons sin; but He will not pardon the will to sin.—ST. ALPHONSUS.

4 It is a fault, not a virtue, to wish your humility recognized and applauded.—ST. BERNARD.

5 Before engaging in your private devotions, perform those which obedience and your duty toward your neighbor impose upon you in such a manner as to make an abnegation of self.—VEN. LOUIS DE BLOIS.

6 The world is full of inconstancy; its friendship ceases the moment there is no advantage to be expected from us.—VEN. JOHN TAULER.

7 There is nothing better to display the truth in an excellent light, than a clear and simple statement of facts.—ST. BENEDICT.

8 Be careful and do not lightly condemn the actions of others. We must consider the intention of our neighbor, which is often good and pure, although the act itself seems blameworthy.—ST. IGNATIUS.

9 He who does not overcome his predominant passion is in great danger of being lost. He who does overcome it will easily conquer all the rest.—ST. ALPHONSUS.

10 To conquer himself is the greatest victory that man can gain.—ST. IGNATIUS.

11 A soul which does not practise the exercise of prayer is very like a paralyzed body which, though possessing feet and hands, makes no use of them.—ST. ALPHONSUS.

12 When you do a good action, have the intention of first pleasing God, and then of giving good example to your neighbor.—ST. ALPHONSUS.

13 The grace of perseverance is the most important of all; it crowns all other graces.—ST. VINCENT DE PAUL.

14 Prayer is the only channel through which God's great graces and favors may flow into the soul; and if this be once closed, I know no other way He can communicate them.—ST. TERESA.

15 To acquire courage it is very useful to read the lives of the saints, especially of those who, after living in sin, attained great sanctity.—St. Alphonsus.

16 The truly humble reject all praise for themselves, and refer it all to God.—St. Alphonsus.

17 Prayer should be effective and practical, since it has for its end the acquisition of solid virtue and the mortification of the passions.—St. Vincent de Paul.

18 We do not keep an account of the graces which God has given us, but God our Lord keeps an account of them. He has fixed the measure thereof.—St. Alphonsus.

19 The more guilty we are, the greater must be our confidence in Mary. Therefore, courage, timid soul; let Mary know all thy misery, and hasten with joy to the throne of mercy.—Bl. Henry Suso.

20 Evil is often more hurtful to the doer than to the one against whom it is done.—St. Catherine of Siena.

21 During life despise that which will avail you nothing at the hour of death.—St. Anselm.

22 He who fails to reflect before acting, walks with his eyes shut and advances with danger. He also falls very often, because the eye of reflection does not enable him to see whither his footsteps lead.—St. Gregory the Great.

23 Sanctity and perfection consist not in fine words, but in good actions.—Bl. HENRY SUSO.

24 As patience leads to peace, and study to science, so are humiliations the path that leads to humility. —ST. BERNARD.

25 Do not disturb yourself with vain curiosity concerning the affairs of others, nor how they conduct themselves, unless your position makes it your duty to do so.—VEN. LOUIS DE BLOIS.

26 The deceitful charms of prosperity destroy more souls than all the scourges of adversity. —ST. BERNARD.

27 The first degree of humility is the fear of God, which we should constantly have before our eyes. —VEN. LOUIS DE BLOIS.

28 He who cheerfully endures contempt and is happy under crosses and affliction, partakes of the humility and sufferings of Our Lord.—ST. MECHTILDIS.

29 He who is resigned to the divine will shall always surmount the difficulties he meets with in the service of God. The Lord will accomplish His designs concerning him.—ST. VINCENT DE PAUL.

30 Consent to suffer a slight temporary pain, that so thou mayst avoid the eternal pains which sin deserves.—ST. CATHERINE OF SIENA.

MAY

1 MARY was the most perfect among the saints only because she was always perfectly united to the will of God.—ST. ALPHONSUS.

2 After the love which we owe Jesus Christ, we must give the chief place in our heart to the love of His Mother Mary.—ST. ALPHONSUS.

3 When we feel our cross weighing upon us, let us have recourse to Mary, whom the Church calls the "Consoler of the Afflicted."—ST. ALPHONSUS.

4 The devotions we practise in honor of the glorious Virgin Mary, however trifling they be, are very pleasing to her divine Son, and He rewards them with eternal glory.—ST. TERESA.

5 There is nothing which is more profitable and more consoling to the mind than to frequently remember the Blessed Virgin.—ST. TERESA.

6 Blessed are the actions enclosed between two Hail Marys.—ST. ALPHONSUS.

7 Let us consider what the glorious Virgin endured, and what the holy apostles suffered, and we shall find that they who were nearest to Jesus Christ were the most afflicted.—ST. TERESA.

8 The servants of Mary who are in purgatory receive visits and consolations from her.—ST. ALPHONSUS.

9 If you persevere until death in true devotion to Mary, your salvation is certain.—St. Alphonsus.

10 He who remembers having invoked the name of Mary in an impure temptation, may be sure that he did not yield to it.—St. Alphonsus.

11 Mary being destined to negotiate peace between God and man, it was not proper that she should be an accomplice in the disobedience of Adam.—St. Alphonsus.

12 Mary having co-operated in our redemption with so much glory to God and so much love for us, Our Lord ordained that no one shall obtain salvation except through her intercession.—St. Alphonsus.

13 He who wishes to find Jesus will do so only by having recourse to Mary.—St. Alphonsus.

14 Mary having always lived wholly detached from earthly things and united with God, death, which united her more closely to Him, was extremely sweet and agreeable to her.—St. Alphonsus.

15 Mary being in heaven nearer to God and more united to Him, knows our miseries better, compassionates them more, and can more efficaciously assist us.—St. Alphonsus.

16 The Virgin Mother, all pure and all white, will make her servants pure and white.—St. Alphonsus.

17 To assure our salvation it does not suffice to call ourselves children of Mary, therefore let us always have the fear of God.—ST. TERESA.

18 Let us offer ourselves without delay and without reserve to Mary, and beg her to offer us herself to God.—ST. ALPHONSUS.

19 Such is the compassion, such the love which Mary bears us, that she is never tired of praying for us. —ST. ALPHONSUS.

20 O Queen of heaven and earth! The universe would perish before thou couldst refuse aid to one who invokes thee from the depth of his heart.—BL. HENRY SUSO.

21 O most blessed Virgin, who declarest in thy Canticle that it is owing to thy humility that God hath done great things in thee, obtain for me the grace to imitate thee, that is, to be obedient; because to obey is to practise humility.—ST. VINCENT DE PAUL.

22 May the two names so sweet and so powerful, of Jesus and Mary, be always in our hearts and on our lips!—ST. ALPHONSUS.

23 Whatsoever we do, we can never be true children of Mary, unless we are humble.—ST. ALPHONSUS.

24 Let us highly esteem devotion to the Blessed Virgin, and let us lose no opportunity of inspiring

others with it.—St. Alphonsus.

25 As a mother feels no disgust in dressing the sores of her child, so Mary, the heavenly infirmarian, never refuses to care for sinners who have recourse to her. —St. Alphonsus.

26 Each of our days is marked with the protection of Mary, who is exceedingly anxious to be our Mother, when we desire to be her children.—St. Vincent de Paul.

27 When the devil wishes to make himself master of a soul, he seeks to make it give up devotion to Mary.—St. Alphonsus.

28 Let us have recourse to Mary; for of all creatures she is the highest, the purest, the most beautiful, and the most loving.—Bl. Henry Suso.

29 Let the name of Mary be ever on your lips, let it be indelibly engraven on your heart. If you are under her protection, you have nothing to fear; if she is propitious, you will arrive at the port of salvation.—St. Bernard.

30 Know that of all devotions the most pleasing to Mary is to have frequent recourse to her, asking for favors.—St. Alphonsus.

31 Let the servants of Mary perform every day, and especially on Saturday, some work of charity for her sake.—St. Alphonsus.

JUNE

1 CAN WE, amongst all hearts, find one more amiable than that of Jesus? It is on His Heart that God looks with special complacency—St. Alphonsus.

2 One must wage war against his predominant passion, and not retreat, until, with God's help, he has been victorious.—St. Alphonsus.

3 An act of perfect conformity to the will of God unites us more to Him than a hundred other acts of virtue. —St. Alphonsus.

4 The love of God inspires the love of our neighbor, and the love of our neighbor serves to keep alive the love of God.—St. Gregory the Great.

5 Live always in the certainty that whatever happens to you is the result of divine Providence; because nothing hard or laborious falls to your lot without the Lord permitting it.—Ven. Louis de Blois.

6 Whatsoever good work you undertake, pray earnestly to God that He will enable you to bring it to a successful termination.—St. Benedict.

7 What is a fruitless repentance, defiled almost immediately by new faults?—St. Bernard.

8 You propose to give up everything to God; be sure, then, to include yourself among the things to be given up.—St. Benedict.

9 If you can find a place where God is not, go there and sin with impunity.—ST. ANSELM.

10 He can not err who is constantly with the visible Head which Jesus Christ has left to His Church, as its foundation, rule, teacher, and defender of the Faith. —ST. ALPHONSUS.

11 The more numerous the gifts we have received from God, the greater the account we must render to Him.—ST. GREGORY THE GREAT.

12 True penance consists in regretting without ceasing the faults of the past, and in firmly resolving to never again commit that which is so deplorable.—ST. BERNARD.

13 We are not raised the first day to the summit of perfection. It is by climbing, not by flying, that we arrive there.—ST. BERNARD.

14 What we do for ourselves during life is more certain than all the good we expect others to do for us after death.—ST. GREGORY THE GREAT.

15 Idleness begets a discontented life. It develops self-love, which is the cause of all our misery, and renders us unworthy to receive the favors of divine love. —ST. IGNATIUS.

16 Have death always before your eyes as a salutary means of returning to God.—ST. BERNARD.

17 If the devil tempts me by the thought of divine justice, I think of God's mercy; if he tries to fill me with presumption by the thought of His mercy, I think of His justice.—St. Ignatius.

18 In time of temptation continue the good thou hast begun before temptation.—St. Vincent Ferrer.

19 In the eyes of the sovereign Judge the merit of our actions depends on the motives which prompted them.—St. Gregory the Great.

20 The benefits to be derived from spiritual reading do not merely consist in impressing on the memory the precepts set forth, but in opening the heart to them, that they may bear fruit.—Ven. Louis de Blois.

21 As clouds obscure the sun, so bad thoughts darken and destroy the brightness of the soul.—Ven. Louis de Granada.

22 To judge rightly of the goodness and perfection of any one's prayer, it is sufficient to know the disposition he takes to it, and the fruits he reaps from it.—St. Vincent de Paul.

23 To commence many things and not to finish them is no small fault; we must persevere in whatever we undertake with upright intention and according to God's will.—Bl. Henry Suso.

24 The perfect champion is he who establishes complete control over his mind by overcoming temptations and the inclination of his nature to sin.—VEN. JOHN TAULER.

25 If the love of God is in your heart, you will understand that to suffer for God is a joy to which all earthly pleasures are not to be compared.—ST. IGNATIUS.

26 The world around us is, as it were, a book written by the finger of God; every creature is a word on the page. We should apply ourselves well to understand the signification of the volume.—VEN. BARTHOLOMEW OF MARTYRS.

27 A man of prayer is capable of everything. He can say with St. Paul, "I can do all things in Him who strengthened me."—ST. VINCENT DE PAUL.

28 Whilst here below our actions can never be entirely free from negligence, frailty, or defect; but we must not throw away the wheat because of the chaff.—VEN. JOHN TAULER.

29 Strive always to preserve freedom of spirit, so that you need do nothing with the view of pleasing the world, and that no fear of displeasing it will have power to shake your good resolutions.—VEN. LOUIS DE BLOIS.

30 Woe to us poor sinners if we had not the Divine Sacrifice to appease the Lord!—ST. ALPHONSUS.

JULY

1 HOW few there are who avail themselves of the precious blood of Jesus to purchase their salvation! —ST. IGNATIUS.

2 O Queen of heaven and earth! Thou art the gate of mercy ever open, never closed. The universe must perish before he who invokes thee from his heart is refused assistance.—BL. HENRY SUSO.

3 Our Faith will never be true unless it is united to that of St. Peter and the Pontiff, his successors. —ST. ALPHONSUS.

4 Short pleasures and long sufferings are all the world can give.—VEN. JOHN TAULER.

5 Learn to be silent sometimes for the edification of others, that you may learn how to speak sometimes. —ST. VINCENT FERRER.

6 Gratitude for graces received is a most efficacious means of obtaining new ones.—ST. VINCENT DE PAUL.

7 To a useless question we should answer only by silence.—ST. VINCENT FERRER.

8 We should not judge things by their exterior or appearance, but consider what they are in the sight of God, and whether they be according to His good pleasure.—ST. VINCENT DE PAUL.

9 Preserve purity of conscience with care, and never do anything to sully it or render it less agreeable to God.—St. Thomas Aquinas.

10 Give not thyself too much to any one. He who gives himself too freely is generally the least acceptable. —Bl. Henry Suso.

11 Affliction strengthens the vigor of our soul, whereas happiness weakens it.—St. Gregory the Great.

12 To acquire purity of the soul, it is necessary to guard against passing judgment on our neighbor, or useless remarks on his conduct.—St. Catherine of Siena.

13 Turn away the eyes of thy body and those of thy mind from seeing others, that thou mayest be able to contemplate thyself.—St. Vincent Ferrer.

14 The brightest ornaments in the crown of the blessed in heaven are the sufferings which they have borne patiently on earth.—St. Alphonsus.

15 We are not innocent before God if we punish that which we should pardon, or pardon that which we should punish.—St. Bernard.

16 Is there any one in the world who has invoked thee, O Mary, without having felt the benefit of thy protection, which is promised to those who invoke thy mercy?—St. Bernard.

17 It is the key of obedience that opens the door of paradise. Jesus Christ has confided that key to His vicar, the Pope, Christ on earth, whom all are obliged to obey even unto death.—St. Catherine of Siena.

18 It is true that God promises forgiveness if we repent, but what assurance have we of obtaining it tomorrow?—Ven. Louis de Blois.

19 We should offer ourselves and all we have to God, that He may dispose of us according to His holy will, so that we may be ever ready to leave all and embrace the afflictions that come upon us.—St. Vincent de Paul.

20 No one has a right to mercy who can not himself show mercy.—Ven. Louis de Granada.

21 We should reflect on all our actions, exterior and interior, and before we commence, examine well if we are able to finish them.—Ven. John Tauler.

22 The reason why the lukewarm run so great a risk of being lost is because tepidity conceals from the soul the immense evil which it causes.—St. Alphonsus.

23 We should learn of Jesus Christ to be meek and humble of heart, and ask Him unceasingly for these two virtues. We ought, particularly, to avoid the two contrary vices which would cause us to destroy with one hand what we seek to raise with the other.—St. Vincent de Paul.

24 The sufferings endured for God are the greatest proof of our love for Him.—St. Alphonsus.

25 It is in vain that we cut off the branches of evil, if we leave intact the root, which continually produces new ones.—St. Gregory the Great.

26 How little is required to be a saint! It suffices to do in all things the will of God.—St. Vincent de Paul.

27 Wouldst thou know what thou art? Thou art that to which thy heart turns the most frequently. —Ven. Bartholomew of Martyrs.

28 When you covet that which delights you, think not only of the sweet moments of enjoyment, but of the long season of regret which must follow.—St. Bernard.

29 They who voluntarily commit sin show a contempt for life eternal, since they willingly risk the loss of their soul.—St. Gregory the Great.

30 It suffices not to perform good works; we must do them well, in imitation of Our Lord Jesus Christ, of whom it is written, "He doeth all things well." —St. Vincent de Paul.

31 Put not off till to-morrow what you can do today. —St. Ignatius.

AUGUST

1 CHRIST Himself guides the bark of Peter. For this reason it can not perish, although He sometimes seems to sleep.—ST. ANTONINUS.

2 Prayer teaches us the need of laying before God all our necessities, of corresponding with His grace, of banishing vice from our heart and of establishing virtue in it.—ST. VINCENT DE PAUL.

3 Take this to heart: Owe no man anything. So shalt thou secure a peaceful sleep, an easy conscience, a life without inquietude, and a death without alarm. —VEN. LOUIS DE GRANADA.

4 If you would know whether you have made a good confession, ask yourself if you have resolved to abandon your sins.—ST. BERNARD.

5 He who does that which is displeasing to himself has discovered the secret of pleasing God.—ST. ANSELM.

6 An ordinary action, performed through obedience and love of God, is more meritorious than extraordinary works done on your own authority—VEN. LOUIS DE BLOIS.

7 Vigilance is rendered necessary and indispensable, not only by the dangers that surround us, but by the delicacy, the extreme difficulty of the work we all have to engage in the work of our salvation.—VEN. LOUIS DE GRANADA.

8 Among the different means that we have of pleasing God in all that we do, one of the most efficacious is to perform each of our actions as though it were to be the last of our life.—St. Vincent de Paul.

9 I have to seek only the glory of God, my own sanctification, and the salvation of my neighbor. I should therefore devote myself to these things, if necessary, at the peril of my life.—St. Alphonsus.

10 Idleness is hell's fishhook for catching souls.—St. Ignatius.

11 Whoever imagines himself without defect has an excess of pride. God alone is perfect.—St. Antoninus.

12 As we take the bitterest medicine to recover or preserve the health of the body, we should cheerfully endure sufferings, however repugnant to nature, and consider them efficacious remedies which God employs to purify the soul and conduct it to the perfection to which He called it.—St. Vincent de Paul.

13 To give up prayer because we are often distracted at it is to allow the devil to gain his cause. —St. Alphonsus.

14 Curb the desire of display, and do nothing from human respect.—St. Vincent de Paul.

15 O Mary, vessel of purest gold, ornamented with pearls and sapphires, filled with grace and virtue,

thou art the dearest of all creatures to the eyes of eternal Wisdom.—BL. HENRY SUSO.

16 We must be careful not to omit our prayers, confession, communion, and other exercises of piety, even when we find no consolation in them.—ST. VINCENT FERRER.

17 Let us leave to God and to truth the care of our justification, without trying to excuse ourselves, and peace will truly spring up within us.—VEN. JOHN TAULER.

18 Read good and useful books, and abstain from reading those that only gratify curiosity.—ST. VINCENT DE PAUL.

19 So great is the goodness of God in your regard, that when you ask through ignorance for that which is not beneficial, He does not grant your prayer in this matter, but gives you something better instead.—ST. BERNARD.

20 Men can use no better arms to drive away the devil, than prayer and the sign of the cross.—ST. TERESA.

21 He who knows well how to practise the exercise of the presence of God, and who is faithful in following the attraction of this divine virtue, will soon attain a very high degree of perfection.—ST. VINCENT DE PAUL.

22 One of the most admirable effects of holy communion is to preserve the soul from sin, and to help those who fall through weakness to rise again. It is much more profitable, then, to approach this divine Sacrament with love, respect, and confidence, than to remain away through an excess of fear and scrupulosity. —St. Ignatius.

23 Let us remember that every act of mortification is a work for heaven. This thought will make all suffering and weariness sweet.—St. Alphonsus.

24 Correction should be given calmly and with discernment, at seasonable times, according to the dictates of reason, and not at the impulse of anger.—Ven. Louis de Granada.

25 There is nothing more certain, nothing more agreeable, nothing richer than a good conscience. —Ven. Bartholomew of Martyrs.

26 God, to procure His glory, sometimes permits that we should be dishonored and persecuted without reason. He wishes thereby to render us conformable to His Son, who was calumniated and treated as a seducer, as an ambitious man, and as one possessed.—St. Vincent de Paul.

27 All that God gives us and all that He permits in this world have no other end than to sanctify us in Him.—St. Catherine of Siena.

28 If you can not mortify your body by actual penance, abstain at least from some lawful pleasure. —St. Alphonsus.

29 One whose heart is embittered can do nothing but contend and contradict, finding something to oppose in every remark.—VEN. JULIENNE MOREL.

30 Without prayer we have neither light nor strength to advance in the way which leads to God. —ST. ALPHONSUS.

31 I have never gone out to mingle with the world without losing something of myself.—BL. ALBERT THE GREAT.

SEPTEMBER

1 HE who perseveres with constancy and fervor will, without fail, raise himself to a high degree of perfection.—BL. HENRY SUSO.

2 An upright intention is the soul of our actions. It gives them life, and makes them good.—ST. ALPHONSUS.

3 You wish to reform the world: reform yourself, otherwise your efforts will be in vain.—ST. IGNATIUS.

4 Let all thy care be to possess thy soul in peace and tranquillity. Let no accident be to thee a cause of ill-humor.—ST. VINCENT FERRER.

5 Humility is a fortified town; it repels all attacks. The sight of it obliges the enemy to turn and flee.—VEN. LOUIS DE GRANADA.

6 The world is deceitful and inconstant. When fortune forsakes us, friendship takes flight.—BL. HENRY SUSO.

7 Perform all your actions in union with the pure intention and perfect love with which Our Lord did all things for the glory of God and the salvation of the world.—ST. MECHTILDIS.

8 An air of meekness and a modest speech are pleasing alike to God and men.—VEN. JOHN TAULER.

9 The saints owed to their confidence in God that unalterable tranquillity of soul, which procured their perpetual joy and peace, even in the midst of adversities. —ST. ALPHONSUS.

10 Look not to the qualities thou mayest possess, which are wanting to others; but look to those which others possess and which are wanting to thee, that thou mayest acquire them.—VEN. LOUIS DE GRANADA.

11 Your heart is not so narrow that the world can satisfy it entirely; nothing but God can fill it. —ST. IGNATIUS.

12 If you wish to raise a lofty edifice of perfection, take humility for a foundation.—ST. THOMAS AQUINAS.

13 It ordinarily happens that God permits those who judge others, to fall into the same or even greater faults.—ST. VINCENT FERRER.

14 Raise thy heart and thy love toward the sweet and most holy cross, which soothes every pain! —ST. CATHERINE OF SIENA.

15 Often read spiritual books; then, like a sheep, ruminate the food thou hast taken, by meditation and a desire to practise the holy doctrine found therein. —ST. ANTONINUS.

16 Love others much, but visit them seldom. —ST. CATHERINE OF SIENA.

17 God sends us trials and afflictions to exercise us in patience and teach us sympathy with the sorrows of others.—ST. VINCENT DE PAUL.

18 Armed with prayer, the saints sustained a glorious warfare and vanquished all their enemies. By prayer, also, they appeased the wrath of God, and obtained from Him all they desired.—VEN. LOUIS DE GRANADA.

19 All souls in hell are there because they did not pray. All the saints sanctified themselves by prayer. —ST. ALPHONSUS.

20 The thought of the presence of God renders us familiar with the practice of doing in all things His holy will.—ST. VINCENT DE PAUL.

21 If we consider the number and excellence of the virtues practised by the saints, we must feel the

inefficiency and imperfection of our actions.—ST. VINCENT FERRER.

22 Prayer without fervor has not sufficient strength to rise to heaven.—ST. BERNARD.

23 The path of virtue is painful to nature when left to itself; but nature, assisted by grace, finds it easy and agreeable.—VEN. LOUIS DE GRANADA.

24 Always give the preference to actions which appear to you the most agreeable to God, and most contrary to self-love.—ST. ALPHONSUS.

25 As the branch separated from the roots soon loses all life and verdure, so it is with good works which are not united with charity.—ST. GREGORY THE GREAT.

26 We should constantly thank the Lord for having granted us the gift of the true faith, by associating us with the children of the holy Catholic Church. —ST. ALPHONSUS.

27 We should not spare expense, fatigue, nor even our life, when there is a question of accomplishing the holy will of God.—ST. VINCENT DE PAUL.

28 Some are unable to fast or give alms; there are none who can not pray.—ST. ALPHONSUS.

29 We meet with contradictions everywhere. If only two persons are together they mutually afford each other opportunities of exercising patience, and even when one is alone there will still be a necessity for this virtue, so true it is that our miserable life is full of crosses.—ST. VINCENT DE PAUL.

30 We should bear our sufferings in expiation for our sins, to merit heaven, and to please God.—ST. ALPHONSUS.

OCTOBER

1 ALWAYS give good example: teach virtue by word and deed. Example is more powerful than discourse. —BL. HENRY SUSO.

2 If thou wouldst glory, let it be in the Lord, by referring everything to Him, and giving to Him all the honor and glory.—VEN. LOUIS DE GRANADA.

3 There is nothing more holy, more eminently perfect, than resignation to the will of God, which confirms us in an entire detachment from ourselves, and a perfect indifference for every condition in which we may be placed.—ST. VINCENT DE PAUL.

4 Prayer consists not in many words, but in the fervor of desire, which raises the soul to God by the knowledge of its own nothingness and the divine goodness. —BL. HENRY SUSO.

5 Let us make up for lost time. Let us give to God the time that remains to us.—ST. ALPHONSUS.

6 When thou feelest thyself excited, shut thy mouth and chain thy tongue.—BL. HENRY SUSO.

7 If it was necessary that Christ should suffer and so enter by the cross into the kingdom of His Father, no friend of God should shrink from suffering.—VEN. JOHN TAULER.

8 We should grieve to see no account made of time, which is so precious; to see it employed so badly, so uselessly, for it can never be recalled.—BL. HENRY SUSO.

9 Every time that some unexpected event befalls us, be it affliction, or be it spiritual or corporal consolation, we should endeavor to receive it with equanimity of spirit, since all comes from the hand of God.—ST. VINCENT DE PAUL.

10 There are some who sin through frailty, or through the force of some violent passion. They desire to break these chains of death; if their prayer is constant they will be heard.—ST. ALPHONSUS.

11 "Thy will be done!" This is what the saints had continually on their lips and in their hearts. —ST. ALPHONSUS.

12 He who would be a disciple of Jesus Christ must live in sufferings; for "The servant is not greater than the Master."—VEN. JOHN TAULER.

13 He who submits himself to God in all things is certain that whatever men say or do against him

will always turn to his advantage.—St. VINCENT DE PAUL.

14 If he be blind who refuses to believe in the truths of the Catholic faith, how much blinder is he who believes, and yet lives as if he did not believe! —St. ALPHONSUS.

15 There is no affliction, trial, or labor difficult to endure, when we consider the torments and sufferings which Our Lord Jesus Christ endured for us.—St. TERESA.

16 Outside of God nothing is durable. We exchange life for death, health for sickness, honor for shame, riches for poverty. All things change and pass away. —St. CATHERINE OF SIENA.

17 If you would keep yourself pure, shun dangerous occasions. Do not trust your own strength. In this matter we can not take too much precaution. —St. ALPHONSUS.

18 After knowing the will of God in regard to a work which we undertake, we should continue courageously, however difficult it may be. We should follow it to the end with as much constancy as the obstacles we encounter are great.—St. VINCENT DE PAUL.

19 In your prayers, if you would quickly and surely draw upon you the grace of God, pray in a special manner for our Holy Church and all those connected with it.—VEN. LOUIS DE BLOIS.

20 Prayer is our principal weapon. By it we obtain of God the victory over our evil inclinations, and over all temptations of hell.—St. Alphonsus.

21 We should never abandon, on account of the difficulties we encounter, an enterprise undertaken with due reflection.—St. Vincent de Paul.

22 Being all members of the same body, with the same head, who is Christ, it is proper that we should have in common the same joys and sorrows.—Ven. Louis de Granada.

23 We should be cordial and affable with the poor, and with persons in humble circumstances. We should not treat them in a supercilious manner. Haughtiness makes them revolt. On the contrary, when we are affable with them, they become more docile and derive more benefit from the advice they receive.—St. Vincent de Paul.

24 Let not confusion for thy fault overwhelm thee with despair, as if there were no longer a remedy. —St. Catherine of Siena.

25 As all our wickedness consists in turning away from our Creator, so all our goodness consists in uniting ourselves with Him.—St. Alphonsus.

26 That which we suffer in the accomplishment of a good work, merits for us the necessary graces to insure its success.—St. Vincent de Paul.

27 We ought to have a special devotion to those saints who excelled in humility, particularly to the Blessed Virgin Mary, who declares that the Lord regarded her on account of her humility.—St. VINCENT DE PAUL.

28 He who wishes to find Jesus should seek Him, not in the delights and pleasures of the world, but in mortification of the senses.—St. ALPHONSUS.

29 Let us not despise, judge, or condemn any one but ourselves; then our cross will bloom and bear fruit.—VEN. JOHN TAULER.

30 It is rarely that we fall into error if we are humble and trust to the wisdom of others, in preference to our own judgment.—VEN. LOUIS DE BLOIS.

31 The best of all prayers is that in which we ask that God's holy will be accomplished, both in ourselves and in others.—VEN. LOUIS DE BLOIS.

NOVEMBER

1 WE SHOULD honor God in His saints, and beseech Him to make us partakers of the graces He poured so abundantly upon them.—St. VINCENT DE PAUL.

2 We may have a confident hope of our salvation when we apply ourselves to relieve the souls in purgatory, so afflicted and so dear to God.—St. ALPHONSUS.

3 The example of the saints is proposed to every one, so that the great actions shown us may encourage us to

undertake smaller things.—VEN. LOUIS DE GRANADA.

4 Let us read the lives of the saints; let us consider the penances which they performed, and blush to be so effeminate and so fearful of mortifying our flesh. —ST. ALPHONSUS.

5 The greatest pain which the holy souls suffer in purgatory proceeds from their desire to possess God. This suffering especially afflicts those who in life had but a feeble desire of heaven.—ST. ALPHONSUS.

6 Death is welcome to one who has always feared God and faithfully served Him.—ST. TERESA.

7 True humility consists in being content with all that God is pleased to ordain for us, believing ourselves unworthy to be called His servants.—ST. TERESA.

8 The best preparation for death is a perfect resignation to the will of God, after the example of Jesus Christ, who, in His prayer in Gethsemani prepared Himself with these words, "Father, not as I will, but as Thou wilt." —ST. VINCENT DE PAUL.

9 The errors of others should serve to keep us from adding any of our own to them.—ST. IGNATIUS.

10 There is more security in self-denial, mortification, and other like virtues, than in an abundance of tears.—ST. TERESA.

11 A resolute will triumphs over everything with the help of God, which is never wanting. —St. Alphonsus.

12 If humble souls are contradicted, they remain calm; if they are calumniated, they suffer with patience; if they are little esteemed, neglected, or forgotten, they consider that their due; if they are weighed down with occupations, they perform them cheerfully.—St. Vincent de Paul.

13 When we have to reply to some one who speaks harshly to us, we must always do it with gentleness. If we are angry, it is better to keep silence.—St. Alphonsus.

14 The two principal dispositions which we should bring to holy communion are detachment from creatures, and the desire to receive Our Lord with a view to loving Him more in the future.—St. Alphonsus.

15 In doing penance it is necessary to deprive oneself of as many lawful pleasures as we had the misfortune to indulge in unlawful ones.—St. Gregory the Great.

16 In raising human nature to heaven by His ascension, Christ has given us the hope of arriving thither ourselves.—St. Thomas Aquinas.

17 It is useless to subdue the flesh by abstinence, unless one gives up his irregular life, and abandons vices which defile his soul.—St. Benedict.

18 No prayers are so acceptable to God as those which we offer Him after communion.—ST. ALPHONSUS.

19 It avails nothing to subdue the body, if the mind allows itself to be controlled by anger. —ST. GREGORY THE GREAT.

20 What is it that renders death terrible? Sin. We must therefore fear sin, not death. —ST. ALPHONSUS.

21 The Blessed Virgin is of all the works of the Creator the most excellent, and to find anything in nature more grand one must go to the Author of nature Himself.—ST. PETER DAMIAN.

22 If we would advance in virtue, we must not neglect little things, for they pave the way to greater. —ST. TERESA.

23 When one has fallen into some fault, what better remedy can there be than to have immediate recourse to the Most Blessed Sacrament?—ST. ALPHONSUS.

24 Afflictions are the most certain proofs that God can give us of His love for us.—ST. VINCENT DE PAUL.

25 Is it not a great cruelty for us Christians, members of the body of the Holy Church, to attack one another?—ST. CATHERINE OF SIENA.

26 The Church is the pillar and ground of truth, and her infallibility admits of no doubt.—VEN. LOUIS DE GRANADA.

27 He who truly loves his neighbor and can not efficaciously assist him, should strive at least to relieve and help him by his prayers.—ST. TERESA.

28 We should blush for shame to show so much resentment at what is done or said against us, knowing that so many injuries and affronts have been offered to our Redeemer and the saints.—ST. TERESA.

29 The reason why so many souls who apply themselves to prayer are not inflamed with God's love is, that they neglect to carefully prepare themselves for it.—ST. TERESA.

30 It is absolutely necessary, both for our advancement and the salvation of others, to follow always and in all things the beautiful light of faith.—ST. VINCENT DE PAUL.

DECEMBER

1 IF WE consider all that is imperfect and worldly in us, we shall find ample reason for abasing ourselves before God and man, before ourselves and our inferiors. —ST. VINCENT DE PAUL.

2 No one should think or say anything of another which he would not wish thought or said of himself. —ST. TERESA.

3 We should study the interests of others as our own, and be careful to act on all occasions with uprightness and loyalty.—St. VINCENT DE PAUL.

4 It is God Himself who receives what we give in charity, and is it not an incomparable happiness to give Him what belongs to Him, and what we have received from His goodness alone?—St. VINCENT DE PAUL.

5 Let your constant practice be to offer yourself to God, that He may do with you what He pleases.—St. ALPHONSUS.

6 It is not enough to forbid our own tongue to murmur; we must also refuse to listen to murmurers.—VEN. LOUIS DE GRANADA.

7 We can obtain no reward without merit, and no merit without patience.—St. ALPHONSUS.

8 No harp sends forth such sweet harmonies as are produced in the afflicted heart by the holy name of Mary. Let us kneel to reverence this holy, this sublime name of Mary!—BL. HENRY SUSO.

9 The life of a true Christian should be such that he fears neither death nor any event of his life, but endures and submits to all things with a good heart.—St. TERESA.

10 We should abandon ourselves entirely into the hands of God, and believe that His providence disposes everything that He wishes or permits to happen to us for our greater good.—St. VINCENT DE PAUL.

11   Regulate and direct all your actions to God, offering them to Him and beseeching Him to grant that they be for His honor and glory.—ST. TERESA.

12   Conformity to the will of God is an easy and certain means of acquiring a great treasure of graces in this life.—ST. VINCENT DE PAUL.

13   Do not consider what others do, or how they do it; for there are but few who really work for their own sanctification.—ST. ALPHONSUS.

14   Today God invites you to do good; do it therefore to-day. Tomorrow you may not have time, or God may no longer call you to do it.—ST. ALPHONSUS.

15   To advance in the way of perfection it does not suffice to say a number of weak prayers; our principal care should be to acquire solid virtues.—ST. TERESA.

16   Humility is the virtue of Our Lord Jesus Christ, of His blessed Mother, and of the greatest saints. It embraces all virtues and, where it is sincere, introduces them into the soul.—ST. VINCENT DE PAUL.

17   It will be a great consolation for us at the hour of death to know that we are to be judged by Him whom we have loved above all things during life. —ST. TERESA.

18   Humble submission and obedience to the decrees of the Sovereign Pontiffs are good means for

distinguishing the loyal from the rebellious children of the Church.—St. VINCENT DE PAUL.

19 The devil attacks us at the time of prayer more frequently than at other times. His object is to make us weary of prayer.—BL. HENRY SUSO.

20 It is an act as rare as it is precious, to transact business with many people, without ever forgetting God or oneself.—St. IGNATIUS.

21 God is our light. The farther the soul strays away from God, the deeper it goes into darkness. —St. ALPHONSUS.

22 True Christian prudence makes us submit our intellect to the maxims of the Gospel without fear of being deceived. It teaches us to judge things as Jesus Christ judged them, and to speak and act as He did. —St. VINCENT DE PAUL.

23 Remember that men change easily, and that you can not place your trust in them; therefore attach yourself to God alone.—St. TERESA.

24 If we secretly feel a desire to appear greater or better than others, we must repress it at once. —St. TERESA.

25 The King of heaven deigned to be born in a stable, because He came to destroy pride, the cause of man's ruin.—St. ALPHONSUS.

26 To save our souls we must live according to the maxims of the Gospel, and not according to those of the world.—St. Alphonsus.

27 Be gentle and kind with every one, and severe with yourself.—St. Teresa.

28 If you wish to be pleasing to God and happy here below, be in all things united to His will.—St. Alphonsus.

29 In proportion as the love of God increases in our soul, so does also the love of suffering.—St. Vincent de Paul.

30 He who keeps steadily on without pausing, will reach the end of his path and the summit of perfection.—St. Teresa.

31 The past is no longer yours; the future is not yet in your power. You have only the present wherein to do good.—St. Alphonsus.

PART VII

Reasonableness of Catholic Ceremonies and Practices

"Let the children of Israel make the Phase in due time . . . according to all the ceremonies thereof"
(Num. 9:2, 3).

Mary, Queen of the Rosary, pray for us.

Reasonableness of Catholic Ceremonies and Practices

"The priest shall be vested with the tunic" (Lev. 6:10).

"And he made, of violet and purple, scarlet and fine linen, the vestments for Aaron to wear when he ministered in the holy places, as the Lord commanded Moses" (Ex. 39:1).

"In every place there is sacrifice and there is offered to My name a clean offering" (Malach. 1:11).

"And another Angel came and stood before the altar, having a golden censer: and there was given to him much incense, that he should offer of the prayers of all saints upon the golden altar, which is before the throne of God" (Apoc. 8:3).

THE CEREMONIES OF THE CATHOLIC CHURCH

THE Catholic Church in the celebration of Mass and in the administration of the sacraments employs certain forms and rites. These are called ceremonies. By these ceremonies the Church wishes to appeal to the heart as well as to the intellect, and to impress the faithful with sentiments of faith and piety.

What is more capable of raising the heart and mind of man to God than a priest celebrating Mass? What more inspiring than some of our sacred music?

How beneficial and how lasting the impression formed by the ceremonies of the Church, the following incident will show:

One of our missionaries once went to visit a tribe of Indians who had been deprived of a priest for nearly half a century. After traveling through the forest for some days he came near their village.

'Twas Sunday morning. Suddenly the silence was broken by a number of voices singing in unison. He stopped to listen. To his great astonishment he distinguished the music of a Mass, and of Catholic hymns well known to him.

What could be more touching than this simple, savage people endeavoring to celebrate the Lord's Day as they had been taught by the priest fifty years before? What more elevating than those sacred songs—the *Stabat Mater*, the *O Salutaris*, or the *Te Deum*—uttered by pious lips and resounding through the forest primeval? What better evidence could we have of the beneficial effects of our ceremonies in raising the heart to God?

And yet few things connected with our holy religion have been more frequently subjected to ridicule than her ceremonies. People scoff at them, laugh at them, call them foolish and unreasonable. Those people do not stop to consider that by doing so they, themselves, are acting most unreasonably. For no reasonable person, no judge, will condemn another without hearing both sides of the question.

These wiseacres, however, flatter themselves that they know all about the Catholic Church and her ceremonies without hearing her side of the case. Hence the misunderstandings and misrepresentations regarding her that exist among well-meaning people.

If people would but learn to speak about that which they knew and understood; if they would accord to the Catholic Church the same treatment as to other institutions; if they would examine both sides of the question before criticising and ridiculing her teachings and her ceremonies; if they would but treat her with that openness, that fairness, that candor, that honesty characteristic of the American citizen when dealing with other questions—what a vast amount of ignorance, of prejudice, of sin would be avoided!

We claim that ceremonies used in the worship of God are reasonable, because they were sanctioned by God in the Old Testament and by Jesus Christ and His apostles in the New Law.

I. CEREMONIES NECESSARY TO DIVINE WORSHIP

THE angels are pure spirits. They have no body. Consequently the worship they render God is spiritual, interior.

The heavenly bodies are not spiritual, but entirely material substances. They render God a sort of external worship according to the words of the prophet Daniel, "Sun and moon bless the Lord, . . . stars of heaven bless the Lord. Praise and exalt Him forever." Man has a soul, a spiritual substance similar to the heavenly bodies. He should, therefore, honor God by the twofold form of worship, interior and exterior.

"God is a spirit; and they that adore Him must adore Him in spirit and in truth" (John 4:24).

From these words of the beloved disciple we are not to conclude that interior worship is prescribed as the only essential, and exterior worship condemned. True piety must manifest itself externally. Man naturally manifests his feelings by outward signs and ceremonies.

The Catholic Church recognizes that man has a heart to be moved as well as an intellect to be enlightened. She enlightens the intellect by her good books, sermons, etc.; and she moves the heart by the grandeur of her ceremonies.

If any one doubts that God considers ceremonies necessary to divine worship, let him read the books of Leviticus and Exodus. Almost the whole of these books treats of the rites and ceremonies used by the then chosen people of God in their public worship.

The 26th, 27th, and 28th chapters of Exodus prescribe the form of the tabernacle and its appurtenances, the size of the altar and the oil for the lamps, and the holy vestments which Aaron and his sons were to wear during the performance of the public ceremonies.

The book of Leviticus treats more particularly of the sacrifices, rites, and ceremonies of the priests and Levites.

"And the Lord called Moses, and spoke to him from the tabernacle of the testimony, saying: Speak to the children of Israel, and thou shalt say to them: The man among you that shall offer to the Lord a sacrifice of the cattle, that is, offering victims of oxen and sheep, if his offering be a holocaust and of the herd, he shall offer a male, without blemish, at the door of the tabernacle of the testimony, to make the Lord favorable to him. And he shall put his hand upon the head of the victim, and it shall be acceptable and help to his expiation" (Lev. 1:1 *et seq.*).

After enumerating all the sacrifices and ceremonies, the sacred writer closes the book of Leviticus with the words, "These are the precepts which the Lord commanded Moses for the children of Israel in Mount Sinai," thus showing that He considers ceremonies necessary to divine worship.

The religion instituted by Our Lord and Saviour Jesus Christ is more spiritual than that of the Old Law. Nevertheless He did not discard ceremonies. In the Garden of Gethsemani He fell upon His knees in humble supplication. He went in procession to Jerusalem preceded by a great multitude strewing palm-branches on the road and singing, "Hosanna to the Son of David." Before He cured the deaf and dumb man, He put His fingers into his ears and touched his tongue with spittle, and looking up to heaven He groaned and said, "*Ephpheta*," which is, "Be thou opened."

At the Last Supper He invoked a blessing on the bread and wine, and after the supper He chanted a hymn with His disciples—ceremonies similar to those used in the Mass. When He imparted the Holy Ghost to His apostles, He breathed upon them. In a similar way they and their successors communicated the Holy Ghost upon others by breathing upon them, laying their hands upon them and praying over them, when conferring the sacrament of Holy Orders.

St. James directs that if any man is sick he shall call in a priest of the Church, who shall anoint him with oil, as is done in the sacrament of Extreme Unction.

We must, therefore, admit that ceremonies used in the worship of God are reasonable, since they are sanctioned by God in the Old Law and by Jesus Christ and His apostles in the New Testament.

All these acts of Our Saviour—the prostration in the Garden, the procession to Jerusalem, the touching of the deaf man's ears, the chanting of the hymn, the laying on of hands, the anointing of the sick—are but so many ceremonies serving as models of the ceremonies used by the Catholic Church in her public worship and in the administration of her sacraments.

II. VESTMENTS USED BY THE PRIEST AT MASS

*B*EFORE entering upon an explanation of the ceremonies of the Mass, which is our principal act of public worship, let us examine the meaning of the vestments worn by the priest during the celebration of that august sacrifice. First, it is well to remember that these vestments come down to us from the time of the apostles, and have the weight of antiquity hanging upon them. Hence, if they did not demand our respect as memorials of Christ, they are at least deserving of attention on account of their antiquity.

The 28th chapter of Exodus tells us the sacred vestments God wished the priests of the Old Law to wear during the public worship. "And these shall be the vestments which they shall make: a rational and an ephod, a tunic and a straight linen garment, a mitre and a girdle. They shall make the holy vestments for thy brother Aaron and his sons, that they may do the office of priesthood unto Me." As God in the Old Law prescribed vestments for the priests, so the Church, guided by God, prescribes sacred vestments to be worn by the priest of the New Law while engaged in the sacred mysteries.

The long black garment which the priest wears around the church in all the sacred functions is called a *cassock*. Kings and officers of the army wear a special uniform when performing their public duties; priests wear *cassocks* and other special garments when performing their public duties. These vestments are used to excite the minds of the faithful to the contemplation of heavenly things.

Who, for example, can behold the cross on the chasuble the priest wears without thinking of all Christ suffered for us on the cross? As the priest in celebrating Mass represents the person of Christ, and the Mass represents His passion, the vestments he wears represent those with which Christ was clothed at the time of the passion.

The first vestment the priest puts on over the *cassock* is called an *amice*. It is made of linen, and reminds us of the veil that covered the face of Jesus when His persecutors struck Him. (Luke 22:64.)

When the priest puts on the *amice* he first places it on his head, thus recalling to mind the crown of thorns that pierced the head of Jesus.

The *alb* (from *albus*, white) represents the white garment with which Christ was vested by Herod when sent back to Pilate dressed as a fool. (Luke 22:11.)

White is emblematic of purity. Hence the wearer is reminded of that purity of mind and body which he should have who serves the altar of the Most High.

The *cincture*, or girdle, as well as the *maniple* and *stole*, represent the cords and bands with which Christ was bound in the different stages of His passion. St. Matthew says in the 22nd verse of the 27th chapter, "They brought Him *bound* and delivered Him to Pontius Pilate, the governor."

The *chasuble*, or outer vestment the priest wears, represents the purple garment with which Christ was clothed as a mock king. "And they clothed Him with purple" (Mark 15:17). Upon the back of the *chasuble* you see a cross. This represents the cross Christ bore on His sacred shoulders to Calvary, and upon which He was crucified.

In these vestments, that is, in the *chasuble*, *stole*, and *maniple*, the Church uses five colors: white, red, purple, green, and black.

White, which is symbolic of purity and innocence, is used on the feasts of Our Lord, of the Blessed Virgin, of the angels, and of the saints that were not martyrs.

Red, the symbol of fortitude, is used on the feast of Pentecost, of the Exaltation of the Cross, of the apostles and martyrs.

Purple, or violet (the color of penance), is used in Advent and Lent.

Green (the color of hope) is used on all Sundays when no special feast is celebrated, except the Sundays of Lent and Advent.

Black (the color of mourning) is used on Good Friday and during the celebration of Mass for the dead.

Thus we see that each vestment and color used has a special significance.

All are calculated to attract our attention, elevate our minds to God, and fill us with a desire to do something for Him Who has done so much for us—to at least keep His commandments.

One word about the use of Latin in the celebration of Mass will perhaps be appropriate here. History tells us that when Christianity was established, the Roman Empire had control of nearly all of Europe, Asia, and Africa. Wherever the Roman flag floated to the breeze the Latin language was spoken, just as English is spoken where the sovereign of Great Britain or the President of the United States holds sway. The Church naturally adopted in her liturgy the language spoken by the people.

In the beginning of the fifth century vast hordes of barbarians began to come from the north of Europe and spread desolation over the fairest portions of the Roman Empire. Soon the Empire was broken up. New kingdoms began to be formed, new languages to be developed. The Latin finally ceased to be a living language. The Church retained it in her liturgy, 1st, because, as her doctrine and liturgy are unchangeable, she wishes the language of her doctrine and liturgy to be unchangeable; 2nd, because, as the Church is spread over the whole world, embracing in her fold children of all climes, nations, and languages—as she is universal—she must have a universal language; 3rd, because the Catholic clergy are in constant communication with the Holy See, and this requires a uniform language.

Besides, when a priest says Mass the people, by their English Missals or other prayer-books, are able to follow him from beginning to end.

The Mass is a sacrifice. The prayers of the Mass are offered to God. Hence when the priest says Mass he is speaking not to the people, but to God, to whom all languages are equally intelligible. Are not these sufficient reasons for the use of the Latin language? Are not good Catholics more attentive, more devout at Mass than others at their prayer-meetings? The good Catholic knows that the Mass represents the passion and death of Christ; that the passion and death of Christ are the sinner's only refuge, the just man's only hope; that it can not but be good and wholesome to turn our minds and our hearts toward this subject; that frequent meditation on Christ's passion will move us to avoid sin, which caused it; and that nothing can more efficaciously cause us to think of Christ's passion and death than the holy sacrifice of the Mass.

III. CEREMONIES OF THE MASS

THE Mass is the great sacrifice of the New Law. It was foreshadowed by all the sacrifices ordained by God in the Old Law. They were shadows; it is the substance.

We learn from Genesis of the fall of man. Universal tradition, as well as Scripture, informs us that the creature formerly became guilty in the eyes of the Creator. All nations, all peoples, endeavored to appease the anger of Heaven and believed that a victim was necessary for this purpose. Hence sacrifices have been offered from the beginning of the human race.

Cain and Abel offered victims; the one the first fruits of the earth, the other the firstlings of the flock. Abraham, Isaac, Jacob, and Melchisedech worshipped this way, and their worship was acceptable to God. Everywhere, even among the heathen, you find the altar, the priest, and the sacrifice. As we learn from Leviticus and other portions of the Old Testament, God Himself carefully prescribed the quality, manner, number, and place of the various sacrifices which He was pleased to accept from the hands of His chosen people. From this fact that sacrifice has ever formed a prominent feature in the worship of all people, we conclude that it belongs to the essentials of religion, and that Christians today should have an altar of which, as St. Paul says, "they can not eat who serve the tabernacle."

The sacrifices of the Old Law were provisional and prefigured the great sacrifice of the New Law foretold by the prophet Malachy. This glorious prophecy of Malachy, "From the rising of the sun even to the going down My name is great among the Gentiles; in every place there is sacrifice, and there is offered to My name a clean offering; for My name is great among the Gentiles, saith the Lord of Hosts"—this glorious prophecy is fulfilled only by the great sacrifice of the Catholic Church. We alone can say with St. Paul, *"Habemus altare."* "We have an altar" and a true sacrifice. Of all the blessings bequeathed by Jesus Christ to His Church, there is none better, none greater, none holier than the holy sacrifice of the Mass. It is the sacrifice of His own body and blood offered to the heavenly Father under the appearances of bread and wine. It was instituted by Our Lord at the Last Supper, when He took bread and wine in His sacred hands and blessed them, saying, "This is My body. . . . This is My blood. . . . Do this for a remembrance of Me."

He instituted the holy Mass in order to represent and continue the sacrifice of Calvary. St. Paul says, in his first epistle to the Corinthians, 11:26, that it was instituted to show the death of the Lord until His second coming. After the consecration, which the priest effects by saying over the bread and wine the same words which Jesus Christ said at the Last Supper, there is no longer bread and wine, but the true and living Jesus Christ, God and man, hidden under the appearances of bread and wine, just as in the manger He was hidden under the appearance of an infant. The priest offers Him up to His heavenly Father in the name of the Catholic Church, or rather He offers Himself up, and we can confidently hope that we will obtain more through prayers at the holy Mass than through our own unaided prayers. In order to have part in the holy sacrifice of the Mass a person should follow the actions and prayers of the priest, especially at the offertory, consecration, and communion; meditate on the passion of Christ; say the rosary or the prayers in the prayer-books, at the same time uniting his intention with the intention of the sacrificing priest.

The sacrifice of the Mass is a true sacrifice, because it is the oblation of a victim to God to represent by its destruction or change His supreme dominion over life and death. It is offered to satisfy our four great debts and wants: in adoration to God on account of His omnipotence, in thanksgiving for His benefits, in atonement for our sins, and to obtain His assistance in difficulties and temptations. The holy Mass obtains for us all graces and blessings, temporal and spiritual.

Since the Mass is the highest act of public worship, it is proper that it should be celebrated with fitting sacred ceremonies. Every ceremony which the Church prescribes has its deep significance. All tend to bring before our minds the mystery of the passion.

The *altar*, which is reached by means of steps, represents Mount Calvary, upon which Christ died with His arms extended as if to enfold all men as brothers. The *crucifix* recalls Jesus dying on the cross. The *lighted candles* are symbols of the faith and devotion which ought to burn in the hearts of the faithful when present at Mass. The *sacred vestments*, embroidered with the sign of the cross, indicate that the priest is the minister and visible representative of Jesus Christ, the invisible priest. The sign of the cross made many times by the priest over the host and chalice reminds us that we offer to God the divine Victim of the cross, and that we ought to unite ourselves to Him by loving the cross, by patience and Christian penance. We genuflect because Our Lord is really present. If we know He is not present on the altar we bow in honor of the place where He sometimes reposes. *Holy water* is used to signify that our souls must be pure if we wish God to answer our prayers. *Incense* is used at solemn High Mass and at Vespers. It is symbolic of prayer, agreeably to the words of the 140th psalm: "Let my prayer, O Lord, be directed as incense in Thy sight." And St. John, describing the heavenly Jerusalem in the 8th chapter of the Apocalypse, says: "Another angel came, and stood before the altar, having a golden censer; and there was given him much incense, that he should offer of the prayers of all saints upon the golden altar which is before the throne of God."

The sacrifice of the Mass, then, is the sacrifice of Calvary, since the same Victim is offered up and by the same High Priest, Jesus Christ. The Emanuel, the God with us, the thought of whom made the prophets tremble centuries before He came, that divine Teacher who loves to dwell with the children of men, the Catholic Church beholds dwelling in the midst of us on our altars. If you have visited some of our ancient cathedrals, or any of our magnificent modern churches, and admired the varied ornaments or artistic wonders therein; if you have ever been present at our religious solemnities and witnessed the gravity of our ceremonies, the beauty of the chants, the piety of the adorers; if you have reflected upon the spirit of sacrifice and self-forgetfulness so common to Catholicism and so unknown elsewhere—that spirit which moves thousands of the young of both sexes to forsake the world and devote themselves to the care of the sick, the education of the young, and to other works of charity—if you have witnessed these things and reflected upon them, you can not but have asked yourself why are such gorgeous temples built; why such magnificent works of art as displayed on the altar, the sacred vessels, paintings, and other things in the church? What prompts such sacrifices? And the answer will be, because the church is the edifice where God in the holy Mass daily renews the prodigies of His mercy, and it can never be worthy of His love; because God, who sacrificed Himself for us, is ever with us in the Blessed Sacrament of the altar, to soothe our cares and answer our prayers. Yes, the grand feature of the Catholic Church is the holy altar. On the altar is the tabernacle for the residence of the Lord of Hosts.

There our "hidden God," Jesus in the Eucharist, dwells night and day in the midst of His people, saying to them with words of love, "Come to me all you that are burdened and heavy laden, and I will refresh you."

The Mass, independent of its sacrificial aspect, consists of the best prayers ever uttered. The priest begins by making the sign of the cross, "In the name of the Father, and of the Son, and of the Holy Ghost." This sign is an epitome of the Christian's belief in the unity and trinity of God and in the incarnation and death of Jesus Christ. After making the sign of the cross he repeats the 42nd psalm, "Judge me, O God," and then makes an humble confession of his sins to God. He ascends the altar and nine times asks God to have mercy on him, *Kyrie Eleison*; then follows the beautiful hymn the shepherds heard the angels singing at the birth of the Saviour, *Gloria in Excelsis Deo*.

The prayer of the feast, the epistle and gospel follow, and then the sermon in the vernacular is usually preached. After the Nicene Creed, *Credo in Unum Deum*, the priest makes the offering of bread and wine. He then washes the tips of his fingers, saying: "I will wash my hands among the innocent," by which he is reminded to be free from stain to offer worthily the Holy Sacrifice.

The preface, canon, and solemn words of consecration follow, during which the bread and wine are changed by the power of Jesus Christ into His body and blood. In a short time he comes to the best of all prayers, the prayer taught us by Our Lord and Saviour Jesus Christ, the Our Father, *Pater Noster*. The *Agnus Dei* follows, then the communion, when he partakes of the consecrated bread and wine, and afterward gives holy communion to the faithful. He then continues the Mass, gives his blessing, and finishes the Mass with the beginning of the Gospel of St. John. Hence you see that, besides the great sacrifice which makes it an act worthy of God, the Mass consists of the best of all prayers.

From what has been said it is evident that ceremonies in the worship of God are reasonable, being sanctioned by God in the Old and New Testaments; that the holy sacrifice of the Mass is the greatest of all acts of worship; and that the Catholic Church in using ceremonies is but following the example of Our Lord and Saviour Jesus Christ and His apostles. St. John in the Book of Revelations tells us that before the throne of God angels stand with golden censers, multitudes from all nations follow and adore the Lamb, while virgins sing the new song which they alone can utter. So, too, before the throne of God on earth we swing our censers, multitudes from all nations prostrate themselves in adoration, the sweet incense of their praise and prayer ascends to the throne of grace, their minds are enlightened by God's word, while their hearts are raised to God by the grandeur of our ceremonies.

The Son of God, after having taught us by His word, shown us by His example, and merited for us by His grace the virtues necessary for salvation, wished to institute the holy sacrifice of the Mass, that He might come Himself in the Holy Sacrament and imprint them upon us. Of these virtues, the most important are *humility*, *purity*, *obedience*, *patience*, and *charity*.

Let us always ask God when present at the holy Mass for a lively faith in His *Real Presence*, an ardent love for Him in the Blessed Sacrament of the altar, and the grace to imitate His humility, His purity, His meekness, obedience, patience, and charity *here*, and enjoy His presence forever *hereafter*.

The following beautiful words of Cardinal Newman show that the Mass is something more than a mere form of words, and that ceremonies are reasonable as well as necessary in its celebration:

"To me nothing is so consoling, so piercing, so thrilling, so overcoming, as the Mass said as it is among us. I could attend Masses forever and not be tired. It is not a mere form of words—it is a great action, the greatest action that can be on earth. It is not the invocation merely, but, if I dare use the word, the evocation of the Eternal. He becomes present on the altar in flesh and blood, before Whom angels bow and devils tremble. This is that awful event which is the scope and the interpretation of every part of the solemnity. Words are necessary, but as means, not as ends; they are not mere addresses to the throne of grace, they are instruments of what is far higher, of consecration, of sacrifice.

"They hurry on as if impatient to fulfil their mission. Quickly they go, for they are awful words of sacrifice; they are a work too great to delay upon, as when it was said in the beginning, 'What thou doest, do quickly.' Quickly they pass, for the Lord Jesus goes with them, as He passed along the lake in the days of His flesh, quickly calling first one and then another; quickly they pass, because as the lightning which shineth from one part of the heaven unto the other, so is the coming of the Son of Man.

"Quickly they pass, for they are as the words of Moses, when the Lord came down in the cloud, calling on the name of the Lord as He passed by, 'The Lord, the Lord God, merciful and generous, long suffering, and abundant in goodness and truth.' And as Moses on the mountain, so we, too, make haste and bow our heads to the earth and adore.

"So we, all around, each in his place, look for the great Advent 'waiting for the moving of the water,' each in his place, with his own heart, with his own wants, with his own prayers, separate but concordant, watching what is going on, watching its progress, uniting in its consummation; not painfully, and hopelessly following a hard form of prayer from beginning to end, but like a concert of musical instruments each different, but concurring in sweet harmony, we take our post with God's priest, supporting him, yet guided by him. There are little children there, and old men, and simple laborers, and students in seminaries, priests preparing for Mass, priests making their thanksgiving, there are innocent maidens, and there are penitent sinners; but out of these many minds rises one Eucharistic hymn, and the great action is the measure and the scope of it."

The Practices of the Catholic Church

I. VESPERS AND BENEDICTION

"Remember that thou keep holy the Sabbath day" (Ex. 20:8).

*T*HIS commandment teaches us that God wills the whole Sunday to be spent in His honor. We should sanctify it by good works, and by assisting at divine service. On that day servile works and improper amusements are forbidden. A salutary rest and moderate recreation are allowed, but never at the expense of duties of obligation. After hearing Mass on Sunday morning, which is obligatory on all Catholics, there is no better way of sanctifying the remainder of the day than by attending Vespers and Benediction.

The Vesper service is a small portion of the divine office, which priests must recite daily, for God's honor and glory. It consists of five of the psalms of David (*Dixit Dominus*, Ps. 109; *Confitebor tibi*, Ps. 110; *Beatus vir*, Ps. 111; *Laudate pueri*, Ps. 112; *In exitu Israel*, Ps. 113, or *Laudate Dominum*, Ps. 116), a hymn, the *Magnificat*, or canticle of the Virgin Mary, from the first chapter of St. Luke, and some prayers. Is it not reasonable thus to praise God in psalms and hymns and spiritual canticles?

Benediction of the Blessed Sacrament usually follows
Vespers. The Catholic Church teaches that Jesus Christ is
really present in the Blessed Sacrament. The reasonableness
of this teaching will be seen in the following article.

Since Jesus Christ is present, He ought to be adored
by the faithful. Faithful adorers frequently visit Him in
the Blessed Sacrament and worship Him in "spirit and
in truth." Hence, the Blessed Sacrament is kept in the
Tabernacle on our altars to soothe our cares, answer our
prayers, and be ready at any time to be administered to the
sick and dying.

Besides our private devotion to the Blessed Sacrament,
the Church has appointed solemn rites to show publicly
our faith and devotion toward the Real Presence of Jesus
Christ. These rites are processions on Corpus Christi,
the Forty Hours' devotion, and, especially, the rite called
Benediction.

When it is time for Benediction many candles are lighted
on the altar. This is done to show our faith in the Real
Presence of Jesus Christ. If He were not present, this display
would be unreasonable, unnecessary, and meaningless. But
the candles we light, the incense we burn, the flowers and
other ornaments we use to decorate the altar, and all that
we do for Our Lord and Saviour Jesus Christ can not be
too much.

Everything being prepared, the priest takes the Blessed
Sacrament out of the tabernacle, and, placing it in the
ostensorium, exposes it on an elevated throne, while the
choir sings in honor of the Blessed Sacrament the hymn

"*O Salutaris Hostia*," "O Saving Host." The priest incenses Our Lord in the Blessed Sacrament, as, according to the Apocalypse, angels do in heaven. Another hymn or a litany follows; after which is sung the "*Tantum Ergo*," "Down in adoration falling," followed by a prayer by the priest. Then in the midst of a solemn silence (except that a small bell is tinkled) the priest takes the monstrance, or ostensorium, containing the Blessed Sacrament, and, turning toward the people, makes with it the sign of the cross over them, thus blessing the faithful with the Most Holy One.

This is certainly a most touching and impressive rite even to those who do not believe in it. Cardinal Newman calls it one of the most beautiful, natural, and soothing practices of the Church. No one will deny that this practice, or rite of the Church, is reasonable, if Jesus Christ is really present in the Blessed Sacrament. That He is really present is our belief. This being our belief, is it not reasonable to light candles as a sign of spiritual joy, and thus to show our faith in Him who is the light of the world? He gave us all that we have. He gave us the beautiful world we dwell upon with its variety of scenery—with its snow-capped mountains, its green-carpeted hills, and its blooming valleys. He has no need of our gifts; for the earth is His "and the fullness thereof." Yet as He was pleased to receive the gifts of the Magi and the precious ointment of Mary, so, too, is He pleased to receive our offerings. And is anything too good, too beautiful, too precious, for Him? Can the altar on which He dwells be too richly adorned? Are the pure candles we light, the sweet incense we burn, the choice flowers and costly ornaments with which we decorate the altar, too much to use in honor of Our Lord and our God? Yes, the Catholic practice or rite of Benediction is dictated by right reason. Everything connected with Benediction is reasonable, beautiful, and suggestive of the *noblest sentiments of the heart of man.*

II. DEVOTION TO THE BLESSED SACRAMENT

"And whilst they were at supper, Jesus took bread, and blessed, and broke, and gave to His disciples, and said: take ye and eat. This is My body" (Matt. 26:26).

*P*ERHAPS no mystery of revelation has been so universally attacked as the Real Presence of Jesus Christ in the Blessed Sacrament of the Altar.

By the Real Presence is meant that Jesus Christ is really and truly, body and blood, soul and divinity, present in the Blessed Sacrament, under the form and appearance of bread and wine.

This teaching of the Church is in perfect agreement with Scripture, tradition, and reason.

If the reader will take up his Bible and read carefully the 6th chapter of the Gospel according to St. John; the 26th chapter, 26th, 27th, and 28th verses of St. Matthew; the 14th chapter, 22nd verse of St. Mark; the First Epistle of St. Paul to the Corinthians, 10th chapter, 16th verse, as well as other portions of the New Testament, he will certainly see that the Catholic teaching and practice concerning the Real Presence of Jesus Christ in the Blessed Sacrament are founded on Scripture. In this 6th chapter of St. John, we learn that before instituting the Blessed Sacrament Our Saviour wished to announce or promise it to His disciples in order to prepare them for it. He first gave them a figure of the Blessed Sacrament in the multiplication of the five loaves of bread by which He fed five thousand persons. After this miracle He told them that He would give them bread superior to that which they had eaten, and that this bread was His own flesh and blood. "The bread that I will give is My flesh, for the life of the world." It is almost impossible to understand these words of Our Lord in any other than a literal sense. He was so understood by those who heard Him. "How can this man give us his flesh to eat?" they said, and many withdrew from Him. It is but reasonable to believe that if He did not wish to be understood in a literal sense He would have told His hearers so, rather than have them leave Him.

This promise of a doctrine so difficult to understand was fulfilled at the Last Supper.

Then Jesus took bread, and blessed, and broke, and gave to His disciples, and said: "Take ye and eat. This is My body." And taking the chalice He gave thanks; and gave to them, saying: "Drink ye all of this. For this is My blood of the new testament which shall be shed for many for the remission of sins."

"Do this for a commemoration of Me."

These are substantially the words of SS. Matthew, Mark, Luke, and of the apostle Paul.

In the 10th chapter of the First Epistle to the Corinthians,

St. Paul says: "The chalice of benediction which we bless, is it not the communion of the blood of Christ? And the bread which we break, is it not the partaking of the body of the Lord?"

Any one of these texts abundantly proves the Catholic doctrine of the Real Presence, and shows the reasonableness of the Catholic practice regarding the Blessed Sacrament. Reflect upon them. Reflect especially upon the words of Christ, "This is My body." Think what an insult it is to the divinity and veracity of Christ to doubt His word, because you can not understand how what appears to be bread is in reality His own body and blood.

If you remember that Jesus Christ is God, that He had the power to make this change, that He could confer this power on others, as the apostles and their successors, that He did so when He said: "Do this in commemoration of Me," and that this change at the present time as at the time of the apostles is made by His almighty power, you will have no difficulty in believing it.

The belief and practice of the Catholic Church of today regarding the Blessed Sacrament is the same as it was in every age since the time of Christ. The history of every century tells us this. The Fathers, Doctors, and Church writers of every age say the same. If it were not so, some one ought to be able to find the time when the doctrine was invented, and the person who invented it. But, since no one has been able to find the inventor of this doctrine and practice, the time or place of the invention, we rightly conclude that they came down to us from the time of Christ, and had Christ for an author. (Berengarius, in the eleventh century, was the first who denied this doctrine.) If, then, Christ is the author, is not the Catholic practice reasonable?

But I don't understand the Catholic doctrine regarding the Blessed Sacrament, some one may say; therefore it is contrary to reason. Dear reader, did the consummate puerility, silliness, foolishness of such an objection ever present itself to you? Do you understand the Blessed Trinity? And is it contrary to reason? No. Although above reason, it is not against it. Do you understand how Jesus Christ is both God and man? Do you understand any mystery? No. If you did it would no longer be a mystery. For a mystery is something above human intelligence. It is something incomprehensible to us, for it pertains to the divine intelligence. And as well might you attempt to pour the mighty ocean into a small hole on the shore, as attempt to hold with your limited capacity the illimitable ocean of divinity. The proper office of reason is to examine the evidences of revelation, and see if God has spoken. But it constitutes no part of its office to dispute the word of God. That God has spoken is evident from the fulfilment of many prophecies and the authority of many miracles. That these prophecies have been fulfilled, and these miracles performed, is as certain as is any historical fact. Reason teaches us this. It teaches us, too, that no one but God (or by the power of God) can prophesy; no one but God can derogate from the order of nature, by the performance of a miracle. Reason teaches us, then, that God has spoken. When we know God speaks, genuine reason will dictate that we humbly believe His holy word. Thus will true reason ever act. And when God says, "This is My body," it will not hesitate to believe.

We all believe that at the baptism of Our Saviour by St.John Baptist, the Holy Ghost appeared in the form of a dove. Now, is it not as reasonable for Jesus Christ, the second person of the Blessed Trinity, to appear in the form of bread as it was for the Holy Ghost, the third person of the Trinity, to appear in the form of a dove? We must therefore admit that the Catholic doctrine of the Real Presence of Jesus Christ in the Blessed Sacrament is reasonable; that it has been believed by the Christian Church of every age from the time of Christ until the present time; and that it is taught by SS. Matthew, Mark, Luke, and John, and by St. Paul in clear and unmistakable terms.

Now, dear reader, since Jesus Christ is really present, is not the Catholic practice regarding the Blessed Sacrament reasonable? Should we not honor Our Lord and Our God? Should we not adore Him as really present in the Blessed Sacrament? Should we not frequently receive Him with pure and contrite hearts? Should we not, when we enter the church, genuflect, bend the knee in His honor? Should we not show Him every mark of respect and devotion? Can we do too much in His honor? Let us, then, adore Our Lord and Our God, for we are His people and the sheep of His pasture. Let us return love for love to the great King of suffering, who was born for love of us, who died for love of us, and who, for love of us, remains ever with us in the Blessed Sacrament. Let us ask that our faith and love may persevere to the end; that loving and adoring Him here in the Blessed Sacrament of His love, *we may be united with Him forever hereafter*.

III. HOLY COMMUNION

"He that eateth this bread shall live forever" (John 6:59)

$\mathcal{H}$OLY communion is receiving the body and blood of Christ in the Blessed Sacrament. The clergy when saying Mass, except on Good Friday, receive under both forms. When not celebrating Mass, they receive only the one kind, the consecrated bread. In the early ages of the Church communion was given to the people under both forms.

The faithful, however, could, if they wished, dispense with one form and receive under the form of bread. This shows that the Church always taught that Christ is entire both under the form of bread and under the form of wine. At one time the faithful received under both forms; now they receive under one form, the form of bread. It is merely a matter of discipline, which the Church could change, if circumstances demanded it. Whether you receive under one form or both, you receive whole and entire the body and blood of Christ. This is clearly taught by St. Paul in the 11th chapter of the First Epistle to the Corinthians, where he says: "Whosoever shall eat this bread, *or* drink the chalice of the Lord *unworthily*, shall be guilty of the body *and* blood of the Lord."

How could a person eating that bread unworthily be guilty of the body and blood of the Lord, unless the body and blood of the Lord were there under the form of bread?

Since Jesus Christ is whole and entire under the form of bread, as well as under the form of wine, the practice of the Catholic Church of giving holy communion under one form is reasonable.

Good Christians frequently receive their Lord and their God in holy communion. He inspires them with feelings of love, gratitude, and adoration. He reminds them to think frequently of their Creator—to give Him their first thoughts in the morning and their last in the evening. He gives them strength to restrain their guilty passions.

Holy Communion is the seed of immortality. "He that eateth this bread *shall live forever.*"

IV. CONFIRMATION

"Then they laid their hands upon them, and they received the Holy Ghost" (Acts 8:17).

*B*EFORE the coming of the Holy Ghost on Pentecost, the apostles were weak and vacillating. One of them betrayed his Master for thirty pieces of silver; another—the Prince of the Apostles, he whom Christ afterward made head of His Church—thrice denied his Lord and his God.

After the descent of the Holy Ghost, what a change! What a wonderful transformation! They who before had been as timid as the lamb, as changeable as the chameleon's hue, became now as bold as the lion, as firm as Gibraltar's rock.

In a similar way does Confirmation act on the receiver. Confirmation is that sacrament in which, by the imposition of the bishop's hands, we receive the Holy Ghost to make us strong and perfect Christians and soldiers of Jesus Christ. It is the second in the order of the sacraments, because the early Christians were accustomed to receive it immediately after Baptism. In the 8th chapter of the Acts of the Apostles we find the first recorded instance of the administering of Confirmation by the apostles. Here we are told that St. Peter and St. John confirmed the Samaritans who had been baptized by Philip. "They prayed for them that they might receive the Holy Ghost. . . . Then they laid their hands upon them, and they received the Holy Ghost." In a similar way does the bishop, the successor of the apostles, administer Confirmation at the present day. First, he turns toward those to be confirmed and says: "May the Holy Ghost come down upon you and the power of the Most High keep you from sin." Then extending his hands over them he prays that they may receive the Holy Ghost.

In the 6th verse of the 19th chapter of the Acts the sacred writer, after telling about the baptism of the disciples at Ephesus, adds: "And when Paul had laid his hands upon them the Holy Ghost came on them." In the 6th chapter of the Epistle to the Hebrews St. Paul mentions Confirmation, the laying on of hands, with Baptism and Penance, as among the principal practices of Christianity.

The sacrament of Confirmation has been administered to the faithful of every age from the time of Christ until the present. We learn this from the Fathers and writers of the various ages. Among them St. Clement says: "All must make haste to be confirmed by a bishop, and receive the sevenfold grace of the Holy Ghost." The practice of administering Confirmation is founded on tradition, then, as well as on Scripture. Is it not reasonable to believe and practise that which the Christian Church of every age believed and practised?

The apostles of Christ administered Confirmation by praying that the faithful may receive the Holy Ghost and laying their hands upon them. The successors of the apostles do likewise. Who will say that this practice is not reasonable? Baptism gives spiritual life; Confirmation increases it. Baptism makes persons children of God; Confirmation strengthens them, causes them to grow, and makes them strong men and soldiers of Jesus Christ.

All the morality of life is implied in the sacrament of Confirmation. It strengthens man, it gives him courage to confess God; and as sin is the denial of God, whoever has courage to confess *God will practice virtue*.

V. HONORING THE BLESSED VIRGIN

"The angel Gabriel was sent from God . . . to a Virgin . . . and the Virgin's name was Mary. And the angel being come in said to her: Hail, full of grace, the Lord is with thee; blessed art thou among women" (Luke 1:26, 28).

"From henceforth all generations shall call me blessed" (Luke 1:48).

*T*HESE words from St. Luke show that the Catholic practice of honoring Mary is scriptural. We alone fulfill the prophecy, "From henceforth all generations shall call me blessed." If Mary was so pure that the archangel Gabriel could salute her as full of grace; if she was so perfect as to be honored, respected, and loved by her divine Son, Jesus Christ, is it not reasonable that we, too, should honor, respect, and love her?

How we honor the sword of Washington! What a cluster of tender recollections clings to the staff of Franklin! Is there a loyal American citizen who does not think with feelings of love and respect of the mother of our Revolutionary hero, or who would not doff his hat at the unveiling of a statue of the sage of Monticello? And why? Is it on account of their intrinsic merit? No. We honor them principally on account of the relation they bear to those three brightest stars in the American firmament. So it is with the honor we show to Mary, the Mother of God. Although she was an example of all virtues, we honor her principally because it was through her instrumentality He was born by whom we achieved not civil liberty, but the liberty of the children of God. She did not draw lightning from heaven, nor the scepter from kings; but she brought forth Him who is the Lord of heaven and King of kings.

The principal reason, then, why we honor Mary is because she is the Mother of Our Lord and Saviour Jesus Christ. This honor consists of love, respect, and veneration. We love her with an interior love, a love proceeding from the heart; nor should we fear to let this love appear outwardly. When others revile her, speak disrespectfully of her, we should shrink from the very idea of acting similarly toward her. We should then remember that she is the Mother of Our Saviour, and should ask ourselves how we would have acted toward her had we lived in her day and been witnesses of the honor shown her by her divine Son. By so doing we will show her that love which is her due. Our respect, our veneration for her, should be affectionate and deep. When we remember that it was her hand that first lifted from the ground and received in maternal embrace the sacred body of Jesus, just born and just dead; when we think how respectfully Elizabeth greeted her; when we recall to mind the reverent salutation of the archangel; when we consider the honor shown her by the apostles and by her own divine Son, can we help feeling a deep love, respect, and veneration for her? You see, dear reader, honoring Mary is scriptural and reasonable.

But if we should honor her principally because she is the Mother of God, we should also honor her because she is the peerless glory, the matchless jewel of her sex. She constitutes a sole exception to a general law. Sin never contaminated, never touched her fair soul. This is what we mean by the Immaculate Conception.

God created the first man free from sin. But he transgressed the law of God, and, by his transgression, all his posterity are born in sin and conceived in iniquity. For St. Paul says: "By one man sin entered into this world, and by sin death; and so death passed upon all men, in whom all have sinned" (Rom. 5:12). But God promised that the woman, Mary, should crush the head of the serpent. Now if she was to crush the head of the serpent, it was fit that she should never be under his power, that she should be pure, free from sin of every kind.

There have been exceptions to all general laws. At the time of the deluge Noe was saved. Lot was saved from the destruction of Sodom. In like manner, the Blessed Virgin is an exception to the general law that all sinned in Adam. Isaias and St. John Baptist were sanctified in their mother's womb. Was it any more difficult for God to sanctify Mary at the moment of her conception, at the moment of the union of her soul with her body? God chose His own Mother. If He had the power to choose her did He not also have the power to preserve her from original sin? And does it not appear to you most fitting that God, the Holy Ghost, should preserve His spouse, and God, the Son, His Mother, from sin of every kind?

"Hail, full of grace," the angel said to her. If she was full of grace, no vacancy was left for sin. Grace denotes the absence of sin, as light denotes the absence of darkness. Hence if Mary was full of grace, she was never subject to sin; she was always pure and her conception immaculate. It is but natural, then, that we arrive at the belief in the Immaculate Conception, at the belief in the sinlessness, the spotlessness of the Blessed Virgin from the very beginning of her existence. If we honor Mary principally because the angel honored her, because God honored her, we honor her, also, because of her immaculate conception and total freedom from sin. She was a model of all virtues. Is it not reasonable, then, to honor Mary, to love her, and to believe that she loves us? If we honor the good and virtuous, where can we find a nobler example of virtue than Mary? What a beautiful model Mary is for Christians, and especially for Christian women! Good Catholic mothers are continually urging upon their daughters the necessity of choosing as a model Mary, the true type of female excellence. In Mary you find all that is tender, loving, constant, and true. In her you find all virtues. In her humility she refused the highest honors; while in patience she endured more anguish and agony than any other creature on earth.

Mary is a creature of God. As the praise we bestow on a beautiful picture redounds to the glory of the artist, so the honor we give Mary redounds to God, since we honor her for His sake. Let us honor her. That person who honors the Blessed Virgin; who loves, respects, and venerates her as the Mother of God; who takes her as a model and imitates her virtues; who prays to her in trials and afflictions and asks her intercession with her divine Son, does not only act in a reasonable manner, but such action is certain to make the path through this world smooth and easy and at the same time safe to a life of *eternal happiness*.

VI. CONFESSION OF SIN

"Whom when He saw He said: Go, show yourselves to the priests" (Luke 17:14).

"Receive ye the Holy Ghost; whose sins ye shall forgive, they are forgiven them, and whose sins ye shall retain, they are retained" (John 20:23).

*T*HE whole of the life of Our Lord and Saviour Jesus Christ may be summed up in these words of the Acts: "He went about doing good." He healed the sick, gave sight to the blind, hearing to the deaf, and raised the dead to life.

The healing of the body, however, was to Him a secondary object. The healing of the soul was His mission on earth. He frequently called the attention of His followers to this. For example, He cured the man of the palsy to prove that as man He had the power to forgive sins. Another example is when He gives us in the cure of the lepers a figure of sin and its cure.

Leprosy has always been considered a figure of sin. As leprosy covers the body and makes it disgusting and frightful to behold, so sin covers the soul and makes it hideous in the sight of God. The Old Law required lepers to separate themselves from society until their cure was certified to by the priests who were appointed for this purpose. Our Lord has been pleased, in the New Law, to institute a similar method for the cure of the more fatal leprosy of sin. The spiritual leper, the sinner, is to show himself to the priest, make known the diseased state of his soul, and submit to the inspection and treatment of the priest, who is the divinely appointed physician of the soul. But should we not go directly to God, since God alone has power to justify us? It is true, God alone can effect our justification; but He has appointed the priest to judge in His place and pass sentence in His name. To the priests He has said: "Whatsoever you shall bind upon earth shall be bound in heaven, and whatsoever you shall loose upon earth shall be loosed also in heaven" (Matt. 18:18); and again: "Whose sins you shall forgive, they are forgiven, and whose sins you shall retain, they are retained" (John 20:23). These two texts clearly show that auricular confession as practised in the Catholic Church was taught by Christ. For how could the apostles and their successors, the pastors of the Church, know what sins to bind and retain and what sins to loose and forgive unless the sins were confessed to them and they were allowed to judge?

No matter how numerous or how great these are, provided they are confessed with a sincere repentance, they will be forgiven. And they will be forgiven by the power of the priest. Properly speaking, God alone has power to forgive sins. But no one will deny that He has power to confer this power on others. He communicated this power to His apostles and commanded them, in turn, to communicate it to others by means of the Sacrament of Holy Orders.

That Our Saviour communicated this power to His apostles is evident from the words of St. John: "As the Father hath sent Me I also send you. Receive ye the Holy Ghost; whose sins you shall forgive, they are forgiven." But sin was to continue till the end of the world. Hence the necessity of the means of forgiving sin being coextensive with sin. As the people receive from the priests the Word of God and the cleansing from sin in Baptism, so also do they receive from them the cleansing from sin in confession.

It is certain that the apostles conferred the power of forgiving sins upon others, if we find that those whom the apostles ordained exercised this power. But we find this to be the case.

From the time of Christ until the present the writers of every age tell us that confession of sins was practised. St. John, who lived until the beginning of the second century, says in the 1st chapter of his First Epistle: "If we *confess* our sins, He is faithful and just to forgive us our sins and to cleanse us from all iniquity."

St. Cyprian, who wrote in the third century, says: "Let each of you confess his faults, and the pardon imparted by the priest is acceptable before God."

St. Ambrose, in the fourth century, wrote: "The poison is sin; the remedy, the accusation of one's crime. The poison is iniquity: confession is the remedy."

St. Augustine, who lived in the fifth century, seems to be talking to some people of the present day, who say they confess in private to God, when he says: "Let no one say to himself, I do penance to God in private, I do it before God. Is it then in vain that Christ hath said: 'Whatsoever thou shalt loose on earth shall be loosed in heaven'? Is it in vain that the keys have been given to the Church? Do we make void the Gospel? void the words of Christ?"

These first five centuries were the golden age of Christianity. All admit that the doctrines and practices of those early centuries were pure and undefiled, as they came from Christ. But among the practices of the time we find confession. Hence it is a reasonable practice, because conformable to Christ's teaching. We might continue quotations from writers of every century from the sixth to the nineteenth, showing that the teaching and practice of confession did not vary through the lapse of ages from the time of Christ until the present day. But this is unnecessary. The quotations from the first five centuries show that the power of forgiving sin was not only communicated by Christ to His apostles, but by them to their successors by means of the sacrament of Holy Orders. What would be the necessity of this power if they could not exercise it in confession? If, as some say, priests invented confession, some one ought to find out and tell us when and where it was invented, and why they did not exempt themselves from such a humiliating practice.

Confession alone, however, will be of no avail without contrition. Contrition is a sincere sorrow and detestation for sin with a firm determination to sin no more. To the truly humble and sorrowful sinner confession is not a punishment, but a remedy for a tortured conscience. The most painful secret to be kept by a heart not yet corrupted by disease is the secret of sin and crime. The soul that loves God hates sin and desires to separate herself from it. To this desire is associated the desire of expiating it. All, from the mother who questions her child about wrongdoing to the judge who interrogates the criminal, recognize in spontaneous confession an expiatory power.

Confession, it is true, is necessarily accompanied by shame and humiliation. This humiliation is diminished by the knowledge that it is of divine origin and that eternal silence is divinely imposed upon him who receives it. Priests never divulge what they know from the confessional. They have been ill-treated, as was Father Kohlmann in this country; have even been tortured and cruelly put to death, as was St.

John Nepomucene, in order to extort from them knowledge they gained in the confessional, but without avail. For what they knew through the tribunal of penance, they knew as ministers of God. And as it is better to obey God than man, no minister of state could force them to divulge that which the laws of God forbid.

Only sinners, who after a thorough preparation, a sincere sorrow, and a good confession, can realize the soothing and beneficial effects of confession, and feel with David, "Blessed are they whose sins are forgiven." If you have ever noticed such after leaving the confessional you could see joy beaming on their countenances, as if a heavy burden had been removed.

Confession quiets the conscience. But this is only one of the benefits it confers upon those who practise going to confession. It has also a salutary influence upon their morals; for one of its necessary conditions is promise of amendment.

The pagans of the first centuries were aware of the guiding and reforming power of the confessional. Voltaire, the leading infidel of the last century, one who made sport of everything Christian, says that "there is, perhaps, no wiser institution, and that confession is an excellent thing, a restraint upon inveterate crime, a very good practice to prevent the guilty from falling into despair and relapsing into sin, to influence hearts full of hate to forgive and robbers to make restitution—that the enemies of the *Romish* Church who have opposed so beneficial an institution have taken from man the greatest restraint that can be put upon crime." While his everyday experience forced these words of praise from the arch-infidel, his hatred of the Church creeps out in the word "Romish."

Confession of sin, as we have seen, is a *reasonable practice*, because it was taught by Jesus Christ, and by His apostles and their successors from Christ's time until the present; but *especially* because it has the power of soothing and pacifying the conscience by freeing it from the torture of sin, the poison of crime. It is not strange, then, that it is so dear to virtuous souls. It is offensive only to those whose hearts are so hardened as to blunt the sting of remorse. Confession is Christianity using its moral power to correct and perfect the individual. In the confessional the minister of God is continually coming in contact with hearts in which reigns an idol that he overthrows, a bad practice that he causes to cease, or some injustice that he has repaired.

Confession is one of the gates by which Christianity penetrates the interior man, wipes away stains, heals diseases, and sows therein the seeds of virtue. The lives and experience of millions are witness of the truth of this. Is it not, then, a reasonable, a beneficial practice? It is only the malicious or the ignorant who calumniate the practice and the consecrated minister who sits in judgment in the sacred tribunal. Those who lay aside their prejudice and study the question soon become convinced of its divine origin. A little study and reflection will show them that confession of sin benefits society by preventing crimes that would destroy government, cause riots, and fill prisons; that it promotes human justice, makes men better, nobler, purer, higher, and more Godlike; that it soothes the sorrowful heart whose crime might make the despairing suicide; and that individuals and families who frequently, intelligently, and properly approach this fountain of God's grace will receive His blessing here *and a pledge of His union hereafter.*

VII. GRANTING INDULGENCES

"Whatsoever you shall bind upon earth shall be bound in heaven, and whatsoever you shall loose upon earth shall be loosed also in heaven" (Matt 18:18).

*O*F THE many practices of the Church, few have been the cause of more controversy than that of granting indulgences. Though not the cause, the granting of an indulgence furnished a pretext for Luther's apostasy. Leo X, who was Pope at that time, desiring to complete St. Peter's at Rome, appealed to all Catholics for financial aid. There was certainly nothing wrong in this. With these alms it was intended that the most magnificent Christian temple in the world would be completed.

"Majesty, Power, Glory, Strength, and Beauty, all are aisled
In this eternal ark of worship undefiled."

All who contributed toward the completion of St. Peter's and complied with the necessary conditions were granted an indulgence.

The alms were not one of the indispensable conditions. Those conditions were a sincere repentance and confession. Hence, those who did not contribute could gain the indulgence. Perhaps the Dominican Tetzel, who was chosen to announce the indulgence, exceeded his powers and made them serve his own ends.

His action in the affair was not approved by Rome. If it is certain that the Pope did nothing wrong in asking for aid to build that beautiful monument to religion, it is equally certain that he did nothing wrong, that he did not exceed the limits of his powers when he granted the indulgence. In order to understand this, we must have a clear idea of what is meant by an indulgence.

You frequently hear it said that it is the forgiveness of sin, or that it is a permission given to commit sin. It is neither the one nor the other. An indulgence is not the forgiveness of sin. In fact, an indulgence can not be gained until sin has been forgiven. One of the necessary conditions for gaining an indulgence is confession.

Neither is an indulgence a license, a permission to commit sin. No one, not even God Himself, could give permission to commit sin. For God is all good, and although all powerful He can not sanction that which is evil in itself. It would be contrary to His very nature. An indulgence, then, is not what it has been painted. Having seen what an indulgence is not, let us see what it is. It is a remission of the whole or a part of the debt of temporal punishment due to sin after the guilt and eternal punishment have been forgiven in the sacrament of Penance.

In the early ages of the Church notorious sinners, after being absolved, were sentenced to long public penances. By sincere sorrow, an indulgence or remission of some of the time was granted them. Public confession and public penances have passed away. These public penances are replaced by pious devotions. Upon the performance of certain pious devotions the Church at times grants an indulgence; that is, a remission of such temporal punishment as is equivalent to the canonical penances corresponding to the sins committed.

Attached to every mortal sin, besides the guilt, is the punishment incurred. This punishment is eternal and temporal. That there is this twofold punishment we learn from various places in the Bible. We have an example in the sin of David. God sent the prophet Nathan to warn him of his guilt. When Nathan rebuked the king, he confessed his sin with signs of true contrition. Then Nathan told him that God had forgiven his sin, but that many temporal punishments would follow. When God forgave the sin, the guilt and eternal punishment were taken away; but temporal punishment remained. Other examples could be cited, but this is sufficient to show that there is a twofold kind of punishment: eternal and temporal. In confession the guilt and eternal punishment are taken away, but not always the temporal punishment. This temporal punishment is what is taken away in whole by a plenary and in part by a partial indulgence.

In a similar manner we have a twofold punishment attached to crime in this world. A man commits a crime. He is sentenced to a term in the penitentiary. After spending his time of punishment he comes back to society, but finds he has another punishment to undergo in being avoided by his friends and others.

The practice of granting indulgences was founded on

many passages of Scripture, both of the Old and New Testament. In the 12th chapter of the book of Numbers we learn that Mary, the sister of Moses, was forgiven a sin which she had committed. But God inflicted upon her the penalty of leprosy. This was a temporal punishment. By the prayer of Moses an indulgence was granted; for God took away the temporal punishment.

Our divine Lord left with His Church the power of granting indulgences, as we learn from His words taken from St. Matthew: "Whatsoever you shall loose upon earth shall be loosed also in heaven." This promise implies the power of loosing not only from sin and its eternal punishment, but also the power of releasing the bond of temporal punishment, of freeing from everything that would prevent the soul from entering the kingdom of heaven. St. Paul granted an indulgence to the incestuous Corinthian, as we learn from the 2nd chapter of his Second Epistle to the Corinthians. By the power and authority which he received from Christ, he granted the Corinthian pardon from performing a certain penance. This penance was a temporal punishment. The apostle took away the temporal punishment. That is an indulgence.

Non-Catholics grant a kind of plenary indulgence to every one by saying that works of penance are unnecessary. The practice of the Catholic Church of granting an indulgence only to the deserving is certainly more conformable to Scripture as well as more reasonable.

Experience teaches us the utility of indulgences. They encourage the faithful to frequent the sacraments, to repent, to do acts of penance, and perform works of piety, charity, and devotion.

A practice productive of such beneficial results is reasonable; it is also reasonable because it is sanctioned by Scripture and the Church of every age. For God would not sanction it nor could the Church practise it if it were *not conformable to reason*.

VIII. THE LAST SACRAMENTS

"Is any man sick among you? Let him bring in the priests of the Church, and let them pray over him, anointing him with oil in the name of the Lord: And the prayer of faith shall save the sick man, and the Lord shall raise him up, and if he be in sins they shall be forgiven him" (James 5:14, 15).

*B*Y THESE words St. James admonishes Christians when sick to do that which Our Saviour had previously directed to be done. This you will learn from the 6th chapter of St. Mark: "And [the apostles] anointed with oil many that were sick."

The historians of the first centuries tell us that the early Christians were as anxious to receive the last sacraments as are the Catholics of our own day. St. Cesarius, in the fifth century, writes: "As soon as a person falls dangerously sick, he receives the body and blood of Jesus Christ. Then his body is anointed, and thus is fulfilled what stands written: 'Is any man sick among you? Let him call in the priests of the Church, and let them pray over him, anointing him with oil.'" What the Christians of the first centuries did, we do; and we do it by the direction of Jesus Christ and of St. James.

Penance, Holy Eucharist, and Extreme Unction are administered to the sick and are known as the last sacraments. The priest first hears the sick person's confession, then he administers holy communion. Afterward he administers the sacrament of Extreme Unction—last anointing.

This sacrament aids the sick to bear their sufferings with patience. It wipes away sin, even mortal sin if the person is unable to confess; and it purifies the soul for its entrance into heaven. The other sacraments assist us in making our lives holy like the life of our divine Model. This sacrament assists in making our death holy, like the death of Jesus. The sacrament of Baptism met us at our entrance into this world; the sacrament of Extreme Unction will be our guide at our departure to the other world. Religion, which rocked us in the cradle of life, will lull us to sleep in the cradle of death.

Go to the bedside of the dying Catholic and you will see the reasonableness of the practice of calling the priest to administer the last sacraments. After the sacraments have been administered, peace and joy and contentment are visible on the countenance of the sick person. He clings no more to the things of earth. His thoughts are centered in heaven. The minister of God consoles him with the thought of immortality and the resurrection of the body. He soon hears the singing of the angelic choir; and breathing the sweet names of Jesus, Mary, and Joseph, his soul takes its flight to the *regions of eternal bliss.*

IX. PRAYING FOR THE DEAD

"It is therefore a holy and wholesome thought to pray for the dead, that they may be loosed from their sins" (2 Mach. 12:46).

*N*O ONE will deny that the practice of praying for the dead is reasonable, if the dead are benefited by our prayers. That our prayers are beneficial to the departed we will endeavor to show. We are taught by revelation that besides heaven and hell, a state of everlasting pleasure and a state of eternal pain, there also exists a middle state of punishment for those who die in venial sin, or who have not sufficiently satisfied the justice of God for mortal sins already forgiven.

The people of God in the Old Law believed, and Jesus Christ and His apostles in the New Law taught, the existence of this middle state. In the Second Book of Machabees, quoted above, we read that the pious general Judas Machabeus having made a collection, "sent twelve thousand drachmas of silver to Jerusalem for sacrifices to be offered for the dead [soldiers], thinking well and religiously concerning the resurrection [for if he had not hoped that they that were slain should rise again, it would have seemed superfluous and vain to pray for the dead], and because he considered that they who had fallen asleep with godliness had great grace laid up for them. It is, therefore, a holy and wholesome thought to pray for the dead that they may be loosed from their sins." If prayers were not beneficial to the dead, God would not have sanctioned them.

This is exactly the practice of the Catholic Church. We pray and offer sacrifices for the souls in purgatory, just as Judas Machabeus did. Even if the Books of Machabees were not inspired, it is historically true that the Jews and almost all nations of antiquity believed in the existence of purgatory and the utility of prayers for the souls detained there. This universal consent is the voice of nature and of God. Hence we see that the practice of praying for the dead is reasonable.

This practice is in accordance with the teaching of Christ. In the 12th chapter, 32nd verse, of St. Matthew, He says: "He that shall speak against the Holy Ghost, it shall not be forgiven him, neither in this world nor in the world to come."

These words teach us that some sins will be pardoned in the life to come. They can not be pardoned in heaven, since nothing defiled can enter heaven; nor can they be pardoned in hell, out of which there is no redemption, for "their worm shall not die, and their fire shall not be quenched." Therefore, there must be a state in the next world where sins will be forgiven, and we call that place or state purgatory. And the existence of purgatory implies the necessity of praying for those detained there. The belief in the existence of purgatory and the practice of praying for the faithful departed have existed in the Church from the time of its foundation.

Tertullian, who lived in the second century, considered it a solemn duty, whose obligation came down from the apostles, to offer sacrifices and prayers for the faithful departed. St. Augustine says: "The whole Church received from the tradition of the Fathers to pray for those who died in the communion of the body and blood of Christ." The dying request of St. Monica, the mother of St. Augustine, is well known. "I request you," she said, "that wherever you may be, you will remember me at the altar of the Lord." And he assures us that he frequently and fervently prayed for her soul.

The teaching of the Church of every age confirms the teaching of the Old and New Testament regarding purgatory and praying for the dead. To one who believes in heaven and hell, a place of eternal pleasure and of eternal punishment, the doctrine of purgatory must appear as a necessity, and the practice of praying for the dead reasonable. For it is certain that nothing defiled can enter heaven. But it is possible that many die guilty of but slight sins. Therefore, it must be said that these are damned, which is impious and absurd; that what is defiled can enter heaven, which is unscriptural; or that there is a purgatory, a state in which such souls are made pure as the driven snow, so that they can enter into the presence of their Maker. For an infinitely just God can not condemn to the same eternal punishment the child who dies guilty of a slight fault and the hardened murderer. No. He will render to every one according to his works.

The doctrine of purgatory, then, is reasonable as well as scriptural and traditional. Reasonable, too, is the practice of praying for the dead, for they are still members of the Church. All the members of the Church, consisting of the church militant on earth, the church triumphant in heaven, and the church suffering in purgatory, are one family bound together by the bond of charity. The members of the Church on earth pray to those in heaven, who love us and pray for us; and we pray for those in purgatory. They are God's friends deprived of heaven for a time. As those in heaven rejoice when one sinner does penance, so those in purgatory hear us, see us, love us, and are helped by our prayers. We love them and never cease to pray for them and offer the Holy Sacrifice for them. Even the unbeliever will stand or kneel by the remains of his departed friend and offer a prayer for him, thus showing that praying for the dead is reasonable and the natural dictate of the human heart.

X. PRAYING TO THE SAINTS

"And may the angel that delivereth me from all evils bless these boys" (Gen. 48:16).

"So I say to you there shall be joy before the angels of God upon one sinner doing penance" (Luke 15:10).

"For in the resurrection they [the saints] shall be as the angels of God in heaven" (Matt. 22:10).

*T*HE saints are friends of God. They are like the angels in heaven. We honor them, not as we honor God, but on account of the relation they bear to God. They are creatures of God, the work of His hands. When we honor them, we honor God; as when we praise a beautiful painting, we praise the artist.

We do not believe that the saints can help us of themselves. But we ask them to "pray for us." We believe that everything comes to us "through Our Lord Jesus Christ." With these words all our prayers end. It is useful, salutary, and reasonable to pray to the saints and ask them to pray for us. No doubt all will admit the reasonableness of this practice if the saints can hear and help us.

That they hear and help us is evident from many passages of Scripture. The patriarch Jacob would not have prayed to the angel to bless his grandchildren Manasses and Ephraim (as we learn he did from Genesis, chapter 48), unless he knew the angel could do so.

We are informed (Luke 15) that the angels rejoice when one sinner does penance. We are also informed (Matt. 22) that the saints are like the angels—*i.e.*, have the same happiness and knowledge.

Hence the saints, as well as the angels, can hear us, can help us, and are acquainted with our actions, words, and thoughts.

It is generally conceded that it is reasonable to ask pious persons on earth to pray for us. St. Paul, in his epistles, frequently asks the Christians to pray for him. "Brethren," he says, "pray for us." It is well known that God was pleased to answer the prayer of Abraham in favor of Abimelech. "More things are wrought by prayer than this world knows of." Now, if we poor sinners here on earth do not pray in vain for one another, will the saints in heaven, the friends of God, who rejoice when a sinner does penance, pray in vain for us? No. We have hosts of friends in heaven to speak a good word for us. And as a child who has disobeyed his parents wisely asks a better brother or sister to intercede with his parents for mercy, so, too, having disobeyed our heavenly Father by sin, we have recourse to others better than ourselves, to our better brothers and sisters, the Blessed Virgin and saints, to intercede with God for us.

Is not this a reasonable practice?

If your mother or sister crosses the sea she will continue to pray for you. And if she crosses the sea of death will she forget you? No. The love she bore you here will continue in heaven. She will pray for you, and the "Lord will hear the prayers of the just." Ask the saints to pray to your God and their God for you. Honor God by honoring His friends and asking their intercession. And all your friends in heaven will unite in praying to the Father of us all that one day all who love God and His friends, the saints, may be admitted with them into the *company of the Saint of saints, Our Lord and Saviour Jesus Christ.*

XI. CRUCIFIXES, RELICS, AND IMAGES

"Thou shalt not make to thyself a graven thing, nor the likeness of anything that is in the heaven above, or in the earth beneath, nor of those things that are in the waters under the earth. Thou shalt not adore them nor serve them" (Ex. 20:4, 5).

*T*HIS first commandment teaches us to adore God alone. It does not forbid the making of images, but it forbids the adoring of them, worshipping them as gods. This would be idolatry. If the making of images were forbidden, it would be improper to have images or pictures of our friends.

It has frequently been said that Catholics are idolaters, because they have in their churches crucifixes, relics, and images of the saints, which they honor. Perhaps many of those who accuse us of idolatry, if asked, could not tell what idolatry is. Idolatry is giving to a creature (whether a crucifix, an image, or any created thing) that honor which belongs to God.

The honor we give those sacred things is a relative honor. We honor them on account of the relation they bear to God and His friends, the saints.

Every Catholic, even the child, is taught the difference between the idol of the pagan and a Catholic image. Pagans looked upon their idols as gods. They thought these senseless objects had power, intelligence, and other attributes of the Deity. They worshiped them as gods and thought they could assist them. Hence they were image-worshipers or idolaters.

Catholics know full well that images have no intelligence to understand, no power to assist them. They do not adore nor serve them. That would be idolatry. It would be breaking the first commandment. They do not say when praying before the crucifix or image of a saint, "I adore thee, O Crucifix"; nor "Help me, O Image," But they say, "I adore thee, O God, whose cruel death is represented by this crucifix," or "Pray for me, O saint represented by this image."

We have images, pictures, and relics of Our Lord, His Blessed Mother, and the saints, for the same reason that we have relics and portraits of George Washington, Abraham Lincoln, or of our relatives and friends. They remind us of the original. Who can look upon the crucifix or upon a picture of the Crucifixion without being reminded of all the sufferings of Our Lord and Saviour Jesus Christ?

And who can seriously contemplate those sufferings, borne for us so patiently, without being moved to pity and to repentance? Such a person will be moved to say with the heart if not with the lips: "Oh, my God, I am sorry for having offended Thee and caused Thee such suffering. Grant that I may love Thee with my whole heart and never more offend Thee."

Catholics, as we have seen, adore God alone. They honor the Blessed Virgin and saints represented by images. They use these holy pictures and statues to beautify the house of God. These pictures are also a source of instruction. They are a profession of our faith. If you enter a house and see on one side of the room a picture of the Blessed Virgin, Cardinal Gibbons, or of Pope Leo XIII, and on the other a picture of Lincoln, Cleveland, or Washington, you will at once know the religious faith as well as the political belief or patriotism of the occupant.

By the aid of the relics of the martyrs we are reminded of all they suffered for the faith. By the use of religious pictures, our devotion is increased and we are stimulated to imitate the virtues of the saints represented.

If it is reasonable to have pictures of our martyred President and relics of our Revolutionary heroes that we may be reminded of their patriotism, it is none the less reasonable to have pictures and relics of Our Lord, the Blessed Virgin, and the saints, that we may be reminded of their virtues. By imitating their virtues here, we may be *happy with them hereafter.*

XII. SOME SACRAMENTALS

"Pray without ceasing" (2 Thess. 5:17).

"Every creature is sanctified by the word of God and prayer" (1 Tim. 4:4, 5).

*B*Y SACRAMENTALS we mean the various prayers, blessings, ceremonies and pious practices of the Church. Here mention will be made of some of the most common of the sacramentals that have not already been treated. Sacramentals, like sacraments, have an outward sign; the latter, however, were instituted by Christ, the former by the Church, and while the latter always give grace if we place no obstacle in the way, the former do not give grace, but excite good thoughts, increase devotion, and raise the mind to God.

The chief sacramentals that have not been mentioned are the books used by the priest in the performance of his sacred duties, the sign of the cross, holy water, blessed candles, blessed palm and ashes, holy oils, scapulars, medals, *Agnus Dei*, prayers, litanies, rosary, the *Angelus*, stations, the funeral service, and various blessings.

The books used by the priest in the performance of his sacred duties are the *Missal*, which contains the Masses for the various feasts of the ecclesiastical year; the *Breviary*, in which is the office recited by the priest every day; and the *Ritual*, where is to be found the form of administering the different sacraments, the funeral service, and the various benedictions.

The sacramental of most frequent use in the Church is the *sign of the cross*. It is used to remind us of the Passion and Death of Our Lord and Saviour Jesus Christ on the cross. The cross is the emblem of the Christian, the "sign of the Son of Man." It is an act of faith in the principal truths of Christianity. When we say the words, "In the name," we profess our faith in the unity of God, which means that there is but one God; "of the Father and of the Son and of the Holy Ghost," are a profession of faith in the Trinity— *i.e.*, that there are three divine persons in one God. The form of the cross which we trace with our right hand from our forehead to our breast, and then from the left to the right shoulder, is a profession of faith in the Incarnation of the Son of God, who became man and died on the cross for our redemption. Tertullian and other writers of the early ages of the Church tell us that before every action, before rising or retiring, before meals, at every step, "we impress on our forehead the sign of the cross." The Catholic Church of today, in accordance with the teachings of Christ, His apostles, and their successors of all time, teaches her children to put their trust in the merits of Jesus Christ's sufferings on the cross, and to do everything "in the name of the Father and of the Son and of the Holy Ghost."

Holy water is water blessed by a priest. During the blessing beautiful prayers are recited. These prayers express the spiritual blessings the Church wishes to follow all who use it. The Church uses holy water in all the benedictions and some of her sacraments. It is placed at the doors of her churches, that all who enter may use it and be reminded of that purity of heart which it symbolizes. Holy water is also kept in the houses of Catholics, to be used in times of trial and when the priest comes to administer the sacraments.

The *blessed candles* used in the service of the Church receive their special blessing on Candlemas Day. We use these lighted candles at different times to remind us of Jesus, who is the "Light of the world." Catholics always keep a blessed candle in the house. The Church puts a lighted candle in our hand at our baptism, and wishes us to die with one in our hand, to remind us to hope in Him who is our Light and the light of the world.

On Ash Wednesday *ashes* are blessed and put on the forehead of the faithful in the form of a cross, with the words, "Remember, man, that thou art dust and unto dust thou shalt return," to remind them that they are only dust and ashes. These are the ashes of burnt *palms* blessed the Palm Sunday of the previous year. These palms are blessed in memory of the triumphal entry of Jesus into Jerusalem, when the people spread palm branches along the way. This palm should remind us to perform faithfully our duty if we wish to enjoy the palm of victory.

The *holy oils* are blessed by the bishop on Holy Thursday of each year. They are of three kinds: oil of the sick, used in the sacrament of Extreme Unction; oil of the Catechumens, used in blessing baptismal water and in the sacrament of

Baptism; and Holy Chrism, used in the preparation of
baptismal water in the ceremonies of Baptism, Confirmation,
and at the consecration of a bishop, of churches, altars, bells
and chalices. The olive oil used should remind us of Our
Saviour's *passion* in the Garden of Olives.

Agnus Deis (blessed by the Pope), *scapulars*, and *medals*
are small articles worn by Catholics to remind them of
Our Lord (the Lamb of God), of the Blessed Virgin, and
of the saints. They are emblems of the Christian, as the
starry banner is the emblem of the American; and as the
flag of our country shows that we are under the protection
of the Government of the United States, so the *Agnus Dei*,
scapulars, and medals show that we are under the protection
of Jesus Christ, His Blessed Mother, and His saints.

Prayer is the elevation of our mind and heart to God to
ask Him for all blessings, temporal and spiritual. Prayer
is necessary to salvation. We are taught in St. Luke (ch.
18) to pray always and faint not. We should pray with
attention and devotion, with confidence and humility.
We are told in the Lord's Prayer to pray for others as
well as for ourselves, and God's choicest blessings will be
granted us through Jesus Christ Our Lord. The best of
all prayers is the one God taught us: the Lord's Prayer.
Other prayers common in the Church are Litanies,
Rosaries, the Angelus, Stations, and the Funeral Service
for the dead. The Litanies most in use in the Church
are the Litany of All Saints, of the Blessed Virgin, of
the Holy Name of Jesus. In these Litanies we ask God
to have mercy on us and the saints to pray for us; but

we ask everything through Jesus Christ Our Lord. Few
practices of the Church are more widespread than the
Rosary of the Blessed Virgin. It consists of the best of
all prayers—the Apostles' Creed, the Our Father, three
Hail Marys, and the Glory be to the Father; then the
Our Father and ten Hail Marys repeated five times. This
constitutes the beads, or one-third part of the Rosary.
During the recitation of these prayers the mind should be
occupied meditating on the principal mysteries of the life
of Our Lord. These mysteries are divided into the five
joyful mysteries: the Annunciation by the angel Gabriel,
the Visitation of the Blessed Virgin to St. Elizabeth, the
Birth of Our Lord, the Presentation, and the Finding in
the Temple; the five sorrowful mysteries: the Agony in
the Garden, the Scourging, the Crowning with Thorns,
the Carrying of the Cross, and the Crucifixion; and the
five glorious mysteries: the Resurrection, the Ascension,
the Descent of the Holy Ghost, the Assumption of the
Blessed Virgin, and the Crowning of the Blessed Virgin
in heaven. Any one of these mysteries furnishes sufficient
material to occupy the mind of man for hours. These
mysteries contain the whole history of the Redemption.
The prayers and meditations of the Rosary satisfy the
minds of the humblest, while they are sufficient to occupy
the attention of the most exalted and most cultivated.
The *Angelus* is a beautiful prayer, said morning, noon, and
night. In Catholic countries the bell is rung, when all cease
their occupations, kneel, and recite: "The angel of the
Lord declared unto Mary, and she conceived by the Holy

Ghost"—a Hail Mary. "Behold the handmaid of the Lord—be it done unto me according to Thy Word"—a Hail Mary. "And the Word was made flesh, and dwelt amongst us"—a Hail Mary. The prayer: "Pour forth, we beseech Thee, O Lord, Thy grace into our hearts, that we, to whom the Incarnation of Christ, Thy Son, was made known by the message of an angel, may by His passion and cross be brought to the glory of His resurrection, through the same Christ Our Lord. Amen." By this beautiful practice we show in a special manner our faith in the Incarnation of Our Lord and Saviour Jesus Christ.

The *Stations of the Cross* are fourteen paintings representing the various stages of the passion and death of Our Redeemer. The faithful pass from station to station and meditate upon that feature of the passion represented by each station. Tradition tells us that from the beginning pious pilgrims were accustomed to tread the path and bedew with their tears the way sanctified by our Saviour on that sorrowful journey from Pilate's tribunal to Calvary's heights. But Jerusalem falling into the hands of infidels, and many being unable to visit those holy places, permission was obtained to erect in churches fourteen crosses and pictures commemorating these sorrowful acts. From these stations all can meditate upon the sufferings of our Saviour, and learn from Him submission to God's holy will, patience, charity, and forgiveness of injuries.

The *funeral service* of the Catholic Church is beautiful, touching, and instructive. After blessing, strengthening, and encouraging us through life with her sacraments; after fortifying our souls for the last great struggle, she follows us beyond the grave with her blessings, her prayers, and her sacrifices. "Eternal rest give unto them, O Lord," she prays; "and let perpetual light shine upon them. May they rest in peace."

There are various other prayers and blessings used by the Church on special occasions. In fact, the Church blesses everything she uses. This blessing of the priest is not such an absurd thing as some imagine it to be; it is rather a most reasonable practice. It is simply a prayer said by the priest, asking God to send His blessing upon the person or thing indicated. People of all denominations say grace before meals, asking God to bless the food they are about to use. This is precisely what the priest does when blessing anything. He uses different forms of prayer ordained by the Church to implore God's blessing upon the water, candles, and other things before using them. This blessing of churches, water, candles, and other things has its foundation on Scripture. We read in the Old Testament of the solemn blessing of the Temple of Solomon. St. Paul tells us that "every creature is sanctified by the word of God and prayer." Churches, water, candles, bells, books, persons, and other things blessed by the Church are creatures. Therefore we are following St. Paul in blessing them, for every creature is sanctified by the word of God and prayer.

We do not claim that those articles that are blessed have any efficacy in themselves; but we hope and pray that God in His infinite goodness and mercy may render those blessed articles beneficial to those using them, may protect them and lead them to *His blessed abode above, where all is peace and light and love.*

XIII. THE CELEBRATION OF FEASTS

"Seven days shalt thou celebrate feasts to the Lord thy God, in the place which the Lord shalt choose" (Deut. 16:15).

"If he will not hear the Church, let him be to thee as the heathen and the publican" (Matt. 18:17).

*F*ROM these texts we learn that besides the Sunday God wishes certain other days to be observed religiously, and that the Church has the power of designating these days.

As the State sets aside certain national holidays in commemoration of its founder or of the Declaration of Independence, so the Church sets aside these holidays in honor of Jesus Christ, the Blessed Virgin, and the saints.

Besides the feasts celebrated on Sundays, there are in this country but six holidays of obligation. Three of these are commemorative of events in the life of Our Lord: Christmas, the Circumcision, and the Ascension; two, the Immaculate Conception and the Assumption, in honor of the Blessed Virgin; and one in honor of God's saints: the Feast of All Saints.

The ecclesiastical year begins in Advent. Advent is a period of about four weeks of penance and prayer preparatory to the great feast of *Christmas* and corresponding to the penitential season of Lent before Easter. During the ecclesiastical year, the first of the feasts of obligation in the order of time is the feast of the *Immaculate Conception*.

It is celebrated on the 8th of December. On this day we commemorate the fact that Mary was immaculate when she first came into being in her mother's womb; that she was always pure; that sin never touched her fair soul. Immaculate Conception, as you will see in the article on the Blessed Virgin, means that she was always free from sin.

The great feast of *Christmas*, in honor of the birth of Jesus Christ, is celebrated on December 25th. This feast is a time of joy and peace to all mankind, and is celebrated by the Church with much pomp and ceremony.

The festival of the *Circumcision* is kept on the first day of the new year. It is commemorative of Our Lord's strict observance of the law by submitting to the Jewish ceremony of circumcision. We solemnly celebrate the day in honor of our merciful Lord, who is our model in all things.

Next in the order of time is the feast of the *Ascension*. It is kept forty days after the grand feast of Easter, and is in honor of Our Lord's glorious ascension into heaven.

The *Assumption* of the Blessed Virgin, celebrated the 15th of August, is commemorative of the glorious taking up to heaven of Mary, soul and body. (This is a pious tradition.)

All Saints' Day is November 1st. Every day is a saint's day. There is not a day that the Catholic Church does not celebrate a feast in honor of some special mystery or saint. But as there are more saints in heaven than could be thus specially honored, she sets aside this one day every year in honor of all the saints in heaven.

There are various other important feasts, some of which fall on Sunday; but these we have mentioned being feasts of obligation to be observed as Sunday, it was thought that it would not be uninteresting to give a short explanation of them.

On them we honor God and His special friends. Let us always, by faith, hope, and love, *bear Jesus in our minds and hearts*.

XIV. INFANT BAPTISM

"Amen, amen, I say to thee, unless a man be born again of water and the Holy Ghost, he can not enter into the kingdom of God" (John 3:5).

*W*HILE most Christians admit the necessity of Baptism for adults, the Catholic Church is alone in insisting upon the practice of infant Baptism. This practice is in accordance with the teaching of St. John, quoted above. It is also in accordance with apostolic teaching and practice.

We read in the 16th chapter of the Acts of the Apostles that St. Paul baptized Lydia "and her household," and that the keeper of the prison was converted and "was baptized and presently all his family." Among these families it is but reasonable to suppose that there were some infants.

Infant Baptism was the practice of the apostles; it was the practice of the Christians of the early Church, as Origen tells us. The Church received the tradition from the apostles to give Baptism to infants, and it has been the practice of the Church from the time of Christ until the present.

St. Paul tells us that Adam's sin was transmitted to all his posterity. "Wherefore as by one man sin entered into this world, and by sin death, and so death passed unto all men in whom all have sinned" (Rom 5:12). Every infant, according to St. Paul, is born to sin—original sin. But as Baptism takes away original sin, and as nothing defiled can enter heaven (Apoc. 21), Baptism of infants is necessary to open for them the gates of heaven.

Baptism may be validly administered by dipping, sprinkling, or pouring. The method practised in this part of Christendom is pouring the water on the head of the person to be baptized, saying at the same time: "I baptize thee in the name of the Father and of the Son and of the Holy Ghost."

The reasonableness of the practice of baptizing infants will be evident if we remember that Christ taught the necessity of baptism for all when He said: "Unless a man be born again of water and the Holy Ghost, he can not enter into the kingdom of God"; and that He declared little children capable of entering into the kingdom of God when He said: "Suffer little children to come unto Me and forbid them not, for of such is the kingdom of heaven."

Now, if infants are capable of entering heaven (and Christ so declares), they must be capable of receiving Baptism, without which Christ says no one can enter the kingdom of God.

While in adults faith and sorrow for sin are required before receiving Baptism, no disposition is required in infants.

They contracted original sin without their knowledge;

without their knowledge they are freed from it.

By Baptism they are made heirs of the kingdom of heaven.

They can be made heirs of property, of a kingdom on earth without their consent; why not also of the kingdom of heaven?

Baptism is the first of the seven sacraments which the Church confers upon man. It cleanses us from original sin (actual sin also if the recipient be guilty of any), makes us Christians, children of God, and heirs of heaven. It prepares us for the reception of the other sacraments. By Baptism we all contracted the obligation of believing and practising the doctrines of Jesus Christ as taught us by the true Church. We fulfill this obligation by *leading a truly Christian life*.

XV. THE MARRIAGE TIE—ONE AND INDISSOLUBLE

"But I say to you that whosoever shall put away his wife, excepting for the cause of fornication, maketh her to commit adultery; and he that shall marry her that is put away committeth adultery" (Matt. 5:33).

"What, therefore, God hath joined together, let no man put asunder" (Matt. 19:5, 6).

*F*EW practices of the Church have been productive of more good to society than that concerning Christian marriage. The Christian family is the foundation of Christian society, and Christian marriage is the basis of the Christian family. Without marriage neither the family nor society could exist. Marriage was instituted by God before society existed, and, as a natural consequence, it is subject not to the laws of society, but to the laws of God and

His Church. The principal law and necessary condition of Christian marriage is its unity and indissolubility. It is the union of *one man* with *one woman* for the purposes intended by the Creator, which union is to last as long as both survive. Such was marriage in the beginning; to such it was restored by our Saviour when He made it a sacrament of His law and a type of His union with His Church.

The practice of the Catholic Church in not permitting a divorce that will allow either party to marry during the life of the other, is clearly taught by Jesus Christ in the 5th chapter of Matthew: "He who puts away his wife maketh her to commit adultery, and he that marrieth her committeth adultery."

No human power can break the bond of marriage. "What God hath joined together, let no man put asunder." It is the work of God. Let no man dare meddle with it. St. Paul teaches the same when he says in the 39th verse of the 7th chapter of the First Epistle to the Corinthians: "A woman is bound by the law as long as her husband liveth; but if her husband die, she is at liberty, let her marry whom she will." The practice of the Catholic Church is conformable to this teaching of Christ, St. Paul, the apostles, and their successors.

In defence of this practice of forbidding divorce, since marriage is one and indissoluble, the Catholic Church has had many a severe conflict. And had she not fought this battle bravely for the sanctity, the unity, and the indissolubility of the marriage tie, Europe and America would today be in as degraded a condition as are the Mahometan and other nations where the laws of marriage are disregarded. For divorces are not only contrary to Christ's teaching concerning the sanctity, unity, and indissolubility of the marriage tie, but are also subversive of society. They sever the marriage tie inasmuch as the law of man can do it. If the marriage tie is loosened, the family is dissolved; and if the family is dissolved, society, the state, falls to ruin. Divorce destroys conjugal love, causes unhappiness, renders the proper education of children impossible, and often leads to terrible crimes. Is it not reasonable as well as scriptural to forbid it?

The Christian husband and wife, knowing the sanctity, the unity, and the indissolubility of the marriage tie, live in love and peace and honor together; together they rear the issue of their union, teaching them to be good children, good citizens, and good Christians; together, after a long, a prosperous, and a happy union, they return to dust; and together they will meet again beyond the confines of the tomb—*yes, they will meet to part no more*.

XVI. RESPECT SHOWN
TO ECCLESIASTICAL SUPERIORS

"We are ambassadors for Christ; God, as it were, exhorting by us" (2 Cor 5:20).

"As the Father sent me, I also send you" (John 20:21).

"Go ye into the whole world and preach the Gospel to every creature" (Mark 16:15).

*T*HE respect Catholics have for the bishops and priests of the Church is often a matter of surprise to those not of the Faith. They do not understand, as Catholics do, that the priests are "ambassadors for Christ" sent to "preach the Gospel to every creature." For Christ instituted the priesthood to carry on divine worship, to govern the Church, to preach His doctrine, and to administer the sacraments.

As in the Old Law God chose His priests from among the family of Aaron, so in the New Law He chooses them from among those whom His apostles and their successors see fit to ordain. Priests and other ministers of the Church receive in the sacrament of Holy Orders the power and grace to perform their sacred duties. If we would but consider seriously for a moment the importance of these duties and the great dignity of the minister of God, we would have no difficulty in understanding the reasonableness of the Catholic practice of showing profound respect to God's priesthood.

The priest is the minister of Jesus Christ, who chose him that he might obtain for himself the greatest good and in return bestow this good upon his fellow-man. Jesus Christ chose him that he might aid Him in the work for which He came on earth. What a noble mission! What important duties! What a great dignity! To aid Jesus Christ in saving souls, to teach them the truths of salvation, to loose them from their sins, to offer the eucharistic sacrifice for them, to pray for them, to minister unto them, and to fill them with Heaven's choice blessings; for such a high mission, for such important duties did Jesus Christ choose the priest. If his duties are so important, his dignity must be correspondingly great.

On the banks of the Lake of Genesareth the Great Teacher chose Peter as His vicar and head of His Church. As the pontiff could not be everywhere, Peter and the other apostles imposed hands on others as the needs of the growing Church demanded. They understood that it was by a living, teaching ministry this work of salvation was to be carried on. For we find it recorded in the 14th chapter of the Acts that Paul and Barnabas ordained priests in Lystra and Iconium.

Paul also consecrated Titus Bishop of Crete, for the express purpose of ordaining others. Thus we see that as Christ was sent by the Father, the apostles by Christ, so, too, is the priest invested with the same power "for the perfecting of the saints, for the work of the ministry and for the edification of the body of Christ" (Eph. 4:12), and that no one but a priest divinely called, rightly ordained, and legitimately sent has power from God to teach God's words to the faithful. He is the ambassador of God, commissioned to do His work with His authority; the vicar of Christ continuing the work He commenced; and the organ of the Holy Ghost for the sanctification of souls. He is ever imitating his model, going "about doing good." He devotes his life to alleviate the sufferings of men. To spend one's life instructing man is but second in importance to alleviating his sufferings. This the priest is ever doing. He rescued us from barbarism; saved for us at the risk of his life the Holy Scriptures, the classics of Greece and Rome, and the writings of the Fathers; founded the great universities of Europe; and is today, as in the past, the greatest educator in the world. He does all this for love of God. Do you wonder, then, that Catholics love and revere their priests?

Nowhere can there be found a body of men or a series of rulers so venerable, so renowned for wisdom, justice, charity, and holiness, as the Popes, bishops, and priests of the Catholic Church in every age, *from the time of Christ until the present.*

XVII. CELIBACY

"He who is unmarried careth about the things of the Lord, how he may please God" (1 Cor. 7:32).

HE Catholic Church recognizes matrimony as a holy state. She recommends celibacy to those desiring greater perfection, and enjoins it on her priests because, as St. Paul says, "He who is unmarried careth about the things of the Lord." It is said that the life of the priest is a hard, lonely one, and that it is unscriptural. Let us see. That his life is one of hardships is certain. His path is by no means one of roses; it is rather one covered with thorns. The young man knows this well before he enters it. With a full knowledge of its duties and responsibilities, he willingly enters the priesthood. He knows well that it is a life full of trials and crosses. He knows, too, that the whole life of Jesus Christ, from the stable of Bethlehem to the cross on Calvary's heights, was one continuous trial, cross, mortification; and that the life of every follower, especially every minister, of Jesus Christ should be fashioned after that of his divine model. "If any man will come after Me," He says in the 16th chapter of St. Matthew, "let him deny himself, take up his cross and follow Me." The disciple, the minister of Christ, is not above his Master; and it is not becoming that the path of the disciple or minister should be covered with flowers while that of the Master was strewn with thorns and sprinkled with His own precious blood.

Yes, the priest's life is one of trials, crosses, and hardships. But the more trials he has to bear, the more crosses he has to carry, the more hardships he has to endure, the greater is his resemblance to his model, Jesus Christ; and if he bears those trials, crosses, and hardships, which he shares with his Master here, with a proper spirit, the more certain he is of sharing with Him a happy eternity hereafter.

But is the life of celibacy unscriptural? No. In fact, few questions are more clearly defined in Holy Scripture than that of religious celibacy. St. Paul, in the 7th chapter of the First Epistle to the Corinthians, says: "I would have you without solicitude. He who is unmarried careth for the things of the Lord, how he may please God; but he who is married careth about the things of the world, how he may please his wife, and is divided. And the unmarried woman and virgin thinketh about the things of the Lord, how she may be holy in body and spirit. But she that is married thinketh about the things of the world, how she may please her husband. Therefore," he concludes, "he that giveth his virgin in marriage doth well; and he who giveth her not doth better." Could language be clearer? Marriage is good; celibacy is better.

"He that is unmarried careth about the things of the Lord, how he may please God." This teaching of St. Paul is the teaching of the Church—that marriage is honorable, is good, but that there is a better, a holier state for those who are called by the grace of God to embrace it.

Religious celibacy is one of the principal reasons why the Catholic priest and missionary will risk all dangers, overcome all obstacles, face all terrors, and in time of plague expose himself to death in its most disgusting forms for the good of his fellow-man.

All are acquainted with the noble examples of numbers of priests and Sisters of Charity who, at the risk of their own lives, voluntarily nursed the sick and dying during the yellow-fever scourge in the South a few years ago. Do you think they would have done so had they families depending upon them? No; they would have cared for the things of this world. Jesus Christ has said: "Greater love than this no man hath, that a man give up his life for his fellow-man." This the good priest is ever doing, ever ready to do. Although death stares him in the face, he never shrinks from his post of duty, never abandons his flock while there is a wound to heal, a soul to save.

When his duty calls him, he is not afraid of death, because St. Paul says: *"He who is without a wife is solicitous about the things of the Lord."*

XVIII. CONCLUSION

"If thou wilt enter into life keep the commandments" (Matt. 19:17).

*W*HEN Jesus Christ died on the cross for us, He did so in order to lead us into life, to open heaven for all mankind. How important our salvation must be, then, for which Christ shed His precious blood. If it is important, He must have taught us how to attain it. This, too, He did by the words, "keep the commandments."

To assist us in keeping the commandments He left a representative on earth. His Church, whose ministers were to teach all nations, is this representative. To her He said: "He that hears you, hears Me."

The night before He died He instituted the adorable sacrifice of the Mass, saying: "This is My body . . . This is My blood which shall be shed for you." He then gave the apostles and their successors power to do what He had just done: "Do this in commemoration of Me." He also gave them power to baptize, to forgive sins, to bless, to be "dispensers of the mysteries of God." He gave them power to confer these powers on others. "As the Father sent Me [i.e., with the same power] I also send you." To these apostles and their successors He spoke when He said that He would remain with them until the consummation of the world. To them and the Church He said: "He that hears you hears Me." What the Church teaches, then, Christ teaches.

As, in the natural order, man is born, grows to manhood, is nourished, and if sick needs proper food and remedies: so, in the supernatural order, there is a birth, it is Baptism;

there is a manly growth, it is Confirmation; there is a nourishing food, it is the Holy Eucharist, the Bread of Life; there is a medicinal remedy against death, it is Penance; and there is a balm to heal the wounds, the scars of sin, it is Extreme Unction. These are some of the channels through which God's grace flows into our souls to assist us to keep the commandments.

The practices of the Church naturally flow from her teachings. She teaches that there is but one God, the creator and Lord of heaven and earth and all things; that man by his reason alone can find out this truth; that the order, beauty, and harmony of the works of nature show God's work; but that there are some truths which the deepest intellect of man can never fathom. Hence she teaches that God has revealed certain truths; such as the mysteries of the Holy Trinity, the Incarnation, and the Blessed Sacrament. When we know that God has revealed these truths we are acting reasonably not only in believing them, but also in showing our belief by practices of respect, adoration, and love.

The Church teaches that we must not only believe, but practise our religion. For faith alone will not save us. "Faith without works is dead." To have these works we must "keep the commandments." We must love God above all things and our neighbor as ourselves. All the commandments are comprised in this. In fact, the essence of Christianity is charity.

Where will you find charity practised in reality except in the Catholic Church? If you wish to see the truth of this, visit our larger towns and cities, and you will find hundreds of hospitals, asylums, schools, and other charitable institutions in which are thousands of the children of the Catholic Church, who have left everything to alleviate every ill that flesh is heir to, and follow the meek and humble Jesus in His mission of love.

The Catholic Church alone teaches, as Jesus taught while on earth, the duty of penance. "If any man will come after Me, let him deny himself, take up his cross and follow Me." According to Christ's teaching, the Church sets aside the penitential season of Lent and other times of mortification.

The Church also teaches that we must not only be faithful in the observance of the practices of religion, but that we must also live in peace and justice and charity with all mankind, and die with a hope beyond the grave. If we love God we will faithfully observe the practices of the Church; these practices will assist us in keeping the commandments, by which we will enter into life.

We have seen that the various ceremonies and practices of the Catholic Church are dictated by right reason; that they are the rational deduction from Christ's teaching; that they obtain for us divine grace, excite pious thoughts, and elevate our minds to God; and that a true Christian is one who not only believes but also practises the teachings of Christ and His Church. The observance of these pious practices of the Church makes us Christians in fact as well as in name. They assist us to keep the commandments and to live in accordance with our faith. By faithfully observing them, we show that we are not ashamed to be Christ's followers. And if we follow Him, who is the way, the truth, and the life, we will not walk in darkness; but will enter by the narrow way into the presence of truth itself, *in the regions of eternal light.*

Additional titles available from
St. Augustine Academy Press
Books for the Traditional Catholic

Titles by Mother Mary Loyola:

Blessed are they that Mourn
Confession and Communion
Coram Sanctissimo (Before the Most Holy)
First Communion
First Confession
Forgive us our Trespasses
Hail! Full of Grace
Heavenwards
Holy Mass/How to Help the Sick and Dying
Home for Good
Jesus of Nazareth: The Story of His Life Written for Children
Questions on First Communion
The Child of God: What comes of our Baptism
The Children's Charter
The Little Children's Prayer Book
The Soldier of Christ: Talks before Confirmation
Trust
Welcome! Holy Communion Before and After

Titles by Father Lasance:

The Catholic Girl's Guide
The Young Man's Guide

Tales of the Saints:

A Child's Book of Saints by William Canton
A Child's Book of Warriors by William Canton
Illustrated Life of the Blessed Virgin by Rev. B. Rohner, O.S.B.
Legends & Stories of Italy by Amy Steedman
Mary, Help of Christians by Rev. Bonaventure Hammer
Page, Esquire and Knight by Marion Florence Lansing
The Book of Saints and Heroes by Lenora Lang
Saint Patrick: Apostle of Ireland
The Story of St. Elizabeth of Hungary by William Canton

Check our Website for more:
www.staugustineacademypress.com

CPSIA information can be obtained
at www.ICGtesting.com
Printed in the USA
JSHW010856081222
34341JS00001B/5

9 781936 639298